LET THERE
BE JUSTICE

LET THERE BE JUSTICE

THE POLITICAL JOURNEY OF IMRAN KHAN

B. J. SADIQ

FONTHILL

To the ageless Imran Khan,
my parents, and Urooj, my ever-forbearing wife

Fonthill Media Language Policy

Fonthill Media publishes in the international English language market. One language edition is published worldwide. As there are minor differences in spelling and presentation, especially with regard to American English and British English, a policy is necessary to define which form of English to use. The Fonthill Policy is to use the form of English native to the author. B. J. Sadiq was born in Pakistan and educated in England; therefore British English has been adopted in this publication.

Fonthill Media Limited
Fonthill Media LLC
www.fonthillmedia.com
office@fonthillmedia.com

First published in the United Kingdom and the United States of America 2017

British Library Cataloguing in Publication Data:
A catalogue record for this book is available from the British Library

Copyright © B. J. Sadiq 2017

ISBN 978-1-78155-637-5

Typeset in 10.5pt on 13pt Sabon
Printed and bound in England

Preface

One of the penalties for refusing to participate in politics is that you end up being governed by your inferiors.

Plato

There are few who believe he is nothing but noise, others believe he is a feckless bore, creating illusions of change and one who relishes public attention, and still others believe he may actually usher in a new era of righteous politics—Imran Khan has been in the spot light again. On this occasion, it is not for his cricket but for his defiant presence on the political canvas of Pakistan. While he is not a starter in politics, exhausting his ribs through roaring public speeches and languishing around for nearly two decades, it is only now that he is being perceived as a serious contender. The age-old status quo can no longer afford to absorb his public barbs with a pinch of salt.

Imran has been in the news since long before my parents had even conceived of having me. His personal life and character has already drawn a lot of coverage. Rising from the depths, his movement for justice party enjoys a strong voice in the opposition, and he has managed to draw huge crowds at voting booths—an uncommon spectacle in Pakistan—reinforcing the wisdom behind voting in an otherwise politically unlettered Pakistani. An irreverent iconoclast, he has also been a recipient of widespread flak. His opponents despise him and, more so, the coverage he gets in the social media. 'Politeness has never been one of his virtues,' concedes an average Nawaz Sharif faithful, rather curtly. His contemporaries may despise him for his open-stage bluntness and tongue-lashing, but the man undoubtedly possesses tremendous persuasive powers to bring about people to his line of thinking: the youth loves him, believes in him, and empowers him; his ideas are revolutionary and prophetic; and, as such, he remains a celebrated figure and a serious crowd puller. For the sake of amusement, his prowess with women is still a hot topic. He could well be the remedy to Pakistan's longstanding political puzzle or could possibly be just another character, conspiring and hungering for power. Nevertheless, he surely is subject of an interesting narrative. Imran Khan's arduous political journey is a territory that deserves to be explored.

This is my first serious study of Pakistan. I have been contributing columns for a number of years, but I have always suspected my book writing stamina. A lover of books, I usually seek refuge in the company of my undersized library at home—that is my way of escaping the vagaries of a disturbing life. Disturbing it surely gets, particularly if one has been plodding through years of economic, political, and social upheaval in Pakistan; a country where I delightfully spent my formative years and a place where I do my search for bread and butter. Pakistan is suspected of being in the news for all the wrong reasons: it is the recipient of bad press and often comes under scrutiny for being a hostile country. Pakistan's survival has also been a subject of much doubt. Several years back, I acquired possession of a book called *Can Pakistan Survive? The Death of a State*; a worthy read, scribbled by Tariq Ali in 1983—he is a well-known left-wing intellectual from Pakistan, who ventured into Europe during the Vietnam War in the '60s and earned a reputation. His prophecies on Pakistan have been heart wrenching.

Unsurprisingly, Pakistan is dubbed to be one of the world's foremost corrupt havens. It is also one of the few places where the gulf between the rich and the poor is of measureless proportions. The elite has a taste for corruption: they move around with an imperial arrogance. Being invincibly loaded, no product on earth ever proves a strain on their pockets. To stay afloat, they have subjected state institutions to the worst version of nepotism. They proudly defy all yardsticks of accountability, control the institutions, and are a law unto themselves. On the contrary, the poor hardly have a life; since justice is a luxury, not many can afford it. Hailing from an educated middle-income household, I have been fed on the stories of how a few rich families in the country have armed themselves with a staggering, below-the-belt fortune—heavily mortgaging their souls to jobbery. Courtesy of an endemic culture of nepotism, all the good people suffer and the bad ones prosper.

The country is no longer safe either: the bearded *fundoos*, until a few years ago, had rocked the nation, and we let them escape without a howl of objection—bombs went off everywhere, no part of the country was spared, and things went haywire. Like many others in my circle, I was on the verge of deciding to uproot myself from the country. However, I stayed back, not fully sold to the idea.

One positive that I have noticed over the past decade is that Pakistan has an extremely vibrant and an able middle class—gradually emerging from the ashes and craving for change. Free marketers by birth, they are richly endowed with all the natural propensities to excel and make an impression. However small and insignificant this middle class may be, it still manages to make a mark globally. Many of them are educated abroad and enjoy positions of significance. Few of them are well-placed in major multinational corporations and financial institutions abroad. As professionals, they have ventured into medicine, finance, marketing, accounting, journalism, and law. They have even meddled with the razzmatazz of the entertainment industry. Therefore, the Pakistan that we see today, despite its unprecedented problems, has managed to trudge along simply on the strength of an extremely ambitious human capital, the fruits of which are slow but still forthcoming. My wife and I go about discussing for hours how a strong leadership may well be the recipe. The political system for years has been wrought with corruption and shadiness, periodically producing governments that administer the country with the same lack of devotion and ineptness. They have fouled the atmosphere, swinging into power by making lofty claims that hardly reap any red-letter dividends for the community down under. This reminds me of a New Testament proverb: 'He who oppresses the poor to increase his wealth and he who supplies gifts to the rich—both come to poverty'. May the transgressors in the land meet their just desserts.

In the middle of this climate walks in Imran Khan, carrying his trademark swagger from the cricketing world. Imran is perhaps the first ever politician we have had who has tirelessly rallied around the theme of social reforms, justice, a corruption-free governance, and stronger institutions. The celebrated cricketer-turned-politician clearly strikes a chord. He has gone from being a single bencher in the parliament to a compulsive public speaker and an unrelenting opposition force. His prospects are a subject of examination. While this book is mainly a biographical account of Imran's political journey that commenced at the twilight of his cricketing career, it will also seek to probe some of the controversies surrounding his meteoric rise as a defiant leader. Interwoven with the chronicles of Imran's political journey is another tale, boldly exposing Pakistan's highly corrupt and lamentable systems.

Without my wife's constant push, I would not have endured the pains of burning the midnight oil, poring over material for this book. Months of writing had thankfully wiped out that unwanted bulge in my belly, and I had also completely lost sense of my time zone. I am not a man of habit and easily get excited over things that I feel I must accomplish, yet my ambitions are usually short-lived and I also do not have a very elevated opinion of my writing ability—though I can identify the difference between good writing and the not-so-good writing. I have harboured writing ambitions since my days as an infant, and I can recount the first time I wrote an English essay; I titled it 'Only the fittest survives' because me and my fellow siblings emerged afresh with an earful from our exhausted mother. While my petrified brothers crouched out of the house to romp in the streets, I began writing. During the course of writing this book, I kept doubting my patience to labour on this project for hours. 'How can I accomplish something like this?' I would repeat to myself. Then, one day, my inconsistent attempts at writing were rescued by Imran Khan— he had called for yet another protest, thrusting his hands in the hornets' nest. His exceptional energy at sixty-four years old became a source of encouragement and kept me going.

List of Abbreviations

ANP	Awami National Party
BBC	British Broadcasting Corporation
Cantab	Member of the University of Cambridge
CIA	Central Intelligence Agency
COAS	Chief of Army Staff
CV	Curriculum Vitae
DNA	Deoxyribonucleic Acid
ECP	Election Commission of Pakistan
FAFEN	Free and Fair Election Network
FATA	Federally Administered Tribal Areas
FIA	Federal Investigation Agency
GDP	Gross Domestic Product
GT	Grand Trunk
HDI	Human Development Index
HRCP	Human Rights Commission of Pakistan
IPO	International Progress Organization
ISI	Inter-Services Intelligence
IUCN	International Union for Conservation of Nature
KP	Khyper Pakhtunkwa
MQM	Mutahida Quami Movement
NA	National Assembly
NAB	National Accountability Bureau
NADRA	National Database Registration Authority
NATO	The North Atlantic Treaty Organization
OGDC	Oil and Gas Development Company
PAT	Pakistan Awami Tehreek
PIA	Pakistan International Airline
PML-N	Pakistan Muslim League Nawaz

PML-Q	Pakistan Muslim League Quaid e Azam Group
PPP	Pakistan Peoples Party
PPPP	Pakistan Peoples Party Parliamentarians
PSM	Pakistan Steel Mills
PTI	Pakistan Tehreek-e-Insaaf
PTV	Pakistan Television
SUV	Sport Utility Vehicle
TV	Television
UN	United Nations
UNDP	United Nations Development Program
UP	Uttar Pradesh
US	United States
WAPDA	Water and Power Development Authority

Thanks must go to Mr Sarwar Khan, PTI's official photographer, who suppled all images.

CONTENTS

1

Why Politics?

We make a living by what we get, but we make a life by what we give.

Winston Churchill

It was an expressive wintry afternoon of Lahore in 1991, and I remember taking a stroll somewhere close to the center of Bagh-e-Jinnah cricket ground—formerly named by the British as Lawrence Gardens. References tied to the site suggest it derives its title from Sir John Lawrence, India's Viceroy during the Victorian age. My father was with me, fondling with my head; I was a minor, hardly eight years old, and unlike other children of my age, I was extremely feeble. My bowels lagged and I used to throw up fitfully. Memories of the early years are usually fragmented, fading away with age, some of them keep snapping back, while most of them perish forever; such is the anatomy of a human brain. However, there is something indelible about that afternoon that failed to escape the defences of my neurons; it is fully etched in my memory, and I never fail at my attempts at recounting the scene. The afternoon was misty, and I was suitably clad for the weather. A few blokes practised their cricket in the nets in one corner of the ground. The grass was emerald green, finely trimmed and perfectly levelled to earth, and the groundsmen had laboured on it ceaselessly. Lawrence Gardens are one of the preserves we have from the British rule, and it is certainly one of the most striking cricket fields in the subcontinent. Its aesthetic expression is an extract from London's Kew Gardens: its Victorian-style pavilion is architecturally captivating, enhancing the decorum of the cricket field, and the sound of bat punching the ball adds that extra zing to its appeal. The pavilion is bounded by a fence on both sides that rings the ground from all four corners. The towering jamun trees lay siege to the park with their dense foliage, guarding the spectators crowding outside the fence from the pelting heat of the summer sun. In the mornings, at first light, huge armies of sparrows and dark crows flap their wings, distinctively settling into the tree branches; at dusk, bats replace them. At times, when the skies are cloudless and the sun commences its descent for the day, the jamun trees would cast a shade that would set parts of the playing field ablaze. A kaleidoscope of sunlight and shadows scatter the ground, creating a rare spectacle; for the spectators, the atmosphere makes for an ideal evening company. Behind the pavilion is a handsome population of trees, with a good profusion of bird life, forming small passages that all lead up to the Jinnah Library—a white marbled structure inherited from the British Raj. On that particular afternoon, I recall a large band of ebullient college girls assembled right by the pavilion, elbowing and pushing each other, their voice pitched as high as their enthusiasm—going bonkers, screaming their tonsils out. As I was constrained by my age, I could not distinguish the most alluring among that animated batch of the opposing gender. Two potbellied guards watched over, preventing the girls from mobbing the field. Subject of their attention was one man standing within in a few yards of the pavilion, although he was trying hard to guard his focus and keep his temper from flaring. That was my first live exposure to Pakistan's favourite son—Imran Khan. Imran, back in his cricketing days, was handled like a rock star; he had a revered following, and the media never tired of giving him coverage. For him going out unescorted would spell disaster as he would draw his fans to fever pitch. I vividly recount that Imran was warming up and prepping for a training session at the nets. Although he was almost forty years old, he appeared to be in great shape, with wide, well-built shoulders, ripped from all angles and without a trace of fat on him. His uncropped hair curled down his neck. At this time, he was wearing a crumply-looking practice uniform that contained a lose pair of bluish trousers and a V-neck polo sweater, hung over his unbuttoned shirt, luxuriantly exposing his overgrown chest hair. Momentarily, he would turn back to have a peek at the girls—a quick survey to determine if any of them was deserving of his approval. The unbuttoned version of Imran often had the babes swooning, leading them into a maddening chorus: '*oh my God kya admi hai*'—'oh my God what a man he is'. Unperturbed with all the attention he drew, Imran buried himself in the nets as he rammed in to hurl his good length deliveries, followed by some clean hitting with the bat. He practised, curled, hopped, bobbed, and weaved as if there was no tomorrow. His bowling had clearly lost its oomph and was hardly anywhere near its skull-crushing best. Fully aware that fast bowlers never make the grade at forty years of age, he had successfully converted into a punishing and prolific middle order batsman. Endowed with the responsibility of leading

Pakistan's cricket team, he would soon be departing to participate in the 1992 Cricket World Cup staged in the kangaroo continent—Australia.

Supplementing Imran's World Cup ambitions was his dream to set up a first-of-its-kind cancer hospital for the people of Pakistan. The motives were extremely novel: no one had ever, in Pakistan's four-and-a-half-decade-long existence, meditated over such prospects—a hospital where the poor and the hapless would receive free cancer treatment. The process of getting the hospital off the ground was excruciating, and for the purpose of my script, draws me into a discussion. As for the World Cup, it transpired that under Imran's command, Pakistan managed to clinch its first ever world title since the inception of one-day cricket in 1971—a notable feat by any measure. His World Cup winning speech to this day is one of the few consoling moments in Pakistan's disturbing history. The round sparkling crystal ball, firmly in the cup of his palms, was something to salvage from the wreckage. 'This trophy should go a long way towards fulfilling my hospital ambition,' pronounced an ecstatic Imran amid a jammed Melbourne Cricket Stadium. While at the time of Pakistan's world cup win, Imran had already managed to make significant progress on establishing the hospital; save for raising enough funds to keep the balance sheet of the institution on its feet, the rest seemed to be on track. By the early '90s, he had trooped up a good team of international experts who had the technical prowess to deliberate on such an experiment. His hospital dream gradually turned into a structure of steel and brick, and it would soon be suspending itself in the skyline of suburban Lahore, but all was not merry in the beginning.

Imran's maiden tryst with cancer's life-shattering impact was some time in the early years of the 1980s, when his mother, with whom he shared a special bond, was tragically diagnosed with the ailment. Until then, Imran lacked any serious stimulus for social reformation. Fully absorbed in his athletic pursuits, he was never personally exposed to the shocking vulnerabilities of life—the naked truth of death or the nitty-gritties of existence. Being a blessed kid, he grew up in a respectable neighbourhood in the heart of Lahore, and no sense of deprivation ever snapped him from the inside. Both his parents were cultivated individuals, bearing a vision for their family and giving uncompromising importance to education. Living off his father's decent stint as a successful civil engineer, Imran was sent to one of the most sought after English schools in the country—the celebrated Aitchison College Lahore—and was later packed off to Worcester for A-levels, followed by the prestigious Oxford University for graduation. At Oxford, he read for a degree in politics, philosophy, and economics, which was an equivalent of the Cambridge Tripos. In brief, Imran's parents had bestowed on him and his four spoiled-rotten sisters all the bounties that one could expect in a young country still finding its feet in the aftermath of independence. His family did not bask in the company of measureless wealth, but it was still a privileged set up by all means. Imran is an Anglophile of sorts, enamoured by the British society and its Victorian sophistication. However, this is not surprising at all as he had moved around in the best of British circles, throbbing the heart of women not only in Pakistan but also in England and the wider English-speaking world. Rubbing shoulders with the English prude, Imran had quickly gained a peerless reputation in Pakistan and India. All the razzle-dazzle and glamour had turned him into a heavyweight attraction, a crowd-pulling sensation, until one day, a tragedy befalling his family switched the course of his life. 'It was the most painful experience for me to see my mother go; the last three months of her life had a huge impact on me,' cuts a helpless-looking Imran years later. His mother was swiftly losing her resistance to cancer by the day. Seeing her enveloped in pain was beyond endurance. The episode was a blow to Imran's otherwise unbothered, easy-going life. There was nothing he could do to mitigate his mother's pain. The concept of pain management for the cancer stricken had not fully taken off in Pakistan. Fits of pain made it all too hard for everyone in the family to swallow. In *Pakistan a Person History*, Imran narrates an incident, which, to this day, continues to unsettle him:

It was sometime in the year 1985; Imran was scanning through his mother's progress with her doctor at Lahore's Mayo hospital. A man suddenly hurried into the room, with tears streaming down his eyes, looking terribly unsettled and carrying a few medicines which he handed to the doctor's assistant. 'Have I brought everything you prescribed or is there anything left?' he sobbed in a frail voice. The assistant pointed out to him the medicines that remained outstanding and also told him the cost. To which, in Imran's words, buried the man in despair and hopelessness as he stuttered out of the room. The incident peaked Imran's curiosity to explore what had gone wrong with him. The doctor disclosed: the man was a poor labourer and had come to Lahore from the North West Frontier Province—now KP; his brother ailed with cancer and was perhaps in an irrecoverable stage. He was spared a small territory in the corridor as the hospital did not have enough beds to fully accommodate all the victims; the labourer would work all day at a construction site nearby and save some money for his brother's medicines. The doctor also informed Imran that the whole city rather the whole country was replete with such cases.[1]

It was Imran's moment of truth as he remained muted in his chair, enveloped in thought. Here he was, the golden boy of the cricketing fraternity, with all the bounties in the world at his feet. Being a celebrated figure, money was never an issue: he could take his mother to the best of specialists round the world and had the best of networks to tap. Yet the vulnerability of the community down under had a humbling effect on him. He began to speculate about them, and there was suddenly a purpose to life—it was all adding up.

Despite Imran's unceasing attempts, he could not rescue his mother from the infirmity of cancer, with her embracing the perpetual silence, breathing her last in 1985. His mother's exit from the world firmed-up Imran's resolve to establish a proper cancer facility in the country—a hospital where free treatment will be sanctioned for the poor. Thus he set the ball rolling, with the hospital dream becoming his unconcealed obsession. He was now fully fixated on the project, though successively deflated by his close aides who kept nagging him on the prospects of the scheme, telling him that the task was beyond the radius of a private individual. People tried to drum sense into him, often calling him a bull-headed Pathan— Pathans being the spitting image of the Sikh nation in India and a long-time source of humour in the subcontinent. He was repeatedly lectured that it was the government's job to provide social services; it was their job to collect taxes; and it was their job to invest in the people. Pakistan already lagged behind in human development standards, and its health and education statistics painted a sorry picture in the early to mid-1990s. It is still one of the most pressing concerns for the government and draws a howl of objection. Presently, Pakistan ranks 146th in the HDI (Human Development Index) rankings of UNDP (United Nations Development Programme). Its infant mortality rates, life expectancy rates, prevalence of malnutrition among children, primary school enrolment ratios, and literacy rates are relatively much lower than its neighbours in the region. The economic model on which it rests its political foundations had either been faulty or the governments had been completely amoral towards its subjects. Well informed of his government's lamentable track record in public service delivery and knowing that turning to the state would not yield the results he wanted, Imran decided to step into the breach and take the matter upon himself. The pep-talking of his chums never struck a chord.

By 1988, Imran was struggling to elicit expert advice on how to line up a ground plan for something that ambitious. Establishing a trust and a board of governors, he called on a meeting and assembled nearly twenty top doctors in Lahore who would wrestle with the idea of proceeding further. To Imran's sheer disappointment, all the doctors, except one, vetoed the initiative, believing that setting up the hospital was one thing, but operating it without hitting any financial snags would be the real challenge. The doctors were not at fault in their assessment. No one had ever thought about a qualified cancer treatment centre in Pakistan, not even the government, who kept dispersing the concept on grounds that the country was fiscally incapacitated and economically on crutches. It is fairly reasonable to assume that these massive undertakings must come from the state in the form of country development schemes or vision plans, with sufficient budgets tied to them. Having a cancer hospital in a low- to middle-income country meant that all the equipment and technical expertise would have to be imported from abroad at exorbitant prices. Next to impossible it surely was. Imran had publicly promised the people that, come hell or high water, the hospital would see the light of day, so back-tracking on his word was entirely out of question. His credibility was at stake. Naysayers were aplenty, with people thinking of it as an inordinately ambitious enterprise—one that may never evolve into a visual form in a botched-up country like Pakistan. Imran himself recounts in *Pakistan a Personal History* one of his most awkward moments when his detractors were attempting to write-off the proposal:

> He was nibbling away at Shezan restaurant in Knightsbridge, London, with a few old friends. Some of them happened to be medical doctors. They needled Imran with technical questions about the project, trying to grill his medical grasp of the subject. They told him that he is a complete novice in this area and must not smother his years of hard-earned reputation. A sudden fit of anger swept across Imran's face as he blew his cool, going ballistic and almost came to blows with them, severing his ties and rumbling out of the restaurant. However, his raging temptations began to taper off, as he recovered himself and nibbled on. His *modus operandi* in life was plain simple: wonderful things in life are a work of perseverance and not luck.[2]

Imran had been doggedly pursuing his fundraising campaign at various platforms. The campaigns had not gathered much steam because, until the late '80s, he had mainly relied on his restricted retinue of friends or other well-endowed rooters from the jet set community of the Pakistani establishment. He had yet to witness the charitable potential of those on the breadline. By the early '90s, he had tapped the huge overseas Pakistani fraternity who had the requisite repertoire of subject knowledge. His coterie of faithful medical gurus was led by Dr Nausherwan Burki, one of his cousins from the maternal line who proved a great hand. At the time, Burki was a professor at the University of Kentucky hospital in the US; he was a man of enormous medical depth and, above all, had the audacity to take the challenge head on and stand by Imran in the heat of the moment. With Dr Burki on board, Imran's worries of getting the right men for the right job began to subside. Manning the hospital was no longer onerous as Burki had taken care of that. The second most teething concern was to rake in the funds needed. Many among Imran's cohorts kept imploring that supplying free treatment would spell disaster for his project and would still the whole effort. However, through some astute marketing advice, Imran launched a nationwide fundraising campaign, this time courting the ordinary citizens of the country. He cruised through the far stretches of the land, convoying from one town to another, visiting schools, colleges, universities, whooping into market places—no stone did he leave unturned—arduously eliciting support for his cause, being flattered by the crowds who responded to him in great numbers. It is during his outdoor expeditions that he really got the opportunity to blend with the people. They would come to him in scores, parting away with whatever grim fortune they had: women undecorated themselves by giving away their jewellery—a portion of their dowries—and children would compromise their strictly measured pocket money. Donations poured in with a big heart. Wherever Imran went, he was decked by a chaplet of flowers that he would remove for reasons of humility and demureness, only to battle the incoming downpour of fresh spongy rose petals loaded with lasting aroma. The clamour of the milling crowd was overwhelming, pelting Imran with unseen hospitality, with several telling him that they were not depositing their grants for him, but only to please their God, while others told him that they donated because they knew how terrible cancer could be.

Towards the summer of 1994, Imran had been endlessly journeying through not only Pakistan but also overseas, ensuring he knocked on as many doors as he could. People in Pakistan, as Imran realized and later quoted in many of his interviews, were lovers of charity and often lent profusely. They were a compassionate lot. I am a first-hand witness of their philanthropic DNA: I remember a few years ago, I rode out with my wife for a quick bite in downtown Islamabad, and we decided to munch away in our weather-beaten 1300 cc 1972 Volkswagen. I beckoned the waiters, strolling around outside the restaurant, and placed the order—two plates of biryani rice (one of the most popular South Asian cuisines with roots in the Mughal culture). Within a few yards of us stood a man, looking totally muffled, frail, and terribly incapacitated. He looked droopy, weakened by the vagaries of old age. By the look of him, one could make out that he was itching for a meal, giving away fleeting glimpses each time the waiter would come out of the restaurant carrying food for the customers. Although he would never say a word, the despair written on his face exposed his craving bowels. Once the waiter returned with our food, my wife advised me to order another plate for myself and give my plate to the old man. I waved at him, he cautiously legged towards us, we gave him the plate, and the despair on his face faded abruptly. He looked up in the heavens, thanked his lord, and left us with a sweet grin and a few light prayers: '*Allah apko lambi umar de*' ('May God bless you with a long life'). Moments later, we saw him sharing his food with four other men, who were feasibly Pashtun labourers working on construction sites in the vicinity. They worked harder than us and survived on a highly measured diet. So dumbfounded was I that my hunger pangs had vacated my belly. Decades of warring, economic exploitation, nepotism, corruption, and plutocracy have failed to erode sentiments of compassion in those who have stinted for survival. They train their bellies to resist their insufficiency. However, despite the most tragically repressed living standards, Pakistan has now managed to establish one of the world's largest social welfare networks. It was a heart-wrenching experience for me, and I am sure it must have been for Imran two decades before.

Within a few months, all the censuring was buried under the weight of Imran's fundraising success. This was clearly a trail-blazing effort, as Imran had kept his body and soul together through a near decade of persistent fund seeking. Shaukat Khanum cancer hospital, named after his mother, finally came to life in the winter of 1994 and became a model of success—in fact, it still is. 'Who ever walks into the hospital must be treated like a human being,' recorded a thrilled-looking Imran announcing his series of moral edicts at the opening ceremony of the hospital. He had an abiding affection towards the poor: 'Here at Shaukat Khanum, there shall be no distinction made between the opulent rich and the trampled destitute'. The audience exploded with an ear-popping round of applause. Such a petition calling to abandon differential treatment in society felt like music to ears. This buries me into an investigation. Why is it that ordinary civilians of Pakistan, venting off their years in gross deprivation, have such a prodigious desire for charity? Yet still, they, with all their destituteness and insignificance, manage to think about the community around them? Why was Imran able to muster up such a huge support, turning heads, and mobilising scores of ordinary men, women, and children, lumping them all together on a common platform? Surely, it was Imran's magnetic appeal as a medal-winning, celebrated household sportsman of the land that pulled the trigger and saved his campaigns from going belly up. Despite his Oxford grandeur, which oozed through every pore of him, people knew that he was genuine and certainly not in it for the moolah, or pointless journalistic publicity. Above all, years of keeping his nose to the grindstone, tossing his butt around the planet, resiliently quibbling about better medication for the poor, had warmed the cockles of the nation's heart. His perseverance was convincing enough, as people began to trust every word that escaped his lips. I trust it is this absence of faith in the system, this trust deficit that Pakistanis have with the agents of power, this disbelief that these petty souls are recurrently tainted with, never fully blending with their governments, who, in turn, have done little to bring any genuine relief to a large section of busted and sorely injured human lives. If one is economical with the truth, it would be fairly safe to assume that these agents of power, having their bums permanently pasted on important government positions, can hardly relate to the materially dispossessed: they do not know how it would feel to go without a meal in a day, investing their holidays in Europe and the Americas, where most of them wallow in the luxury of their large, princely, sprawling estates. Little of what they do or talk about resonate with the ordinary countrymen. Their taste in music, food, and entertainment is all western. Living like *rajahs* (monarchs), they have a relay of servants at their beck and call, tendering to their daily needs, and they go about in their ritzy, exquisitely priced roadsters to make a statement. Immune to the pains of inflation, these are the people who mostly belong to the thick-skinned political nobility. The landed aristocracy is another clique notorious for their ostentatious display of wealth. There hoity-toity manner is akin to those of the political elite. Cocooned with huge egos and kingly treasures, they go about throwing their weight on every state institution. When the country's institutions are heavily under the influence of a narcissist elite—merciless and uncompassionate—then economic activity only captures a minor section of the population. There are hardly any trickledown benefits for the community down under. This explains the flood of social issues inflicting the country. Pakistan is dubbed to have a huge economic potential with its massive human capital base, but that population instead of becoming its strength has become its excess baggage. The entire state machinery is wrought by a mafia. This undermines the ability of the state to collect revenue, implement reforms, create incentives for new industries to sprout, and, above all, invest heavily in developing a dynamic human capital through education and health programs. Anatol Lieven, a London-based journalist, paints an accurate picture of the system:

> Whenever a political party is sworn into power, it takes some short-term measures to pacify the electorate. These measures may come in the form of massive big ticket infrastructure projects with greater visibility. They usually don't have a long-term development agenda for the population they rule. Once into power, these individuals invest more time and money in rewarding those who supported the political party in its ascendancy to the highest offices. These rewards may come in the form

of tax breaks, infrastructure contracts and particularly state loans which are never paid back. The state loans are facilitated to the business elite in return for large favours. The infrastructure contracts given to favoured industrialists is a source of kickbacks and fat commissions. Politics has therefore become a business platform. The end result is that the common citizen of the country never appears in the equation—and remains under the thumb. The growth that takes off is not inclusive enough to benefit a wider section of the population. This explains the yawning gap between the rich and the poor.[3]

Private Citizens or NGOs attempted to fill that space, but were constrained by the authority they possessed over the land. Not being the enforcers of law, there was only so much they could do. Imran's hospital initiative supports my argument. Why is it that one man, only on the strength of his unflinching conviction and grit, managed to establish one of the finest state-of-the-art cancer facilities in the country, yet the government machinery remained reticent all those years? In situations like these, usually third world governments would try to dash social initiatives carrying a mass appeal because they view such developments as a threat to their own law-giving profile. Imran himself resents his experience with the government as he never received any serious backing from them during his fundraising operations. He concedes that, just as the hospital project began to show signs of maturity, most politicians in the country started perceiving him as a serious political opponent: his phones were tapped and he was tailed in public; undercover agents milled around his residence in Lahore; and Moeen Qureshi, a former World Banker and caretaker Prime Minister of Pakistan in 1993, had also tried to tap Imran's frenzied public following by offering him a ministerial rank. Imran brushed off the temptations. 'I know I am not meant to be a politician; I know my limitations full well,' confessed a reluctant Imran, candidly ruling out his prospects in politics. Instead, throughout the course of 1994, he was receptive to the bidding of the ISI front man General Hameed Gul, who wished to join hands with him to create a pressure group. The group was to work more like a civil society watchdog for the government. It never lasted long as Imran felt he was expected to perform the role of a doormat and had a bitter fall out with the general.

With Gul out of the scene, another clique of well-meaning retired generals, headed by Mujeeb-ur-Rehman (former information secretary of President Zia-ul-Haq and a compulsive talker), started making their pitch to Imran. Throughout the autumn and winter of 1995, Imran had a series of confidential meetings with the generals' emeritus in what proved to be his first brush with politics. No official announcement of a political party came, but Imran was more alert to the suggestion. All of a sudden, Imran had become so central to the two leading political parties in the country—the PPP led by Benazir Bhutto, Imran's Oxford colleague, and the PML-N under the supervision of Nawaz Sharif. The two parties kept deploying tactics to woo Imran. Attempts made by the PML-N leadership to win Imran's loyalty were ceaseless. At a function hosted by Sharif to honour the Pakistan cricket team on their return from Australia, journalist Richard Carlton buttonholed the premier: 'If Imran gets into your party, will he not be a nice addition to your team?' Sharif smirked a reply, twitching Imran by the sleeve, 'I had offered him a prospect long time back but I don't know why he refused. My offer is still valid though.' A restrained laughter ensued. Much to the chagrin of the Sharifs, Imran repeatedly repulsed their overtures. Known for his ready opinion—Imran always had a reputation for exposing his mind, mainly on matters to do with the politics of his country—he understood full well the flaws that abounded the political system of Pakistan and had been vehemently fulminating corruption like a maverick on the loose, even before he made his final call of gambling into politics. His ideals of statesmanship descended from the magnetic Muhammad Ali Jinnah, founder of Pakistan. He sought inspiration in the welfare state established by the great seventh-century Islamic caliph, the even-handed Umar bin Ibn Khattab, and he had an abiding passion for Iqbal's penetrative and stirring verses.

Having a mind of his own, he knew that only an honest leadership could purge the country of all its freckles. Ratifying the existing order would be tantamount to breaching his own conscience, and knowing that Sharifs were corrupt to the bone, he would have smothered his own credibility by joining forces with them. Imran had another option: one of his closest friends had advised him to court Benazir Bhutto and her husband, Asif Ali Zardari, as, at the time of the hospital inauguration, Benazir was in power. This option was equally dodgy as Benazir was also embroiled in a variety of corruption scandals. Zardari is now an icon of corruption in Pakistan, having money laundering cases pending against him in the Swiss courts. He is, as a friend scowled, 'the Al Capone' of Pakistan's muffed up politics, amassing a huge fortune during Benazir's two elected terms in the '90s. Not only that, Imran was rumoured of being romantically linked with Benazir during their days together at Oxford, a possibility that Imran curtly rules out. Imran's earlier playboy image had raked in considerable wealth for the media. Malicious reporting on his personal life has always sold like hot cakes. Rumour mills warmed up and began grounding out news of Imran's possible engagement with Benazir. His adventure with Benazir, however, was later spared further scrutiny and was suppressed by the media. Years later, Imran blasted all such accusations, burying the whispers and ensuring that they were just good friends. The controversy never had much impetus to begin with. Whatever happened in Oxford, there were clearly more reasons to keep a distance from the PPP contract. Rejecting both Sharif and Benazir meant that Imran had motives of his own, which, quite explicably, steamed up both the parties. It was during the latter part of his hospital campaigns that he realised how significant a role he could play in politics. Although his plans to actually set foot in politics were obscure, he was beginning to muse over the possibility. His connection with the people and his experience in dealing with the government was a rude awakening; he knew that there was an opportunity up for grabs, and if he managed to expend the same hospital vigour in his political aspirations, he would have had more momentum within the scene and would have been a force to be reckoned with. Moreover, the frustration among the educated urban youth ran fairly deep, with an outrageous flight of human capital from the country, fortifying Imran's belief that there was something tragically wrong. However, Imran must have failed to realise at the time that politics in Pakistan would be a ball-and-chain exercise. Taking on the status quo would prove to be a journey too rugged for him.

By the winter of 1995, Imran fully understood that the old structures of the political system would never let Pakistanis achieve their true social potential. The official launch of his party, however, had to wait for another few months, but he had sent the ball rolling and began evaluating résumés to establish his team of believers. Imran had yet another purpose to his life: he was now willing to grind his leadership skills in the trade of politics, defying the forecasting of most of his cricket contemporaries, who usually settled as well-paid cricket commentators. As the word of Imran's debut in politics began to toss around in the press, he once again faced a barrage of criticism as his detractors flooded him with admonishment. This time, they told him that politics was not his cup of tea. Imran, however, did not give a fig about them. The hospital project was another feather in his cap and his meteoric rise in the public eye had stepped up his determination. Obscurantism had given way to sound judgement. He had a few more miles to go before he could bury his head in the sand, and a few more fences to mend. The cricketer-turned-social activist would now battle it out on the political canvas—Pakistan's iffiest quarters.

2

Humble Beginnings

There comes a time when one must take a position that is neither safe, nor politic, nor popular but he must take it because conscience tells him it is right.

Martin Luther King Jr

'Don't you dare ever brood over prospects of bringing me a *gori* (white) daughter in law from England,' said Imran's mother. She had her concerns and fully understood Imran's flamboyance, his ready eyeballs for good-looking women and his impulsiveness more than anyone else, and she did not hold back her fears, while packing off her only son for studies to the British Isles. She thought it best to let Imran know that any attempt to dislodge her trust would not be favourably absorbed. Shaukat Khanum was a caring mother and loved Imran hugely. Being a South Asian mother, it was all but natural for her to fume at prospects of Imran's matchmaking in foreign lands. Twenty-four years later, when Imran contemplated at the idea of tying the knot to Sir James Goldsmith's and Lady Annabel's daughter, Jemima Goldsmith, the words of his mother must have reverberated during the dead of the night. With the pains of getting the cancer hospital off the ground behind him, Imran was now looking to move on. Running the hospital without any snags would obviously have been a sapping exercise, but by the summer of 1995, he had the backing of his well-endowed donors, somewhat easing the burden on his shoulders. Imran, as accounted earlier in the book, moved in the best of British circles, something which many other Anglophiles of our origin have failed to enjoy. He had made a lasting impress on the English minds. I remember how, during my initial days at Cambridge, I went about its gothic landscape, trying to absorb its smell of fresh breeze, the jingling of church bells, the occasional whiff of fresh beer, and the scattered fortresses of learning. There, right along the shores of the River Cam—famous for its punting—I bumped into my Hughes Hall lodge mate, Roger (his surname escapes my memory) and his parents. The moment I told them that I came from Pakistan, Roger's dad was rapid: 'Oh, you mean the land of Imran Khan.' I smiled, but before I could construct my sentence, he went on:

> You see when Rog was a toddler, I was posted to Sussex. One of our next-door neighbours was this charming, budding, page three starlet and I don't recall her name. On weekends Imran, then a mainstay of the Sussex cricket line up would pull up in his well-scrubbed car, all spruced up—dressed to kill, in an unwrinkled black avatar. The petite looking, scantily clad diva would scamper out of her lodge in her minis and the two would take their stance nudging and snogging each other before sputtering off for late night partying.

It was then that I realised that Imran's bedding of well-proportioned British girls was a more sellable tale for the English than his darting late in swingers. His off-the-pitch carnal exploits yielded more publicity than his in dippers on damp, grassy wickets could ever fetch. The English clearly accepted him with great fervour. In all honesty, many of our ancestors here were deeply obsessed with the English society. To them, the high world of the English aristocracy, peppered with a fine queen's accent would be God's greatest gift to humanity: English sounded crisp, new, and placed at a higher pedestal. Even now, those who handle the English language best enjoy high-point positions in the country. The English language and customs had a lasting impact on Hindustan. During the pinnacle of the Mughal rule, sometime in the seventeenth century, the British began making inroads into the subcontinent, and within half a century, they had virtually subjugated the entire region. Their culture was rousing and the technology they brought with them was a revelation. They were fully in their pomp and on the rise: universities and colleges of some repute sprang up; writers like Khushwant Singh and Rabindranath Tagore would exalt the British for giving them *angrezi* (English); and Jinnah, Nehru, Gandhi, and, more recently, the Bhuttos were all products of the British renaissance of Hindustan. The English spell was captivating, as the stubbly old Khushwant Singh believed that by reciting 'Ode to Nightingale', he could lodge into any English babe's heart. He assumed that a few doses of English poetry were enough to flatter an English girl, even going as far as expressively imagining what it would feel like to bed a *gori* woman—extensively fantasising over their bed behaviour. Such was the furore surrounding the English society in our desi minds. The frenzy persisted even after the partition of Hindustan. Those of us who managed to rub shoulders with the British elite were either looked upon with envy or exalted with pride. The English on the other hand behaved like royals, although not all of them—a few of them attempted to mingle, but there was never a genuine meeting of the hearts between the rulers and their subjects. Still, I recount that in my days in England as a student, I personally did not find them frigid at all, making many lasting friends within the English community and never am I reluctant in dispelling all those prejudices as concoctions or myths. Perhaps in my times things had changed—I trust for the better.

In a climate like that when Imran embraced the British society as one of his own, it positioned him in a different league altogether. His Oxford education and adventures with English women were finger-itching tales for the press in Pakistan. For the general public, it was a source of malicious gossip. The *fundoos* in Pakistan must have hated his escapades in England as he became the only international icon of a young country such as ours. Though never a lover of booze, and certainly not into cracking bottles at London's Soho square, Imran still enjoyed going to parties, meeting people, and occasionally shaking a leg. In one of such visits, while dipped in a heavy dose of discussion with Lady Annabel, Imran made a pass to a strikingly young, charming looking girl who happened to be Annabel's daughter—Jemima Goldsmith. Jemima had some presence. To those who knew her well, she was a great wit. She was tall and slender, with a high forehead, a firm chin, and a prominent cheek bone. Brought up under the care of her mother, she was tailor-made for the cameras. Gifted with extremely photogenic features, she was an attractive lass, exuding an air of sumptuousness. To top it all off, she was blessed by dense brown hair that enhanced her glaring beauty. At the time, she was leading an important life in England, enrolling at Bristol University to read for a degree in English literature. Imran and Jemima began exploring each other, reciprocating mutual attempts of flattery. Soon, they both drew closer. In a matter of weeks, their relationship invited gossip. For Imran, nightmares of his dead mother rebuking his affection for Jemima must have been a recurring theme until he gave his final declaration: the couple decided to advance their relationship without wasting much time and vowed to marry each other. Jemima was only aged twenty-one, while Imran was a seasoned man of forty-three. There was reluctance on both sides, but no serious obstacle came in the way. On 16 May 1995, in a two-minute ceremony in Paris, the couple tied the knot. Five weeks later, at Goldsmith's large mansion in London's Ormeley Lodge on the edge of Richmond Park, the couple observed another august ceremony. The ceremony was a close affair, restricted to a small coterie of friends. The pair would soon be departing for Pakistan where Jemima was expected to expire her remaining years. This was a huge undertaking for a young British girl, venturing into a land with a culture so different from her own strikingly liberal life style. Their marriage invited a lot of commentary not only in London, but also in Pakistan. Some of it was good, some of it not so good. The general concern in London was the survival of young Jemima in a world that was completely different from her own. Some in her circle dreaded at the prospects of her wearing a jet-black *burka*—a black dress that covers a woman's frame and all her charming assets from head to toe. Others wondered how Imran would be as a husband. Imran at the time was claiming to reinvent his long-lost interest in religion, openly discussing the Sufi aspects of his religion and how deeply he was influenced by them. This gave the English media more reasons to suspect the chances of their marriage carrying any real distance. A few London-based tabloids started branding Imran as the new *fundoo* on the bloc. Back home in Pakistan, the media was stunned, and the response was mixed. The more liberal newspapers did not create much fuss, while others saw in their marriage the possibility of a Zionist plot to take over Pakistan. This was the time when Pakistan was just fresh out of the Soviet war, and religious bigotry was rampant and the political elite had made a hash out of democracy. Jemima was half-Jewish, which fumed the more extreme sections of Pakistan's society. With Imran increasingly getting serious over his political ambitions, the media and the political elite vowed to target his marriage and, in the process, nip Imran's rudimentary political advancements in the bud. Despite all the media clamour, Imran and Jemima tried to honour their pledge and settle down in the former's ancestral house in Zaman Park, Lahore. The couple got on well together. A few searches on the internet yielded significant amount of coverage of the couple's early days in Lahore. Jemima in her interview to one of the western correspondents—dressed up beautifully in her brown *shalwar kameez*, with half of her head sheltered with a brown scarf and the other half lay bared for the cameras—spoke highly of her husband's conviction and verve. Imran inspired her: she adored his focus, seemingly coping well with Imran's household and even taking Urdu lessons to assimilate fully into the local culture.

Once all the rioting over Imran's marriage had somewhat abated, he was back in his groove. This was the time when Imran had firmly made up his mind to enter politics but did not know how to organise a qualified political party. His conviction got him through the hospital campaign, but here the challenge was tougher, as in politics, he felt out of his zone. 'Pakistan's politics is a dirty world,' one of his friends from the Aitchison College had repeatedly cautioned him. His mates from the cricketing fraternity were also stunned by his decision, while many others were petrified at the possibility of him being rattled by his opponents. It was widely believed that politics was surely not his territory. Observing Imran's life from a distance, two versions come to mind. Firstly, Imran had an explosive temper—he still has that. He was not very calm in dealing with hordes of people around him, often retiring to the mountains in the north of Pakistan to stay in complete solitude except from the company of exotic birds and dense forests, and the mountains fascinated him. He is a good pen too and loves his reading and writing, and by the mid-1990s, he had already scribed a couple of books. A reticent personality, he liked to stay within himself and did not let anyone draw too close to him. This made for a poor case for someone who dared to challenge the political status quo in a country like Pakistan, a country where you require the gifted oratory of Zulfiqar Ali Bhutto to charm the audiences and stir them towards you. His sisters would have contended him, drawing the line after his hospital was up and running. Secondly, Imran was not known for his oratory skills— he was certainly not cut out for addressing scores of people or leading a populist movement. Public preaching was something he had to hone to stay firmly rooted in politics and keep himself afloat. Most orators in Pakistan have their roots in the Urdu-speaking culture that bloomed in the areas around Delhi, Agra, and Lucknow in Uttar Pradesh province, now in India. One needs a certain measure of softness and crisp language skills to woo the audience, and Imran did not have that. He was cold and brusque at times, brushing off his fans whenever they broke into a frenzy and hunched upon him. He obviously relished public attention, like any well-known celebrity would, but he valued his solitude far more than any other privileges of life. Public speaking is a skill and one is usually born with it. Abraham Lincoln's Gettysburg address in 1863, during the height of the American Civil War, was only a few minutes long, but it is still revered for its lasting impact, it is still a subject of discourse at American colleges and universities. Martin Luther King Jr's 'I have a dream' speech altered the fate of the black populace, who had been battling for their rights in America for over a hundred years. He created waves that still reverberate in the political circles around the globe. Malcom X was another gifted speaker. Winston Churchill, with his fiery wartime speeches, infused an unmitigated spirit in the supporters of the Allied forces during the Second World War. He would charge up his audiences and bring them to fever pitch, and his speeches are widely praised to this day. Churchill handled his speeches with such precision that US President John F. Kennedy said that Churchill mobilised English and sent it to the battlefield. Endowed with all the stimulating powers, Churchill controlled his audiences to the limit possible. In my part of the world, we had Jinnah, the founder of Pakistan, whose speeches are still exalted. An astute lawyer, Jinnah was a wonderful communicator, and conversationalist. Zulfiqar Ali Bhutto was yet another political figure gifted for giving pompous speeches, stirring the population in droves and driving them into a chorus. His oratory is perhaps the only redeeming factor of the political party that he founded in the late 1960s. As for Imran, he lacked this very basic ingredient to launch himself into a political career. During his hospital campaigns, Imran would journey round the far reaches of his country to raise funds. Inevitably, he would find himself with a mic in his hand, expected to announce the purpose of his campaigns and the cause he attempted to champion. He would speak too timidly, causing a few giggles in the audience. In one of his partisan speeches he gave in Lahore, sometime in 1996, at the opening of his party's first office, his performance was dreadful: the speech was full of interludes of excuses made for having a bad throat. There were too many pauses in between and hardly any authority when he spoke against the malfeasance of the status quo. The thought of a public address brought him nightmares and a bowlful of sweat. This was a bothering situation as he had threatened to blow the lid of corrupt politicians, announcing his commitment towards the people, who in turn expected wonderful things from him. Despite his few misfits for the job, the climate in which he launched his political pilgrimage was ably suited to his idea of a nationwide drive against corruption. Imran officially launched his political party on 25 April 1996, naming it '*Pakistan Tehreek-e-Insaaf*' (Movement for Justice Party). Including him, there were in total seven founding members. The choice of the party's name was well-reasoned, and the intuition behind it, as I infer and mildly conclude from the party's preamble, bears the courage of Imran's conviction:

> While the elite of the country moved around ravaging the law of the land, looting and plundering the national kitty with impunity, no systems under the sun could hold them accountable or try them. The courts and all institutions of accountability fell under the weight of the debauched elite. Corruption had killed all sense of national responsibility amongst those in power—amassing fortunes within a span of a few years. The poor on the contrary were in an appalling state. And if the poor, out of their utter frustration committed even a petty crime, they would be sent to jail and left there to rot for years. Imran pushed for a movement, with this tragic public slaughter in mind.[1]

The idea was tempting and the timing was spot on. 'There shall be no peace for the wicked,' warned Imran repeatedly. No one before Imran had ever damned corruption, fulminating it and so vociferously using it as part of his campaign to rouse the electorate. It was a step in the right direction;

however, it would be some years before his movement really picks up any momentum. The entire power structure at the time was under the sweeping control of the two leading political syndicates of the country, the PPP and the PML-N. It is imperative that we understand the nature of Pakistan's democracy back in the years that preceded Imran's movement calling. This we must do to comprehend the hash some politicians had made out of the democratic order, and also to get the hang of the climate in which Imran found himself.

In the winter of 1988, a vast section of the society was somewhat petrified at the news of General Zia-ul-Haq dying in a plane crash. The crash not only killed Zia, but also killed the US Ambassador to Pakistan Arnold Lewis Raphel. People to this day see in their death a working of a serious conspiracy. The conspiracy was not allowed to ripen further as the authorities rapidly inferred that there were issues in the engine of the plane. In December 1988, Pakistan was back to its democratic ways, elections were held, and the PPP achieved a sizeable majority. Zulfiqar Ai Bhutto's first born, Benazir Bhutto, arrived in her convoy at the Islamabad secretariat as the first female Prime Minister of Pakistan, setting a precedent for the entire Muslim world. This development invited good press from around the globe. Her rise to power was widely celebrated as people thought that this could be it. She had an educated shoulder on her heads, and her Oxford and Harvard background could mean that Pakistan was in wise hands. Sadly, few months into her government and Ms Bhutto was already in the news for all the wrong reasons: she wanted control over finance; her chief counsel was her husband, Asif Ali Zardari, a Sindhi land baron who spent his teenage strolling around his father's cinema house in Karachi, sozzled up, and wasting away his youthful loins on the best harlots in town. His biggest qualification was that he could never go straight and was capable of humiliating his opponents in every way possible. So, a long period of turmoil began as the two partners got into their groove. They started violating the constitution and committed corruption at a scale that Pakistan had hardly ever seen before. This forced the President of Pakistan Ghulam Ishaq Khan to deploy his constitutional powers and dissolve the National Assembly. Benazir was gone by November 1990, with charges of corruption, nepotism, and despotism levelled against her. Her husband was bundled into jail, whisked straight out of the parliament. Another bout of elections was held that year and this time Nawaz Sharif's party PML-N had a sweeping majority. Benazir was asked to confine herself in the opposition. Sharif, another important character in the political set up, waggled his way up to the highest office in the country. He was the first Prime Minister from the industrial elite and, since his inception, seemed to hunger for absolute power. Sharif was of Kashmiri descent, and he was the first child of his father—a steel baron with pre-partition roots in the Indian state of Punjab. This family was fond of a large life, and above all other affinities, they relished eating. Grapevine suggests that they also love women. Sharif had already tasted success by being the Chief Minister of Punjab during Benazir's first term in office. His flunkeys in Punjab behaved like the army of Genghis Khan, wielding unmitigated power in the country's largest province. He even tried to gain a two-thirds majority in the parliament to strike off the constitutional powers of the President, but his attempt to accomplish this did not gain much backing. He, much like his predecessor, was also accused of snooping with the state machinery and trying to amass a fortune unknown to man. Always wanting to have his own ways, Sharif even bypassed the will of the President on certain matters of state importance. The President could not stomach his excesses and once again tapped his constitutional perks to get rid of him in October 1993, advertising for yet another election; this was the third election in five years of democratic hodgepodge. Clearly, the politicians were not acting responsibly and making a mishmash of their authority. Things went haywire, with Benazir rising to power a second time. Sharif and Benazir were seemingly taking their turns, and although they publicly displayed retribution towards each other, there were reasons to believe that they collaborated behind closed doors.

While many expected Benazir to have learned from her misadventures during her first term, she trooped inside the parliament along wither her groom, resuming their ravaging from where they had left. Her second term turned out to be a greater nightmare, and corruption scandals against them crashed through the ceiling. The investigation agencies of Pakistan and Europe managed to unearth important documents, which traced the couple's indulgence in laundering millions of dollars into Swiss bank accounts. These records revealed misadventures of monumental proportions. Most of the couple's energy was spent in plotting their criminal adventures, doling out corrupt infrastructure contracts in return for kickbacks. How on earth were the poor people to benefit from any of this? The revelations from their underworld ventures are aplenty, but a few come abruptly to mind. In a bid to support the gold industry of Pakistan, the couple courted one Middle Eastern goldsmith, granting him a monopoly to import bullion into Pakistan, in return, raking up kickbacks to the tune of roughly $10 million paid into their Citibank accounts, allegedly maintained by companies owned by Zardari. Zardari and his associates spared no opportunity to rob the state treasury. In another revelation, the infamous couple was accused of generating $1.5 billion through kickbacks and state loans in virtually every stream of government activity. Western publications, including *The New York Times* and *The Sunday Times*, girded up and cannoned heaps of allegations towards the controversial pair in power. Zardari was notorious for raping the system and was a terror of sorts, particularly in Sindh—his long-time fortress. Call him Al Capone or the gilded multibillionaire Escobar of Pakistani politics, Zardari has been the ultimate racketeer, scooping the national kitty, godless to his bone and always on top of his game. In all my born days, I have perished the thought of seeing him rule the roost, licking from the plate of privilege until it is gleamingly tidy. To make matters worse, Murtaza Bhuto, Benazir's younger brother, was brutally massacred, point blank, along with his convoy of around six people in front of his house. The police stood there unfazed, watching the spectacle with cold eyes. That name, Zardari again, was tossed around, rumoured to be the man behind the killings. However, the real causes remain inscrutable. Corruption, racial violence, abuse of state authority, drug trafficking, human trafficking, poverty, street crime, and dampened economic prospects were some of the problems that Pakistan was left to deal with. Compounding these was another party called MQM, controlled by a Hindustani import from the UP province, Mr Altaf Hussain. Hussain had allegedly turned Karachi into a blood bath, instigating a 'never-seen-before' communal violence in the streets of Karachi—the entire city was petrified.

This was the climate in which Imran Khan had unfortunately landed in, one as horrid as a cyclonic Bay of Bengal. It is no wonder that his friends repeatedly harped that politics in this land of the pure is a game too impure to fiddle with. Here was Imran, fully girded up to launch an offense through a nationwide movement, with absolutely no idea on how to organise the party at the grass root level. He was buoyed by years of heroism as a cricketer and social activism through his hospital project. These were the only accomplishments he had to support his foray into politics—a résumé not good enough if you do not have an infinite fortune to do your bidding in Pakistan's bungled up politics. Politicians backed with booties from a despotic tenure in the centre have the privileges to buy off large swathes of unschooled rural population, and Imran lacked these credentials. His only chance was to push for a movement. By the summer of 1996, Imran started campaigning in major urban centres all over the country. By the autumn of that year, the country was in the grip of serious rallies, mainly prompted by the religious parties against the corruption scandals of Benazir and her controversial consort. This lured President Farooq Leghari, handpicked by Benazir, to make use of his constitutional permits and sack the government. For the second time, Benazir ended short of her full constitutional term. Fresh elections were planned in early 1997. Imran, being the quintessential believer in his theme of justice and parity, saw in these events the opportunity for his party. Yet this was deemed too overambitious, considering that his party still operated at a fairly embryonic stage. PTI also did not have enough cash in its bank to sustain a proper election campaign. As Imran was deprived of any serious grass root presence and organisational reach, he would have to ride his volunteers' coattails to keep the campaigns rolling. In brief, Imran's party was not yet ready to take on the larger players in the game. Elections in Pakistan can be a costly affair as campaigns demand a lot of expense. The execution of the Election Day in particular is vital. For once, the ignorant, unlettered electorate is handed a kingly reception—escorted into buses with care and fed a plateful of exquisitely cooked local cuisine. It is common knowledge that the polling agents are subjected to the temptations of bribery, and those who resist are either abducted or killed. All this may happen under the nose of the law enforcement agencies, who for their own share, dust the story under the carpet. All this Imran knew, and he could foresee a crushing defeat in his first public examination as a politician. Imran's views on instigating any serious policy reforms were also vague. He did speak doggedly against corruption but lacked depth, once expected to produce a comprehensive course for the future of the country. Inexperience had taken a toll on him, and many in his party had advised him to withdraw from the elections as a defeat could bring about a permanent end to his political prospects. Unaffected by the proposal, he went in with great self-belief. Sadly, the results were unsurprising; Imran was subjected to a disgraceful routing—the drubbing was dreadful. Out of a total of 207 seats of the National Assembly, PTI failed to win a single one. By the press accounts, PTI could only secure anywhere between 130,000 to 160,000 votes. This was less than 2.2 per cent of the electoral force of roughly 19.3 million. PML-N emerged with a sweeping majority and formed the government for the second time in less than eight years. The loss was indeed a learning experience for Imran as few of his party associates jumped ship. They were perhaps misled by the huge crowds they saw at Imran's election rallies. Imran later conceded that his defaulters were perhaps never with him for the long haul.

Imran's campaign, much like his election results, never really made an impact. His rallies, barring a few, never got off to a rollicking start. That election year, Imran seemed to have fallen out of favour with his God— not only did the election results panned out worse than he had expected, but the months preceding the election were torturous. PML-N, together with other opposition parties, had launched 'a defame Imran' campaign to thwart his election ambitions, and their attempts to ridicule him bore fruit. They started by targeting the celebrity couple's marriage, labelling it as a Zionist scheme to destabilise Pakistan. They even went as far as publishing a blurry copy of £40 million cheque in a local English tabloid, supposedly doled out by James Goldsmith and bound for Imran to fund his electioneering. This stirred a negative sentiment in the public, even sparking protests outside the couple's residence in Lahore—a nerve-racking experience for Jemima. Never before had she witnessed such shredding of one's self esteem and character. She was petrified and Imran was furious. 'Because I was taking on the corrupt elite, my wife became a soft target,' stated a revolted and huffed-up Imran. Imran's past playboy image was another soft target. By the government, Imran was a fun-loving epicure, who considered himself peerless and a careless public seeker who was also anti-Islamic. His escapades with foreign women conveniently became an easy target in a Muslim majority country. The Jewish conspiracy was itself enough to soil his image. Other than this personal onslaught, reports of rigging on the Election Day by the usual suspects was a final nail in the coffin. Imran was not ably equipped to handle an offense of that measure, especially at a time when his party was not even fully grounded in the system. A twelve-member team of 'The International Progress Organisation (IPO)', entrusted with the responsibility of monitoring the elections, came out with some disturbing findings. By their account, one gentleman from Karachi, a polling agent named Muhammad Haneef, was severely pounded by unknown assailants. Tragically, Haneef failed to survive the thrashing and died. In another incident, a bus full of PTI supporters arrived at a polling station only to be told that they should return an hour later; once they did, they found that the polling station was shut down, showing no trace of life. Administrative mishandling was widespread, undermining the state's responsibility to ensure free and fair elections.

The political culture in Pakistan demands that the ruling party must continue to focus its energies on disgracing the opposition, and in the most atrocious of manners. A year down the elections, Imran and Jemima were planning to move into their own residence, pursuing site selection for an expansive villa perched high on top of a hill, a few miles in the outer wilderness of Islamabad proper. The couple finally saw an opportunity to move out of their ancestral house in Lahore and have a life of their own. While they were in the process of confining themselves to the foot hills of the Himalayan range, Jemima had already started to think about casting her aesthetic spell on the house. Bani Gala is a small town on the outer edges of the capital city; at the turn of the century, it was nothing but a coterie of sparse villages, a dense forest, and a convergence of birds of a varied species coming together in splendid harmony—it was wild life at its purest. I remember visiting the area as a teenager; it was a handsome-looking forest, extremely informal in character. There was an abundance of wild existence, free from human infiltration. On a windless sunny day, I remember the forest would be as silent as the grave. Nights were dead and ghostly. As the climate was variable in nature, monsoon breezes would cause the trees to wiggle their branches and dance. Winters were blue and full of frost. Imran and Jemima are wild life enthusiasts and loved the virginity of the place. The hill they planned on acquiring overlooked Rawal Lake, which stretches miles into the heart of Islamabad. The lake was set against a background of Margalla hills. Watching birds descend on the lake surface was no ordinary spectacle. Even more captivating was the view of the sun just as it dipped below and went into hiding behind the cover of low mountains, leaving behind a cloud of evening mist that hovered over the city. For a moment, it would seem as if the sun would drown in the lake. Directly beneath the hill was a small valley, naturally draped with lofty mature eucalyptus trees that invaded the lake shore from all directions. Some of the trees had their protruded branches prostrate over the lake water. Certainly a sight for sore eyes. This was the company that the esteemed couple envisaged on keeping. Jemima took keen interest in the designing of the house. Fully preoccupied with her aesthetic ambitions, she started visiting vendors to buy some material for the construction. In one of these visits, she purchased some blue tiles for the house. At the time of purchase, the vendors informed her that the tiles were manufactured in Pakistan and bore no archaeological significance. A few months down the line, Jemima decided to ship the tiles to London with the hope of giving a Persian feel to London's Ormeley lodge. However, to Jemima's disgust, the tiles were scrutinised and held by the customs officials in Lahore, swiftly drawing to a conclusion that exporting artefacts bearing a heritage value was a crime as per the local law. They suddenly discovered that the tiles dated back to the reign of Mughal Emperor Shah Jahan, and they had adorned the courtyard of his wonderful mosque in Thatta Sindh. The authorities latched onto the opportunity and soon got Imran hooked up in a court case. The accused was now embroiled in a wasteful exercise, attending hearings incessantly at the Lahore high court. The accusation carried a seven-year imprisonment penalty if proven guilty. This was a deliberate attempt to sabotage Imran through his wife, and it proved too much for Jemima—the experience was nerve wrangling. First, she had to put up with all the pre-election onslaught and rallies around the theme of her being a Jewish conspirator, followed shortly after by the fuss over the tiles. She soon left for London to regain herself. Meanwhile, Sharif went about finding the constitutional legitimacy to subdue the President. He did not want a repeat of 1993, but the flabby-looking steel baron somehow gets it wrong. This time he took on the COAS (Chief of Army Staff), the dapper-looking General Pervez Musharraf. Nawaz and Musharraf were already at loggerheads over the issue of Kargil war with India since April 1999. Tensions between them pitched to boiling point in October, when

Musharraf was hopping back to Pakistan after concluding a foreign trip to Sri Lanka and learned that he has been surprisingly suspended by the premier. In a bid to bide some time, Musharraf's plane was not even allowed to land in Karachi, forced to circle the air space for a few minutes—by some press accounts, it was running out of fuel. Now, you do not rouse the COAS of the Pakistan Army with such an unwise dispensation—that was unbecoming. Musharraf, without wasting much time, ordered his troops to raid the premier's office. In a matter of hours, Sharif's administration was history, with him and his entourage rushed to jail. It was 12 October 1999, a day of mourning, not so much for the people of Pakistan, but most certainly for the democratic elite who saw their eleven years of good living smothered once again by the armed forces. Pakistan was back to its garrison ways. As for Imran, he was relieved from the political molestation of Sharif. A military takeover would give Imran's wrangling a new turn; his party was young, already dampened by the humiliation it suffered in the 1997 elections, but Imran remained as zippy as ever, elevating himself and plodding on in what would prove to be an extremely trying journey ahead.

3

Out of the Frying Pan, into the Fire

I am not bound to win, but I am bound to be true. I am not bound to succeed, but I am bound to live by the light that I have. I must stand with anybody that stands right, and stand with him while he is right, and part with him when he goes wrong.

Abraham Lincoln

The bumbling Sharif had once again teared apart his political prospects through his careless handling of the nation's foremost commander. Sharif was like an ox going to the slaughter—few of us wondered that it was the end of his story. A cultivated political scientist who taught at Government College University, Lahore, forecasted Sharif's choking at the gallows. That prophecy, however, never came to pass as Sharif escaped his tryst with the afterlife by being confined to a hard-walled jail in Attock—a small city located close to the point where Punjab snogs with KP. Musharraf, now firmly in control of the scheme of things, had kept Sharif in breathing condition until he figured out what to do with him. More important matters begged for his endorsement.

Five days after Sharif's fall from grace, Musharraf announced his treatise, suggesting solid ingredients for the economy's turn around—like most leaders in Pakistan do soon after taking charge of the control towers in Islamabad. Going through the same motions as the governments of years past, Musharraf created a lilt of economic urgency. By him, the country was in need of repair as he reminisced in his personal account:

We stood at the brink of being declared a failed state, a defaulted state, or even a terrorist state. Economic growth had come to a standstill. The central bank was bankrupt, with only ten days' worth of imports in foreign exchange remaining. Nawaz Sharif had to freeze private foreign currency accounts after $11 billion of deposits went unaccounted for. Over one trillion rupees, around $20 billion, had been invested in development over eleven years, but there was almost nothing to show for it except solitary 230-mile (370-kilometre) highway. Sectarian terrorism was on the rise, with Shias and Sunnis being killed regularly. The police were totally demoralised, lawlessness was rampant, and the law courts were overwhelmed. The public was also demoralised and beginning to display signs of hopelessness in the future of the country. The people had lost their honour and pride in being Pakistanis.[1]

There is little denying of Musharraf's assessment of the economic mishmash. The country was indeed robbed bone dry and the corruption we witnessed in the eleven-year democratic rule made even the angels blush. Musharraf presented his seven-point patchwork:

1. Reviving national confidence.
2. Strengthening the federation.
3. Restore investors' confidence.
4. Ensure law and order.
5. Rescue state institutions.
6. Transfer authority to the grass roots.
7. Upgrade accountability standards.

In addition, the general was bent on stripping the robbers of their spoils. In other words, baring their lousy bottoms and spanking them hard until they turned blue. Musharraf's maiden brush with state level governance suggested that he was genuine—establishing NAB, which would be entrusted with the gall to take on the narcissist elite. NAB was navigated under the lordship of General Muhammad Amjad, Musharraf's trusted cohort and a reputably *saaf admi* (clean man). Other point-scoring remedies of the general included establishing a national reconstruction bureau; establishing a local government ordinance to strengthen the institutions down at the grass roots; and giving considerable liberty to the electronic media—unlocking the sector's potential and paving the way for the setting up of private TV channels. Within a few months, broadcasting limits of the country transcended the pointless tittle-tattle of the long-time state television: PTV. The media market sprouted a variety of options. Chief among them were late night talk shows on current affairs, perhaps more dramatic than the usual mother-in-law–daughter-in-law scuffling shown in local plays.

Imran viewed these developments as a welcoming change in Pakistan. His initial assessment of Musharraf was of a man who was purposeful and most importantly hard-nosed to the bone in his dealing with second-rate politicians—legislators who had been racketeering their way up in the parliament. In Musharraf, Imran saw someone who would lay the course for Pakistan to have genuinely stronger institutions and a democracy friendly system. Musharraf spoke vociferously of his intentions to plant a legitimate democracy, a system where all hanky-panky was brought to audit and the politicians elected were barred from any fooling around. All this resonated well with Imran's antidote for a fast-decaying Pakistan. The press began calling Imran the new accomplice of the Pakistani Military establishment. The incessant yakking of the reporters was soon repulsed by Imran as he provided his rationale of supporting the general. Speaking candidly to the reporters in Lahore, Imran gave his two cents:

> The reason why we are backing General Musharraf is because we hope that he will keep the crooked politicians at bay. Neither the election commission nor the apex courts in the country have been able to achieve that. We have had four elected governments since 1988 and each time they have been dismissed on charges of corruption. So, I hope Musharraf manages to keep these phony politicians out of the electoral process.[2]

This was a period in which Imran and the general had a number of behind-the-curtain meetings to pan out ways of mutual cooperation. To ingratiate himself with Imran, Musharraf began soliciting benefactors for Shaukat Khanum Hospital in Lahore. In a few months, Musharraf registered himself as a good Samaritan in Imran's books. What gave Imran hope was Musharraf's repeated statements of relinquishing state authority and retreating to the barracks in due course.

With Pakistan being supervised by khaki-uniformed, puffed-up generals for most of its existence, any political leader found extoling the army was rewarded with an unforgiving scuffle. As Imran publicly went about confessing his exclusive membership of Musharraf's Coffee-Klatch, he was invariably summoned by the media to clarify his position. Hooked up in a heated wrangling with a well-known journalist in early 2002, Imran expounded, beginning with a refresher course on Pakistan's botched-up electoral politics:

> People have lost faith in our democratic system. The voter turnout in the elections of 1970 was 60%; it subsided to 50% in the elections of 1988 before retreating to a shameful 20% in the elections of 1997. This only shows that people are fed up of the conventional political parties and are pleading for change. We are supporting Musharraf because he is hitting all the right buttons and making all the right noises. From day one, he

has been fulminating the incorrigible breed of politicians our system has manufactured over the years past. If I had an appetite for power, I had all the overtures on my plate to satiate my hunger; Zia courted me for a ministerial position in his cabinet and Nawaz Sharif offered me thirty seats in the National Assembly at a time when my party was less than six months old. I give no hoot about people who scrutinize my loyalty to the country. Musharraf's honesty is the only reason why we are backing him.[3]

My own mind, however, reads the situation differently. Pakistan's constitution has been the most tampered piece of script, sustaining all possible modifications conceivable. All political parties celebrate this document as their Old Testament, yet when in power, they infringe its various clauses to justify their mishandling of the national till. This constitution was promulgated on 14 August 1973 by the ungainly land baron Zulfiqar Ali Bhutto, widely known for his snooty Oxford manners and his brusque temperament towards his political opponents. Sadly, the constitution lost its virginity in no time. Four hours after it was hatched, and even before the ink dried, Bhutto, through a gazette notification, stripped the people of Pakistan of their constitutional rights by having scores of his opponents seized and locked up in cells throughout the country. Between 1973 until his slump from authority in 1977, Bhutto had enforced a spate of amendments in the constitution. Years later, his petulant daughter, Benazir, and her co-conspirator, Nawaz Sharif, fiddled with the constitution at an even a higher rate. In a brazen violation of the constitution in 1997, Sharif even had his rowdy hoodlums scale the walls of the Supreme Court, when the Chief Justice of Pakistan had the audacity to summon the Prime Minister for a hearing. All the fuss about democracy went out of the window. Then, in the autumn of 1999, came Musharraf, in his khaki-printed glad rags, bearing the cockiness of a typical Pakistani general, once again demeaning the land's official book of conduct. Through his provisional constitutional order, the general had himself exonerated from the sin of thrusting a *coup d'état*—Pakistan's fourth official tryst with martial law. Musharraf had his team of brown-nosing judges on call to sanction all his moves without an audit. Surely, he was no different from the dictators of the years past, and clearly Imran had hurled a half volley, as they say in cricket—he had erred sorely in his assessment of the general's ground plan. His untamed impulse often landed him in trouble. The more gallant Punjabis among his ranks invariably adjudicated him as the bull-headed Pashtun—the one who acts without reason. The good thing about Imran, which enabled him to recover from his awkward fluffing, was his good nature to take a stock of his own foibles. A trait that eluded most politicians in the country.

Musharraf's first two-year spell in Islamabad had yielded a small cabinet of no more than ten people. Some of the major portfolios went to men who knew their trade well. The Finance Ministry went to Shaukat Aziz—a tastefully dressed international banker, fully cognizant of the local economy and the challenges it weathers. The Commerce Ministry was given to Razzaq Dawood—an astute businessman who had expanded the tentacles of his enterprise to the oil rich Gulf States. Dr Ishrat Hussain, the Pakistani version of Alan Greenspan, was to take charge of the banker's bank—the State Bank of Pakistan.

In April 2002, Musharraf presented himself for his first public examination through a referendum. His appeal in the public eye had suddenly taken off. An overwhelming 70 per cent of Pakistanis voted in the general's favour. This meant that Musharraf could extend his lawgiving in the centre for another five years—this time as the president of the country. Anti-dictatorship clamour rented the heavens, calling for Musharraf to divest himself of his military uniform should he intend to pursue his presidential occupation. Musharraf dismissed all that hurly-burly as utter nonsense and was determined to implement his reform agenda. To do that, he had to think through his options in first dealing with the Sharif family. Option one could possibly have been a high-profile trial of the steel barons, but that bore a risk of a damaging outbreak in Punjab, Sharif's long-time fortress. Option two was more judicious: rusticating the entire lot of them to a foreign land and prohibiting their political operations for at least a decade. Being in the middle of Sharif's fate-sealing puzzle, King Abdullah of Saudi Arabia offered to host the Sharif family. Musharraf, without wasting much thought, endorsed his majesty's proposal and sent the Sharifs packing. With Sharifs out of the scene, the stage was set for Musharraf to begin surveying the leftover crop of politicians in the country. The game plan was then to fortify his grip on the system by launching a political party that would compete in the elections of October 2002. The president was willing to throw in his lot with the Chaudhrys of Gujrat and have them launch their party, PML-Q, in August 2002. The few months prior to the elections had enduringly strained Imran's relationship with Musharraf. The general had always thought of Imran as an upright, above-suspicion politician, and felt that Imran's nascent political career was in need of a godfather, as is normally the case in Pakistan, where military regimes extend their terms in the centre by implanting new politicians in the parliament: Ayub Khan, Pakistan's debut martial law administrator, had nurtured Zulfiqar Ali Bhutto under his wings; Zia presented us with Nawaz Sharif; and now Musharraf was reinventing the wheel by rearing the Chaudhrys of Gujrat, and possibly Imran as well. Years later, the forbidden Musharraf, now in London, expiring his remaining years in exile, declared his version of negotiations with Imran:

As we neared the elections of 2002, I was assessing Imran's vote bank. As per our evaluation of Imran's electoral appeal, he would have raked up not more than 8 to 10 parliamentary seats. Imran however overestimated his prospects and was expecting a ground swell, collecting a tally of nearly 100 seats. I told him that he was too optimistic and that his only chance to survive was to subscribe to our coalition government. But he remained mum over my overtures as our paths diverged.[4]

Imran's version of his divorce with Musharraf was more radically sarcastic. 'The Generals are mentally impaired to size up the requirements of a democratic system,' scoffed Imran, appearing to be in a light mood while addressing the Asian society in New York, primped in a nicely pressed black suit—his only alternative when he was asked to put on something other than his snow white *shalwar kameez*. He confessed to be in error in his flagrant backing of the general. Generals, he felt, were too mechanical in their approach towards running the country—it was simply not one of their fortes. What really damaged Imran's affection for Musharraf was the general's endorsement of the Chaudhry gang. The Chaudhrys, as per Imran, were no different from the Sharifs, likewise having a history of schooling under military regimes. Imran's version is more sellable. The most prominent predecessor of the Chaudhrys of Gujarat was a sallow-complexioned man, sporting jet black whiskers—Chaudhry Zahoor Elahi. Zahoor Elahi for most part of his early life sulked at his destiny as an ordinary third-rate police constable in Amritsar (now in India). His fortunes went through a sudden reversal during the partition of Hindustan in 1947, when he pleaded the new government of Pakistan for compensation against his overstated pile of real estate possessions in Amritsar, which seemingly became a casualty of the 1947 incision. The partition undoubtedly had more losers than winners, but Zahoor Elahi could easily be placed in the latter category. He had an abiding passion for real estate. Soon, he consolidated his position in Gujarat and other nearby dung heaps of Punjab. Years later, he joined Ayub Khan's Muslim League and firmed up his prospects in Pakistan's rogue driven politics. Later, he was widely classified as the military cohort—a reputation that he passed on to his progeny, Chaudhry Shujat Hussain, Imran's adversary in the elections of October 2002. For Musharraf to sign a contract with Chaudhrys meant that he had already fixed up the elections. Imran's scowling was not out of place. He already rode on the strength of a disastrous run in the elections of '97, and clearly pre-empted another routing in October 2002.

Call it Musharraf's mindless scheming or his ambitious consolidation of power, Imran remained resolute in rescuing his near moribund political party. The only way through which he could keep his political career inflated was to pull himself up through his own bootstraps, spinning life and appeal into his election rallies, and extending his reach to a greater number of the voting population. Being an idealist, he never underestimated his electoral potential. His second full public examination yielded another drubbing, but failure was always the least of his worries. Jemima, twice the bearer of his progeny and by now passably well-versed in Urdu, revved up to take part in the election rallies. All that clamour over her Jewish ancestry came back to haunt, but six long years of conjugal vows in a hostile atmosphere had hardened her significantly. Despite the entire state machinery playing to the tune of the President Commander and his chums in PML-Q, Imran declared his optimism. Speaking to the BBC, he seemed animated:

> One factor they don't have and I have is credibility. The fact that every year I raise millions of rupees from Pakistani people for a charitable project makes me the only politician who can do it, who people trust. That's what's lacking in Pakistan, people don't trust the politicians.[5]

He stressed that people were tired of having the same crop of politicians ruling the roost. Imran's self-belief in his electoral prospects never translated into visible results—his assembly of faithful disciples was only restricted to the metropolises of Karachi, Lahore, Islamabad, and a few industrial hamlets in Punjab and Sindh. The rural agrarian majority failed to subscribe to his compulsive talking, mainly because his party still lacked any real grass-root existence. Worse, many among the breadline community still regarded his bygone sexcapades as an unforgiving sin. In *The News*, the country's most-read columnist Ayaz Amir stated: 'Imran was a great cricketer, a great playboy and a charismatic charmer. But he does not have that political thing which sets the bellies on fire. People respond to him with great admiration but they just don't react to his politics'. Imran was fully aware of these snags and willed to alter his public image. He sharpened his manifesto and toned it down to three specific prescriptions for the country's fledgling population: provision of justice; promotion of human values; and self-respect. A packed schedule of nationwide campaigns was brainstormed. Karachi, Pakistan's economic nerve centre, was chosen as the venue for Imran's maiden rally of the season. His speech making had notably improved, with thousands thronging to Nishtar Park in the heart of the city to listen. After he had exhausted his routine acerbic vocabulary, he presented an out of the box solution to upgrade the country's shaky accountability standards—a national council manned by the honest retired judges, lawyers, journalists, intellectuals, and other men, steadfast in their loyalty to the country. This, in Imran's assessment, would preserve the accountability of the system. Next, his rallying proceeded to interior Sindh, to a small town called Khairpur, known for its baking heat. After setting the tone in Karachi, Imran's Khairpur outing went through the same genuflections. For the umpteenth time, he blasted the corruption misadventures of his adversaries and shored himself up as the most suitable boy for the electorate. Imran then penetrated Punjab, meandering from one town to another, nit-picking at the Musharraf–Chaudhry contract. The Chaudhrys defended themselves by poking Imran for his haram— forbidden encounters with an endless list of attractive women. Character assassination escalated to a whole new level, and things got ugly. Unfazed by all the flak he was being showered with, Imran proceeded to KP, then NWFP. There at Hangu, some 100 kilometres south of Peshawar, Imran rustled up his memory of Islamic jurisprudence. An interesting blend of Islamic theology and fulmination of the notorious rulers made for an absorbing afternoon:

> Allah says in the Koran that he does not revive the fortunes of a nation until they strive for it. I appeal to all of you to step ahead and support our cause. We can't change your lives till we purge the country of these crooked politicians. They have amassed a fortune, stashing all their spoils in foreign accounts, leaving you all to face the music through hunger and poverty.[6]

The crowds exploded into a chorus. That was all very well, but Imran's estimation of a parliamentary majority was still out of his range. His performance at the opinion polls was hardly encouraging. Experts incessantly panned him as a one-man show. Musharraf and his gang of Gujjars were in the saddle, well and truly running the spectacle. By October, the election results came in and they were unsurprisingly predictable. Musharraf's king's party was in the driving seat; however, no political party secured an absolute majority. In the centre, PML-Q scored seventy-one seats, PPPP reaped sixty-two seats, and the traditionally out-of-favour Islamic parties secured the third spot with fifty-one seats. Together, these three parties formed a coalition in the centre. Prophecies of Imran's routing were met with approval as he could only improve upon his previous duck scoring by a margin of one seat. The town that responded to his overtures of change was Mianwali—a place that Imran claims to be his fortress. His lineal bondage with Mianwali helped him wade through any possibility of ballot manipulation. Disappointed as he was, Imran still managed to absorb the defeat by boasting a jaunty tone, as he was officially admitted to the national parliament following a decorative swearing in ceremony in Islamabad. His debut oath taking in the parliament opened a new window of opportunity, as he began censuring the ruling administration's unpopular foreign policy. Between 2002 and 2005, Imran became known for his writ large commentary on the US-led War on Terror in the rugged gorges of Afghanistan and Waziristan. He brazenly called US interference in Waziristan as foolish, wildly slogging at Musharraf for doing the bidding of the US. Using pejorative terms like bootlicking of *Amrika* (America), or in other words, loosening the grip on Pakistan's already dodgy sovereignty over its western frontiers. Imran spared no platform to give the general a dress down. His bickering over the issue was not unbecoming. Disgusted by Musharraf's support to the US, the weird bearded *fundoos* dawned on Pakistan, a never seen before violence, killing and maiming ordinary civilians to make a point. Since the beginning of 2002, the tumult has escalated *ad nauseam*. It all started with a spate of unlucky strikes aimed at dispatching Musharraf from existence. This was followed by the abduction of the ill-fated New York-based journalist Daniel Pearl. Daniel, known for his inquisitive journalism, earned his bread and butter by serving as the South Asia Bureau Chief of *The Wall Street Journal*. His method of curious reporting—stripping naked the shady bonding between the intelligence agencies and inherent terrorist cells—invited his own death warrant. Picked up while on his way to a well-known restaurant in Karachi, Pearl was transported to an unknown address, where his throat was slit and his body was then mutilated, chopped into nearly a dozen pieces. Waves of terror rippled across the globe. If this was not sufficient, scores of Shia slaying incidents were engineered across the country. In Karachi, the after-winter season of 2002 was the deadliest. Press reports were replete with stray episodes of target killings: in Saddar—a long-time business centre of Karachi, one Shia shop owner was sprayed with bullets; a Pakistan Steel Mills security officer, Syed Adil Hussain, was sliced and dumped on a highway; a pan-shop owner was stabbed; an employee of a pharmaceutical company was gunned in public; and a sizeable tally of other ordinary remnants of the city were wounded. Worse, the brother of the Interior Minister in Islamabad was killed, followed by the torching of a well-preserved church in the restricted section of Islamabad. These were no mundane matters. Pakistan was changing by the day: radicalisation of the youth ran fairly deep and Imran fired his shafts of insult vocabulary at both Musharraf and the US. Using his anti-war rhetoric, he began prescribing the remedies to what he labelled as a foolish war yielding no winners. The electronic media latched onto Imran's ceaseless public venting, blessing him with sufficient coverage. By 2005, resentment against the war had hit the ceiling; I kept a close watch over the affairs in Pakistan, sitting miles away, sorely wrapped up in my demanding tutorial lessons at Cambridge. Searching for a good excuse from my unsparing schedule of sifting through lecture handouts or forbiddingly sending a tumbler of Scottish wine down my entrails, I was relieved to learn that Imran was scheduled to address a full house students' convention at the London School of Economics (LSE). Enveloped in excitement, I took the early morning train to London's King's Cross station. There at LSE, amid the usual paparazzi that Imran elicits, he entered the hall with his trademark ramrod open-chested stance, exuding a tone of valour. He looked proper, all spruced up, good enough to get the chicks in the audience ogling. An odd-looking young English boy with feminine features—a bulgy pair of eyes and overinflated lips—took control of the rostrum, wasting a good ten minutes in riffling through Imran's resume—telling us something we already knew. Moments later came Imran, beginning with his standard extolling of the British judicial system before proceeding to a fleeting remark about his team's recovery from a near-doomed outlook in the 1992 Cricket World Cup. After alluding to his brush with philanthropic obligations in Pakistan, Imran finally ruminated in good detail over the bungled up 'War on Terror'. Resuming his tongue-lashing of *Busharraf*— an amusing concoction of Bush and Mush, and a term used widely in the heydays of the global war on terror—Imran played to the gallery, enslaving us all with his irresistible commentary:

> This moronic War on Terror has spelt disaster not only for Pakistan but for the US as well. It is flat out hypocrisy. Twenty-five years ago, Zbigniew Brzezinski, that cold-blooded National Security Adviser of President Jimmy Carter, while wandering over the invisible Pak-Afghan border, addressing a whopping assembly of bearded mullahs, garlanded them for waging Jihad against the infidel soviets. He preached that by driving the red army out of their holy lands, a decorated after life awaits them in paradise. A master of compulsive speech, Brzezinski invited Afghan warlords over to the White House in Washington and drew their comparisons with the founding fathers of America. Now, twenty-five years downstream, the same heroes of the Soviet expulsion have become terrorists. Both the US and Musharraf are not well versed in the history of Afghanistan. It is well documented that this is a nation that has never been receptive to the idea of foreign occupation. From Alexander the Great, down to Maharaja Ranjit Singh, Afghan Pashtuns have been uncontainable.

After almost forty-five minutes of captivating expression, Imran took his leave. Just as he strode out of the hall, he lured all the women towards him like a babe magnet. Few even crossed the line, stretching out their arms and tugging him by the elbow. Sycophants also seized the opportunity as

they lured towards him like flies drawn to a jar of honey. Imran, like a
true charmer, guarded his poise, hopped in his car, and fled the scene. His
assessment of the Pashtun resistance had me enthralled until he finished
reeling off his War on Terror recital. This reminded me of an account by
Dr William Brydon, the fortunate lone survivor of the British exodus from
the rock-laden Afghan gorges: in the snow pattering winter of 1842, nearly
17,000 British soldiers fled Kabul towards the direction of Peshawar,
treading through an intimidating terrain and an ill-fated journey having
death written all over it; few miles short of Jalalabad, the crew ran out
luck, bumping into a band of raging Afghan warriors who had crowned
themselves on top of a hill with their muskets craving for English blood.
In a few days, all but one gentleman, Dr Brydon, were killed. Afghan
retribution against foreign occupation can get sorely nasty. The Americans
are sure to realise this in due course.

By 2006, just as Imran rolled up public support in the opinion polls,
his personal life had gone through some tragic roller-coaster ride. Having
completely renounced his nuptial vows with Jemima, he was now set to
regress his remaining years both in politics and in the solitary constraints of
his large mansion in Islamabad—retreating to his bachelor existence. His
kids were gone: Suleiman and Qasim were now permanently grounded in
England, under the wings of the Goldsmiths. Two summers earlier, in June
2004, following nine years of fatiguing through pointless tattling over her
Jewish connection, Jemima finally pulled out of the marriage. Years later
while compiling notes for his personal history, Imran confessed that the six
months preceding his divorce and the six months after it were the hardest
times of his life. Worse, pangs of separation with Jemima had become even
more nerve-racking as Imran's bygone illicit exploits with a woman named
Sita White invited ugly press. Imran's allegedly undisciplined libido levels
and his frequency of ogling at London's night clubs yielded him three
months of shacking up with Ms White—daughter of a British billionaire,
Lord Gordy White. The union with Sita led to a daughter called Tyrian.
For months Imran escaped the controversy, brushing off proposals for a
DNA test. However, soon after Sita's tragic demise—succumbing to dope
addiction and robbed of her share in her father's infinite fortune—Imran
developed a soft spot for the child. Though he never publicly sanctioned
his claim over Tyrian, he made calculated confessions. Years later, while
being probed by a well-known journalist in Islamabad, Imran ingeniously
handled the investigation, sparing little room for suspicion; 'I have never
claimed a sinless life. We all struggle with our fair share of foibles,' said
Imran, breaking into a stutter. That was it, he was candidly honest and
no further quizzing ever flared up as the controversy tapered off. Further,
a few online tweets by Jemima, alluding to her step daughter, laid all

remaining suspicion to rest. Tyrian, however, remains an enigma to this day, but all grapevine campaigns tied to her have taken a backseat.

By the early months of 2007, Imran had expanded his relief work by soliciting funds for a well-endowed college—a knowledge city built on western patterns in the remote barrens of Mianwali. The enterprise was dubbed to lock horns with the more settled and less humble colonial institutions in the country: the Aitchison College, Lahore, and the Government College University, Lahore. It was a good move, lessening the under-supply of quality academic seminaries in the country. This was the time when Imran's ceaseless squabbling with Musharraf had bagged significant media coverage. By March 2007, the general's abiding passion for unbridled control slumped his public image to the bottom. At around the same time, battling the plummeting temperatures breathed into Cambridge through a violent East Anglia sea breeze, I, along with a small gang of fellow British Asians, seemingly absorbed by the events unfolding in Pakistan, shared our loathing for the President over a flask of late night coffee and tumblers of mild cocktail. An hour or so into our dialogue, one of them, acceptably under the spell, elevated in spirits, and reeking of alcohol, erupted *'yeh Musharraf pagal ho gaya hai'* ('this Musharraf has gone bonkers'). Unnerved by the passion of the new Chief Justice—the disfigured-looking Iftikhar Chaudhry—Musharraf, in the most unceremonious of ways, handed a pink slip to the principal judge, trampling the reputation of his office. A few bold rulings by Chaudhry led to this rupturing: he had cancelled the shady privatisation contract of the Pakistan Steel Mills; had called for a regulation of the commodity prices; and dauntlessly demanded the government to produce all terrorism affiliated missing persons who had been framed and sent packing somewhere for torture. All this was enough daring for the general as he wasted no time in robbing the Chief Justice of his position. As with all dictators, Musharraf was equally intolerant of free-minded judges. Soon, a never-seen-before anti-dictatorship buzz rented the atmosphere. Lawyers, political parties, journalists, human rights activists, and all other categories disapproving of the general marched out to hunt him down through some profane cursing. Imran also sharpened his cussing and joined the ranks. Following three months of pandemonium and buckling under the pressure, Musharraf reluctantly re-employed Chaudhry as the country's supreme judge. Soon after taking charge, Chaudhry resumed his snooping over Musharraf's under-the-counter deals with pliant politicians to validate his extension as the president for another term. That October morning was tragic for the luckless Pakistanis—the exact date of which escapes my mind—as Musharraf and his flunkeys forged a deal with all ostracised politicians, including the Sharifs' and the Bhuttos. Skimming through the papers that arrived with my early morning tea in Cambridge, I determined the details of the scheme. The National Reconciliation Order they called it, giving a clean passage to all the faithless politicians thankfully in exile for years to sadly return and waggle their way to the top offices. Imran was utterly dismissive of the project, fulminating its execution. The Chief Justice was in his stride again, vetoing Musharraf's desperate bargaining tricks. Inflamed by the Chaudhry's oversupply of arm twisting, Imran's routine tongue lashing, and the media's mudslinging, Musharraf called for an emergency rule, suspending the constitution, on 3 November 2007. The judges were given the axe for the second time in less than eight months. Within hours, thousands of political activists and journalists were picked up and detained. Similar orders were issued for Imran. In a surprise police raid at his ancestral residence in Lahore, Imran demonstrated his old, fast-bowling vigilance by leaping across a 10-foot wall in the back yard and fleeing from the scene. For the next few days, he stayed largely undetected, barring a few interviews that he gave to send a message to his group of admirers. More drama ensued: Imran decided to abandon his underground musing and hand himself over to the local police in his attempt to sully the general's global reputation. All geared up for a protest at Punjab University—territorially, the country's largest academic institution—Imran was roughed up by a gang of bearded misled *mullahs*, allegedly doing the general's bidding. A day later, he was sputtered off in a decaying truck to Dera Ismail Khan, home to the country's shoddiest jail. In his memoirs, Imran draws a detailed sketch of what was to follow:

> The jail smelt of garbage. Nearly fifteen people squeezed together in every cell. I was allotted a cell in the hospital wing. It contained a fragile bed and a soiled bathroom. In the mornings, I was permitted to sit outside and bake myself under the sun, whereas in the evenings I was confined to my jurisdiction. I could not eat to my fill as I was in need of exercise. Several years of exercise had conditioned my frame in a way that it demands regular physical occupation. Failure to do so, makes me weak in the bones. It was torture as I thought I would expire out of sheer boredom.[7]

Imran's celebrity stature saved him from any further humiliation as protests against his detention rumbled across the world. Eight days of internment and hunger pangs suddenly made him look a good ten years older. Wrinkles formed around his cheek bones, and with his unrefined stubble, he looked completely exhausted. His spirit, however, remained as inflated as it was before his nabbing. Moments after his release, and speaking to the reporters in his usual baritone voice, Imran slammed

Musharraf: 'The upcoming elections in January will again be fixed up and the way Musharraf has ravaged the law of the land, I find no other parallel examples in the history of this country. I call upon all political parties to boycott the upcoming elections'. As Musharraf's unpopularity crashed through the ceiling, he discontinued the emergency project, restored the constitution, and surrendered his army chief title. He had finally settled in the role of an ordinary civilian president, which was a much humbler position than being in the saddle, backed by over a 1-million-man army. The shock was not over. The year that began with the termination of the beastly looking judge concluded with the shocking assassination of Benazir Bhutto in the garrison town of Rawalpindi. The nation was stunned, with an eerie silence prevailing. More appalling was the widower Zardari's assertion that his deceased companion had bequeathed the party to him and his progeny. *'Bura waqt aney wala hai'* ('ugly times ahead') foretold a friend who knew that Zardari was back to his Al Caponing. 'You will see that Zardari's PPP will rob the mandate in the next electoral conquest,' growled my friend, suspecting a clear pattern in the way things were turning up. So right was he when Zardari and his team of organised ravagers routed the elections of February 2008. Imran's careless boycotting of the polls yielded another faithless parliament, which was a decision that he later came to regret as he began multiplying his repertoire of insult vocabulary at a rate of knots, including new terms like swine and *kutta* ('dog') to an already comprehensive swearing directory; he was clearly disgusted by Zardari's stroke of luck in the centre.

4

That Night in Lahore

If you're going to kick authority in the teeth, you might as well use two feet.

Keith Richards

Nonplussed at late Ms Bhutto's chief benefactor—widower Zardari's binge to an honourable position in the government—my good friend, surnamed Mufti, and I would go about venting our spleen. How shameful was it to be identified as natives to a land whose voters had approved the biggest known thug and his henchmen to resume their fleecing of the national exchequer? Even more disgusting was Zardari's grin, which seemed a permanent feature of his appearance. His prodigious smirking often exposed his well-polished, gleaming teeth—another good indicator of his ravaging plans for the national kitty. He was on cloud nine. Manipulating ministries from his plush estate in Dubai, Zardari took a few bold steps. Chief among them was clipping the wings of ISI—Pakistan's version of the CIA. Then, most of his yes-men from his days in jail were shamelessly placed on important positions. Supplementing his official cabinet was an unofficial one, full of debauched, faithless, and pliant small-time technocrats. One amusing nomination came in the form of Hussain Haroon, whose CV was considered most befitting to be Pakistan's official representative to the UN. Mr Haroon's college education is dicey, so is his experience for the illustrious positon. Similar appointments were made in literally every stream of government activity to rob the state down its bones.

Many years in jail had made Zardari vindictive. It was payback time now. Sadly, the onus of Zardari's riling on the top was consumed by the ill-clad beggarly, who unfortunately had no share in the game of thrones that Zardari so flawlessly champions. Zardari's latest upgrading in life must have been nightmarish for Imran. Imran's flaky, devil-may-care decision making cost him and his party a stint in the parliament, allowing a clear passage to Zardari and his loyal bidders to rule the roost. There are plentiful accounts of Imran's instinctive and rash judgement, but one of them described in good detail by Ikramullah Khan Niazi—Imran's late father—comes abruptly to mind:

> I was buried in work at my office when the news of Imran's falling from the stairs reached me. I hurried back home and realized that it was no accident. In his attempt to belittle his older cousins through a flagrant advertisement of his courage, the five or so year old Imran had jumped off a lofty staircase, cracking one of his arms. The best part came later. Knowing that he was grossly at fault, he concealed his pain and refrained from weeping.

Even more hellish for Imran was Zardari's appointment as the president of the republic in early September 2008. Fearing impeachment, Musharraf divorced his presidential office and retired to a life of book reading and golf swinging in his exorbitantly priced apartment on London's Edgware Road. Most generals, high-point bureaucrats, and politicians, ill famed for their blotchy tenures, secure an afterlife in London, somewhere in Europe, or, more recently, in Dubai. During Zardari's presidential election, he was guaranteed a victory by securing 481 votes, far above the 352 tickets required to ratify the appointment. The presidential occupation meant that no law of the land could prosecute Zardari over his corruption charges, exonerating him from his past skimming of the national vault. Such embarrassment he caused me when I was working as a financial journalist in London. None of my fellow colleagues, passably well-versed in Pakistan's nerve-boggling politics, spared me the shame: 'You folks have elected a robber as your President'. Another one said: 'How does it feel to be governed by a glorified rogue?' I was ghastly humiliated. Worse, Zardari, for the next year, spent more taxpayer notes in trotting round the planet and soliciting more loans and grants than any of his predecessors in the past. Even more detestable was his flirting overtures to Sarah Palin—a good-looking Republican and then Governor of Alaska. When Zardari's father was savouring the fruits of ten long years in prison, how could his progeny, Bilawal—the surprising heir apparent of the Bhutto dynasty—skip all the fun? Bilawal, behaving like a genuine prince in waiting, went on his own lewd course when he and the charming, middle-aged, and attractive cabinet minister, Hina Rabbani Khar, were caught *in flagrante*. The sordid encounter was rapidly brushed away. On performance, Zardari's qualified workers earned nothing more than well-printed spoofs in one of the state's leading English tabloids. One of my favourites, published in early 2010, shows a turbaned Zardari enclosed in a tall bulletproof rostrum topped with a hilarious caption: 'After three years there will be no shortage of electricity, water, gas, petrol and jobs'. Two unsullied-looking spectators in the milling crowd below panicked: 'He is suggesting we should wait for the next government'. Another gut-busting spoof, appearing in the same papers roughly around the same time, showed Zardari's ungainly interior minister Rehman Malik holding a press conference and walking the reporters though the eight wonders of the world: the eighth wonder, quite mockingly, being Zardari's visit to a hospital in Karachi to inspect victims of a terrorist attack; a visit that was widely considered to be less of a bounden duty and more a means to blow his own trumpet and invite journalistic exposure, such was the indifference towards the real issues the country faced. Zardari's casual approach towards his job had well and truly crossed our threshold. This was also the period when anti-US sentiments had reached their summit. For Imran, the high point of treachery was when Zardari conferred the country's highest civilian award on Mr Joe Biden, the US Vice-President, famed for his flagrant expounding of drone strikes in the frontier gorges of Pakistan. In protest, Imran robbed himself of his civilian award, willingly returning it to the government. Steadily coming into his fold, Imran was now riding the tide of public discontent. Zardari's negligence had supplied Imran with ample themes to work with: a wobbling law and order; unbounded down pouring of US drones; sharp increase in inflation; the insolvent state of education and health; and, lastly, the infinite plunge into darkness—load shedding. Imran bickered over these issues over every platform, large or small. Such brazen open-stage vilifying of Pakistan's unfaithful lawmakers had always been his rallying cry. Imran had roasted their reputation in public on several occasions by this point, and in one of his budding rallies more than a decade ago, he even charged Zardari with the murder of Benazir's brother. The years of Imran being overcritical had become too much for a few pro-administration publications. One of them revolted with a regular blurb aimed at turning Imran's mutinous behaviour into a laughing stock. The spoof, titled 'Im the Dim', was a weekly fantasy, a fictional diary of Imran himself. One of the wittiest extracts from a long catalogue, to what Imran's paladins rule out as blasphemy, reads:

> As you know everyone's waiting in a queue for Zardari to go. Foremost in this queue is myself and my friends and relations, followed by honourable judges, some hacks and hackettes and other bits and bobs. When Zardari is turfed out, I will hold a grand dinner party at my baronial palace in Islamabad. Of course, I never serve booze at my

dinners. So people start sozzling up the minute receive my invitation with the result that I have very drunken dinners. I am thinking ill stop serving food too and that way people can bring their own lunch boxes and we can all sit together and eat them. As soon as Zardari's taken care of, I am going to form a government. For that, I'm preparing by standing in front of the mirror and practicing standing on a truck and waving to the non-existent masses and by imagining myself scribbling on a pad during cabinet meetings and by sitting at the United Nations listening to myself making a brilliant speech. For my cabinet, I've started looking for honest, upright and highly stupid people of the male variety. This has resulted in my brain going into overdrive. At the best of times, my brain is not known for its activity and alacrity but with this cold wave it's somewhat jammed and frozen.[1]

For reasons of strategy, as one notable political analyst had told me, Imran's ranting was more severe on Nawaz Sharif than any of his prolific list of adversaries. This could be because Sharif wielded uncontested power in the country's largest province of Punjab. In the local bodies' elections of 2010, Imran's party was knocked out by Sharif's office-seekers. Sorely irked by the blow, Imran was quick to fulminate the voting results by identifying the number of bogus votes in the voters' list. He even accused the Government of Punjab's officials for acting as the polling agents during the balloting process. It was later reported that the matter was being handled by the FIA. However, the investigation remained vague and un-fateful.

By August 2010, Imran's prattling over the government's gerrymandering was diverted to a more serious cause: the ill-fated floods. This, as many believed, was Imran's real breakthrough in trekking up the opinion polls. No one that year had forecasted a lethal monsoon: the skies were parched by the beaming sun, the earth set aflame, and the branchless trees thirsted for water. Then there was an abrupt change in the fragrance of the air above the far edges of the Himalayan horizon, thick blobs of nimbus clouds blotted out the sun; deadly winds shamelessly uprooted thatched roofs in the rural dung heaps, and steady rains gradually turned into a flood, overflowing the shores of rivers and streaming away the rural produce southwards towards the Arabian ocean. Within a fortnight, approximately 2,000 people embraced death and over 20 million lives were forced from their homes. Economists did their maths and came up with unexaggerated loss figures ranging in the billions (not rupees, but dollars). Sadly, team Zardari was suspected of having a good time in the Chief Executive's baronial fortress in Normandy. A dim-looking Imran slandered the status quo for their callous, cold-blooded treatment and informed the press of the launching of 'Imran Khan Flood Relief Drive'. He set out on a plane, riding around the globe and soliciting relief funds in what proved to be the biggest natural calamity since the battering of the tsunami in 2004. Imran and his die-hard representatives had set up relief camps in every major urban metropolis in the state. We were impressed. 'Kudos!' shrilled a fellow female colleague and Imran fanatic, jumping over her seat and shaking her flat booty in joy.

In the six months that followed, Imran's public acceptance had hugely scaled up. Zardari's knack of humbugging, his joyriding in foreign lands, and his amoral temperament towards the ill-clad, ill-bread community he was supposed to govern had shredded his already riddled public reputation. Zardari's initial three years in the centre was widely regarded as the most trying phase in the country's sixty-year life. I have, for the purpose of this book, sat down and documented opinions coming out of ordinary Pakistanis—the voiceless commoners who are never heard (from retired bureaucrats and retired Army officials to rickshaw operators, and from wise and rational-thinking students to traders, professors from leading universities, artists, labourers and other petty workers desperately trying to make their ends meet, but who are somehow compromised given the economic constraints heaved upon them). Najeeb, a small-time owner of a grocery store, somewhere on the fringes of Islamabad, wishing to keep full his identity undisclosed for this account, befittingly synopsised Zardari's tenure:

> When nothing in the country is moving in the right course and the entire system is infested with corruption, you cannot expect men of piety and grace assuming important positions of power. Zardari's rise to parliament only shows that our system has failed. We all know that he is brutally corrupt and has laundered millions of dollars from Pakistan but still the system supported his election. We must all, in equal measure, shoulder the blame for Zardari's raping of the country.

Growth wise, Pakistan trailed behind every other neighbouring country, putting up a lacklustre average GDP figure of around 2.9 per cent between 2008 and 2011. This was well behind India's 7.8 per cent, Bangladesh's 6.8 per cent, and Sri Lanka's 6.1 per cent. Economists the world over prescribed a sustained GDP figure of nearly 6 per cent for growth to effectively funnel down to the base of civilization. Inflation was painful and fluctuated between double digit numbers. Energy shortages had crippled economic prospects and incentivised capital flight. As a result, foreign investors pulled out their bets on the economy. Many small-time textile owners ceased their cloth weaving and looked to venture abroad.

Foreign reserves dwindled, and tax collection posted mediocre digits. Worse, suicide bombers were rampant, brazenly loitering about and infiltrating every part of the country. Relations between the centre and the tribal areas remained as strained as ever. One episode was particularly disturbing. In January 2011, an American intelligence contractor, Raymond Davis, shot dead two people in Lahore but was secretly escorted out of Pakistan without a trial. In May the same year, US officials claimed to have hunted down Osama bin Laden, sadly confined in the mountains of Abbottabad—a lovely hamlet, nearly 30 miles to the north of Islamabad. To top it all up, Hussain Haqqani, a foreign diplomat, then ambassador to the US and to many a stooge of the PPP government, came under attack for writing a controversial letter to the American Government, proposing them to protect the PPP regime from the military establishment. All that insanity and more only strengthened Imran's anti-government clamour, assuming nationwide dimensions. Imran sensed that his time had come. He was no longer a man of few words, evident from the growing crowds that his rallies were drawing. He, as a source close to his mansion in Bani Gala informed me, was always on the run, enslaving himself to a tight speech-making schedule. 'He had no tolerance for shirkers,' exclaimed a party worker. All of his rallies proved a smashing hit, but we had not the foggiest of idea that the late October session he summoned in Lahore would transform him from being a humble fortune seeker in politics to the land's most suitable boy.

Lahore was Special!

It was an eventful evening in Lahore on 30 October 2011, a defining moment in the history of Pakistan. A quick survey of the crowd revealed people of all ages, regressing their lives without hope for a better tomorrow. The stage set was at Lahore's famed Iqbal Park, formerly known in the local vernacular as Minto Park, an unkempt, sparsely green and garbage-laden landscape where inland tourists straddle to take their selfies in the company of *Minar-e-Pakistan*—a cherished monument. It was not a place for nature watching, but certainly the site for a refresher course in Lahore's Mughal relics. Imran's choice of location was astute. Iqbal Park has been home to many popular rallies in the past and it was here in the spring of 1940 that the All India Muslim League officially announced the Pakistan project. Late in the afternoon, just as the sun began to lose its colour and plunge into a pit of darkness, PTI supporters in great numbers charged out of their nests in what is traditionally the PML-N stronghold, chanting out slogans for their new leader. Access roads in the vicinity of Iqbal Park were quickly filling up, and soon, all arteries leading to the venue were clogged to capacity. The scenes were dramatic, nothing short of a carnival. People were dancing in their submission to PTI anthems, yelling ho-ho hosannas to the Imran miracle who promised them a better world. Songs that provoked the patriot. The people came in throngs, like a roaring ocean invading the shore. Autumn had set in and the mercury significantly plummets in the evenings; however, the elated pack of Imran believers was indifferent to the vagaries of a cold evening. After a few motivational speeches by Imran's party members, in came Imran himself amid a loud of thunder of hymns and hooting, with a touch of swagger about him, as if still on a cricket field. Beginning with his usual cutting remarks aimed at his adversaries, Imran promised the assembly a world they had only dreamt of. 'Im the Dim' prepped up its wits, lampooning Imran for being the military man. The confidence with which Imran kicked off his oratory for the night was exhilarating: he spoke at great length about his motivation to enter politics, a turf where only the landed aristocracy or the industrial elite had traditionally dared to enter. His fifteen-year wrangling was now paying him dividends. Raising a full-fledged political party out of the depths and catapulting it into the mainstream was no small feat. I insist, it was no small feat indeed, particularly in a convoluted political system like Pakistan. Imran walked his audience through his struggles as a cricketer and his doggedness as a social activist, repeatedly citing verses from the Koran and combining them with *verba de futuro* to a crowd that was clearly falling under his spell by the minute. He knew that he had set the stage for a perfect address as the crowd responded well to his overtures. Words like 'Tsunami' and *'Naya Pakistan'* ('New Pakistan') were latest revelations and struck a chord, turning the event into an overnight frenzy. *'Tabdeli aa nahin rahi, tabdeli aa gayi hai'* ('change is not just approaching, it is already here'), screamed Imran cutting a triumphant note. Coinages like these have been rare in Pakistan, and the last time Pakistanis absorbed anything remotely similar, or were overwhelmed by emotions of nationalism, was when Zulfiqar Ali Bhutto promoted his *roti, kapra, makan* (bread, cloth, roof) crusade in the late '60s. The next morning, *'Naya Pakistan'* and 'Tsunami' made it to the press, receiving widespread coverage. 'We had not anticipated that the Lahore rally would be such an overwhelming success,' declared a startled leading journalist of the state. Sitting miles away in her Richmond mansion in London, Jemima followed the events in Lahore keenly. Failing to resist the spasms in her fingers, she tweeted her blessings: 'Everyone is talking about this PTI Lahore rally and how it is being a game changer in Pakistan. *Inshallah* [God willing]'.

5

The Festive Ballot

A politician thinks of the next election. A statesman, of the next generation.

James Freeman Clarke

He would sacrifice a goat every day for his master to ward off any possibility of an evil spell, and he would live within the presidency as a trusted counsel. This was President Zardari's personal *pir* (spiritual healer), his bringer of fortune, his best man, licking his chops and entrusted with the responsibility of keeping the president guarded from all misfortune. The president's role was to go out and do his job. The *pir*'s job was to protect the president from anything troubling that drew near him. These religious healers, *sadhus*, or priests have enjoyed elevated positions in the structures of power. They are everywhere in the country, particularly more pronounced in the Sindh province. You may find scores of them in interior Sindh, with their wild overgrown, unkempt hair, exploding stubble, untrimmed finger nails, unpolished slovenly set of gums yellow with ages of ignorance, unshaven moist armpits, exuding an offensive stink, and breaching all etiquettes of hygiene. They are often adorned with beads hanging round their necks, reciting verses from the Koran that sound more like *sadhus*, muttering prayers from Hindu Sacred Scriptures, frivolously theatrical, particularly when they wiggle their heads hollering *hak hoo hak hoo* . Products of religious bigotry and an obvious obstruction in the way of modernisation, they have worked their charms on vast tracts of rural Pakistan. Those incapable to reason turn to them for solace and guidance. They have managed to captivate even the landlords and local tribal heads. The seekers turn to them, hoping for prosperity. One often ignores their importance as religious figureheads. They were important back in Rome, in the Ottoman courts, in the Mughal era, even in Muslim Persia, and they surely have cut out a role for them within the political realm of Pakistan and India. Aamir Khan, a global Indian icon, revered for his out-of-the-box motion pictures, attempted to explore this South Asian cult in his movie titled *PK*. Khushwant Singh, the famous Indian satirist, in his book *God and Godmen of India*, discusses India's obsession with the supernatural, and describing in good length various versions of *sadhus* that abound in India. Courtesy of Google, I came to pass an interesting video of former deceased premier Benazir Bhutto in the company of a *pir*, her head lowered in humility as she had completely subjected herself to the edicts of her spiritual master. One may wonder for the sake of amusement if the smirking Zardari really got through his term in the centre because of his *pir* bondage. I gave much thought to it, but then felt like kicking myself in the gut. The *pir*, with all his magical wonders, sorcery, tricks, and non-stop muttering of inaudible prayers, could not butter up the people of Pakistan. Zardari, with all his subscription to religious cults, remained an unpopular figure as his administration proved curtains for the country.

Zardari's five-year occupation in the centre has drawn a heap of negative press. The poorer his party performed, the more conveniently Imran worked his way up in the opinion polls. Imran's 2011 Lahore speech, as reviewed in the preceding chapter, was fresh in the minds. Throughout 2012, he rallied around the country to strengthen his position. His theme of a *Naya Pakistan*, a corruption free governance, and his calls for bringing the loot back to the countrymen boosted his political appeal. Soon after the Lahore *jalsa* (rally), and seeing the mounting hysteria surrounding Imran, opposition parties began courting him to forge an alliance, to which Imran graciously nodded, but only on the condition of them sharing details of their assets. To most opposition parties, this was an inappropriate demand. Politicians in Pakistan guard their wealth to their graves. It is, after all, their life's work and bears sanctified importance. Later, in 2011, Imran held similar rallies in Karachi and then proceeded to the resource rich Baluchistan in the north-west. He spoke about matters that, normally, politicians in Pakistan are awfully uncomfortable with. Discussing themes like police reforms, judicial reforms, local government system, and strengthening of the institutions. The word 'corruption' was never subscribed by any political party in any of the rallies in the years past, and especially not with such fervour. People saw in Imran a liberator. This was perhaps the first time in the country's history that the mood preceding the national elections had grown into a frenzied affair. Imran was upbeat about his prospects in the upcoming elections, scheduled for 11 May 2013. He had decided to pack a punch with his rallies, his only chance in a country where election results could be conveniently massaged and manipulated through money and power. Zardari's tenure even got the religious parties charged up. Never in the history of the country have religious parties managed to survive the electoral competition on their own, always pushing for an alliance to stay afloat. Yet on that occasion, even the religious parties were hopeful. Punjab was never threatened by Zardari because, there, PML-N enjoyed absolute authority. Zardari had not only eroded the economic prospects of the country, but had also inhibited the political chances of his own party. In KP, parties like ANP (Awami National Party), the religious gangs, and Imran's PTI sensed an opportunity. Baluchistan, however, with its lower representation in the electorate, remained in the hands of independent tribal leaders, who would need to forge an alliance to keep going. Karachi, the nerve centre of Pakistan's economy, was controlled by MQM. However, with the city's large Pashtun population and a disappointed youth, PTI was optimistic. The conditions seemed too ripe for PTI to cultivate its impact. Two chief reasons, briefly examined earlier in the book, explain PTI's sudden bulge.

First, PPP had a dismal five-year economic and political scorecard in the centre. Pakistan's economy, which had enjoyed a period of sustained economic growth courtesy of a few liberalised policies by General Musharraf, was once again found wanting. The period between 2008 and 2013 was marked by persistent failure. It was a period of stagflation, a term coined by economists who wish to sound more disturbing. It meant that Pakistan struggled with depressingly low growth rates and abnormally high and unmanageable levels of inflation. Zardari failed to provide any relief to the common man, and no serious reforms ever saw the light of day. The annual UNDP report, printed in 2013, painted a nasty picture. By the report, Pakistan even fell below some of the poorest countries in Africa on human development standards. Out of a total of 186 countries, it ranked at 146th—a shameful statistic by any measure. A further nail in the coffin came when it was highlighted that Pakistan spends lower than even the Democratic Republic of Congo on social services like health and education. Worse, around 49 per cent of the population survived below the poverty line. This was a little consoling when compared to the rate of India, which was higher than 50 per cent. Yet India is a much bigger country and is endowed with a much larger industrial base as well. Furthermore, the report also suggested that Pakistan's politics was controlled by a total of 100 elite families—mafias, I would call them. These are the families who, through their oligarchic practices and control over the state institutions, have impeded economic progress. The PPP's regime saw increasing levels of fiscal deficit as major sectors of the economy remained virtually untaxed. Pakistan, as a result, had one of the poorest tax to GDP ratios. The energy sector particularly invited poor press coverage as it had badly choked the economy. I remember working for a large multilateral organisation at the time, which provided policy advisory services to the Ministry of Water and Power. Countless wrangling with government secretaries over pointless power point presentations consumed my days. Nothing really moved: no major efforts to revive the paralyzed sector came to the fore; the gap between energy supply and demand kept widening; theft of electricity by various customer categories went unnoticed; neglecting the energy sector spelt disaster; widespread load shedding was reported in the entire country; and even major urban centres like Karachi, Lahore, and Islamabad drowned in the dark for more than eight hours a day. For rural Pakistan electricity was a privilege. Without energy, the large-scale industry was poorly affected as their production levels dipped; exports were badly hit; and many textile owners decided to shut down their operations and moved their units abroad. Law and order was bizarrely poor. In 2009, the Sri Lankan team touring Pakistan was attacked by a group of bearded diehards, right outside the Qaddafi Cricket Stadium in Lahore. Thankfully, the players escaped, sustaining just a few injuries. Foreign cricket teams have since then ruled out prospects of touring Pakistan. To this day, the nation stands deprived of the only source of entertainment it ever had. No major foreign investment came in. All major state institutions, including PIA, PSM, OGDC, and WAPDA, were falling apart. By late 2012 and early 2013, this was the weather that Imran's PTI had inherited. Zardari's misadventures in the centre provided the stimulus—ideal conditions for someone who is riding a populist agenda to barge into the corridors of power. With only a few months short of the next national elections, Imran had already started touring various leading universities of the country, convincing students that any prospects of him aligning with the existing corrupt politicians was out of court—already kicking off his soft campaigning for the elections.

My second version that explains Imran's staggering growth was the youth hysteria. How real and penetrative was the youth frenzy and what were the reasons? Pre-election reports churned out by the print media suggested that nearly 48 per cent of the 85-million-strong electoral force were aged between eighteen and thirty. It clearly seemed from the periphery that it was not just noise. I personally vouch for the bulge. As the elections drew near, my employer, a US firm, funding development initiatives across Pakistan, decided to dispose me off to various small towns in a bid to collect some data. They planned a mid-term evaluation of their various development schemes, ranging from energy to health to education, etc. I have always been a politically animated person, and saw those travels as an opportunity to see how earnestly people were looking forward to the elections. Besides, many of the towns I was bound to visit were new to me, as I had until then mostly shuffled between the comforts of urban Islamabad and Lahore—something I am definitely not proud of. My first trip was to the town identified as Imran's ancestral root base, Mianwali. Mianwali is located on the north-western strip of Punjab and is a gateway to the frontier Pashtun region. Throughout history, the city has attracted traders and thugs from both Afghanistan and Central Asia. As I reached Mianwali, I saw lampposts along the roads, shrouded with posters of Imran's ever-determined face, with rage written all over and his fists firmly closed, jabbing the air. The hoardings were also teemed with his publicity. The anthems of Imran's party bustled the streets, drawing crowds to fever pitch. Posters of Imran's adversaries struggled for spaces. In fact, I saw a few of them trampled by a raging student cavalcade of PTI supporters. It was Imran everywhere. Wherever I went, I encountered PTI's roaring expression. Mostly young men and children dancing in small processions. The entire city had lit up. I did my data collection and retired for the day at a small hotel. At night, I dallied around to absorb the city and the Imran mania that had swept across. I dined at a restaurant and met a young waiter, freshly employed, aged not more than twenty-one, delightfully telling me, 'We never believed in the need to vote. My parents have stopped voting. But now with Imran Khan emerging, we see hope. He promises us a new world. My parents will also vote now to change our future.' The next day, I resumed my journey. From Mianwali, I journeyed back into interior Punjab. I went to Sargodha, Chakwal, Faisalabad, Gujranwala, Multan, and finally Lahore. Wherever I went, I confronted feverish exaltation of Imran Khan. Young men and women shedding their old party loyalties with youthful abandon. The streets rippled with music. Youthful enthusiasm had not only gripped the young, but also the old in the majority of the urban areas I trotted. The mood was overwhelming. Imran's newfound popularity binge wrested on some of the initiatives that he had taken during the course of the past few years.

On corruption, Imran had been consistent right from the beginning. In December 2012, NAB (National Accountability Bureau), an autonomous state body, put into place to ensure transparency in government functions, announced through a report that corruption of around 12 billion rupees per day has been committed in Pakistan during Zardari's tenure. The report blamed the senior politicians for being the real suspects, followed by the bureaucracy that controlled the state machinery. None of the political parties took the report seriously. However, Imran repeatedly harped on the issue in his various interviews and public speeches. At a function organised in Lahore by PTI's Insaaf Lawyers Forum, Imran seemed unimpressed:

The report speaks volumes about the performance of the current regime. Once we are in power, we will save 4,000 billion rupees every year. The

total expenditure of the government comes to around 3,300 billion
rupees per year. In Punjab alone, corruption was 65% of the GDP.

Imran bluntly undermined the VIP culture that had found permanence in
the parliament house. He gravely resented the narcissist, fortune lovers of
the Pakistani political elite, censuring the huge expenses incurred by the
official convoys on their foreign trips. 'This is all state money,' protested
Imran, gallantly educating everyone. Such commentaries on state's 'above-
the-law' behaviour were unheard of in the political dimensions of the
country. No state level politician prior to Imran had ever objected to the
luxuries, state authorities afforded themselves at the tax payers' expense.
I have read about Zulfiqar Ali Bhutto's populist politics, but even he was
known to lead a pompous life. Endowed with regal etiquettes, he was
a typical landlord controlling vast tracts of rural lands and the people
living in them. This was the attitude that Imran hoped to quash once in
power. He also questioned the authenticity of the wealth piled up by the
leading political figures in the country. In one of Imran's election rallies
in Peshawar in the spring of 2013, he accused all major party heads of
corruption and vowed dragging them to books. Imran's earlier attempts
to officially declare Altaf Hussain a state terrorist had already earned him
a reputation of an non-compliant politician. MQM powered themselves
on thug culture that has, for years, subjected the ordinary Urdu-speaking
fraternity of Karachi. No one prior to Imran had ever had the limbs to
take them on.

Imran also suggested that he was a disciple of righteous politics and
preached supremacy of law, rallying around a number of themes that
resonated with people, among them was a dream to build a country where
a peasant's son can also become a prime minister. He was inspired by the
politics of Nelson Mandela and the contents of western-style democracy,
hugely borrowing from the life of Mandela and often exalting him in his
interviews. He repeatedly stressed on the need for strong institutions,
drawing examples from Europe. Youth and urban class activism may
have been a new spectacle in Pakistan, but has a rich history in Europe
and the Americas. The 2012 Quebec protests in Canada created waves.
The 2006 youth activism in France in opposition to a bill being passed
to deregulate labour is also a classic example. Going back a few decades,
Martin Luther King Jr's movement for civil rights had penetrated in
the corridors of power and found a voice. Imran wrestled with these
ideas and employed them effectively in the context of local political
culture. His aggressive campaigning throughout the country had hiked
expectations to an inestimable measure. His stance on dynastic political
culture received lamentations full of praise. In November 2012, while

addressing a gathering of roughly 5,000 students in Peshawar, Imran had announced that a quarter of the tickets to contest the upcoming elections would go to the younger members of the party. He also said that his party provided a stable platform for the younger generation to contest intra-party polls. The intra-party elections of PTI were held in the autumn of 2012. These elections sent a positive message out. Imran, through his numerous interviews, resented the undemocratic nature of political parties in Pakistan. Political parties in Pakistan are usually family controlled, warding off any possibility of lower-middle-class party workers rising through the ranks and making a statement. 'In other political parties if you do not bear the name of Bhutto or Sharif, you will never be allowed a leadership role in politics. Only PTI will provide such an opportunity,' exclaimed Imran, cutting a triumphant note while addressing the students' convention. Imran was confident that his intra-party elections would pave the way for a genuine democratic culture in the country. He believed that political parties, who themselves evaded a democratic process within their ranks, could not deliver on their promises. PTI's vice-chairman and former PPP designee Shah Mehmood Qureshi was also a member of the addressing team, emphasising that PTI was youth friendly, and that without the youth, the party's prospects would fade rapidly.

On matters of justice, social security and female empowerment, Imran had already called for a few steps prior to the elections to strengthen his campaign. He spoke vociferously in favour of a strong local government system. He championed the idea of a decentralised political system, stating that speedy justice in remote areas can only be delivered through small courts established in villages. The women in particular would stand to benefit as they were the most vulnerable sitting ducks of rural life. Imran promoted the idea of women contesting intra-party elections and rising through the party ranks. He also promised female empowerment through education, speaking at length about promoting female entrepreneurship through special loans and also improving logistical support for the working women. He also believed that through a local government system, people would be able to take control of their education and police structures. Imran supported development at the grass root through community organisations: pledging to uplift the standards of education and health and focusing all his energies in increasing the education and health expenditures from their current depressingly sinking levels. Equality was another aspect he preached, and his proposals descended upon the youth as sheets of rainwater following the height of a scorching summer. He prescribed a uniform syllabus for all, dreaming of a country where the poor man's son and the rich man's son would share the same syllabus. The youth, who until then simmered under the weight of the old political culture that thrived on nepotism and favoured the elite, were beginning to gain some sense from Imran's tutorials.

It must also be noted that the security climate in the year preceding the elections was horrendous. There was widespread retribution across the country towards the US-endorsed unmanned drone strikes in the tribal areas. Drones have been a recurring theme of the US foreign policy in recent times. In response to the drones, the *fundoos* were out of their bases and rocked Pakistan with impunity. The politicians in power had little to offer. The armed forces struggled to contain the situation, and public outcry was outrageous. The *fundoos* targeted mosques, Sufi shrines, and other places of worship, turning the country into a blood bath. It was a homicide of Everest proportions. In October 2011, around sixteen suspected militants were killed by a drone attack in Buland Khel—an area of Orakzai agency on the fringes of the Waziristan border. Numerous other incidents of severe drone pounding were being reported. To make matters worse, a survey carried out by the Pew Research centre, based out of Washington earlier in June 2012, revealed that 62 per cent of the Americans favoured the drones. The survey also suggested widespread unrest and discontent among the Muslim world towards the US wars in Afghanistan and Iraq. Popular sentiment in the Obama circles was that drones have done more good than harm. Some press accounts in the US had also ruled out chances of anti-American sentiments showing signs of abating, should the drone strikes be called off completely. A few noises of drone fulmination from left-wing media outfits and other peace activists in Europe and the Americas did emerge, but hardly made any impact. Unfortunately, Pakistan became the biggest casualty. In response, the banned terrorist outfit TTP (Tehrik-i-Taliban Pakistan) had cut loose. A bomb explosion was reported in KP and Baluchistan provinces literally every few days, and Shia processions and political rallies became soft targets. In December 2012, a suicide bomber raged through a meeting of ANP senior politicians in Peshawar, killing former ANP minister Bashir Bilour. A few days later, a bomb went off in a bus that was carrying participants to a MQM rally in Karachi. Amid that butchery of public faith in the law enforcement agencies, the Zardari regime came under severe scrutiny for not doing much to calm things down. It was carnage. No howl of serious protest ever went up. It was Imran who struck a dismissive note, played his cards, and publicly slandered the US drone transgressions. Imran was already well-known across the western press as a stout critique of US adventures in Afghanistan, Waziristan, and Iraq. On a number of occasions, he blasted the US attacks and made no bones about how sorely these strikes were destroying life in his country. He consistently pushed for a political dialogue as the only measure to mitigate tensions. He had already given a spate of interviews to foreign media channels and publicly expressed his disapproval. Seeing little progress, he finally decided to lead a peaceful procession to the war-rattled south Waziristan town of Kotkai. The peace march was slated to take place on 6–7 October 2012. His move drew some support from the international human rights community. In early October 2012, a few rights' activists from abroad reacted on Imran's call for a peaceful march by descending on Islamabad and bracing themselves to troop into the tribal hinterlands with an uncurbed enthusiasm. Chief among them was former US ambassador and peace activist Ann Wright, an old decrepit lady, bearing a cross of wrinkles over her face and cropped beige hair that hardly drooped pass her bent shoulders. Ms Wright was heading a nine-member party called 'Women for Peace'. The activist looked unbending, despite her government issuing a travel advisory that warned all US citizens against touring Pakistan. The peace march was surely the first of its kind attempted in Pakistan to send out a clear message to the US administration. Speaking to a group of journalists in Islamabad, an unshakable Ms Wright seemed loyal to the cause: 'We are going to South Waziristan to witness the destruction and apologize for the killings. The US is violating the sovereignty of your country'.

For Imran, it was a symbolic move. He did not receive the blessings of his government; in fact, it turned out that the ungainly Zardari attempted to unsettle Imran's marching plans by delaying visas to interested foreign peace activists. No other mainstream party had ever visited Waziristan before, so clearly it promised to be a landmark excursion. Shoring up Imran was another US-based anti-drone campaigner, the skinny faced Stafford Smith. Mr Smith thought that the march would enlighten the people in the West, who to this day remain blinded by the anti-extremism campaigns of the US government. The truth, he believed, must be told. The Mehsud, Bhittani, and Burki tribes of the Waziristan belt had also welcomed Imran's move and promised security to the marchers. It was now 6 October 2012, and the day of the march had opened auspiciously for Imran. He had the unwavering support of his party workers, and even the women in his party wanted to accompany him to the rugged gorges of Waziristan. However, knowing the Afghan temperament towards the free thinking, freely dressed *aurat* (women), Imran tactfully brushed them out of the excursion. An early riser by habit, Imran preferred to start his daily routine through a sweat-belching workout. His early morning workout addiction is household knowledge in Pakistan; no matter how pushed he is for time, his body would cease to cooperate without an early morning run. He therefore makes a conscious effort of keeping himself in shape. By 8 a.m., his workers started descending at his villa in Bani Gala. After treating himself to a healthy vitamin-rich breakfast, usually dominated by oranges plucked off from his own diverse plantations, Imran slipped into his traditional spotless white *shalwar kameez*. He then made a swift inspection of his entourage, took measure of their spirits and jumped onto his jet-black bulletproof SUV. His convoy left the villa at lazy speeds, streaming its way down the hill and along the bumpy curves, often obstructed by onlookers aiming to catch a glimpse of their leader. The convoy had a subdued presence by the time it left Bani Gala, but it gradually gained momentum as it entered the heart of the capital. In around half an hour, the procession had managed to speed through Islamabad to reach the outer end of the city, where more supporters awaited with bated breath, showering Imran's sleek V8 with rose petals. Imran reciprocated with his fist lifted high above his shoulders in an unswerving display of courage and bravado. By the afternoon, Imran and his fellow campers had attracted enough strength that they were beginning to cause traffic disruptions. They reached Talagang, a small town in district Chakwal, nearly 150 km away from the country's capital in Islamabad. The crowd chuffed up, and yelling, chirping, and chanting was all that one could hear against a background of music played at an ear-popping pitch. By the evening, the convoy had laid siege to Imran's home town Mianwali before proceeding to Dera Ismail Khan, where fellow party workers had made arrangements for overnight encampment. The next morning, Imran's safari, now a hefty 5,000 and growing, was obstructed by the administration through whale-sized containers and teasing roadblocks. Journeying arduously and quite obviously exhausted, Imran protested: 'We would even go to America to get the drone attacks stopped. If the drone strikes do not stop, I will give a call for a march on Islamabad'. The crowds flared up into a heaven-soaring chant.

Moments later, once his raging temptations had given way to controlled thinking, Imran decided to halt the journey and gather the crowds in Tank, some 41 miles short of his planned destination. Donning a white turban in line with the tribal traditions, Imran announced that they had already succeeded in sending out the message loud and clear. He once again lauded the persistence of the youth and congratulated all those who supported the cause. Families of victims from north Waziristan had also made the journey, carrying images of innocent children and people who were killed by the drones. Interestingly, other leading political parties scoffed at Imran's wearisome journey, calling it nothing more than a picnic outing and a scheme to score political points. In my saner opinion, the peace march did prove to be a point-scoring decision. The youth particularly saw it as a good move, especially at a time when the government in control was paying lip service to the matter and had not made any conscious effort to alleviate the problem.

The marching plan of the PTI was well-received for another reason. The march took place against a backdrop of widespread protests across the Muslim world. Resentment for the West compounded when a trailer of an anti-Islamic movie, titled *Innocence of Muslims*, was uploaded on YouTube earlier in the summer, sparking off a series of protests across the Islamic world. Millions had taken to streets, and the protests turned sorely ugly. The liberals in the West shielded behind the contents of freedom of speech. Many Western peace activists expressed solidarity with the Muslims and called for a restraint on sensitive matters. Two weeks prior to PTI's march, its secretary, Dr Arif Alvi, demanded an immediate removal of the controversial video and advised against repeating such vexing in the future. In fact, this was the only matter ratified by all major political parties, as the authorities concerned decided to ban YouTube for an indefinite period.

The election season was finally inching closer. A lot of prophetic surveys came to light. With nearly half of the electoral force between the age of eighteen and thirty-five, Imran went about with boisterous optimism. He had full faith in the youth as he had seen a vast ocean of them turning up at his rallies. His tsunami, he believed, would see him through and make history. Buoyed by the success of his aggressive point-making rallies over the past fifteen months, Imran made several trips to universities and colleges across the country—also tapping the ever-growing social media. His speeches were fiery and his agenda of change was reverberating in the far stretches of the country. However, men of letters within my extended household and the wider circle, especially the ones well-versed in the dynamics of an election, suspected Imran's chances and doubted his claims of a clean sweep; this was because most of the Imran hooting emerged from the urban youth-ones, who had access to modern instruments of social media. The Imran bulge, many believed, may have failed to penetrate the more interior agrarian parts of Punjab and Sindh. That is where large clusters of the country's population hole up. To court that segment, one must have a grass root presence. A problem that Imran grapples to this day. In a constituency based political set up, there may be other forces at play. For example, the spine to manipulate the local courts and tribal *jirgas*. Imran's populism it seemed was restricted to the urban youth and the urban lower, middle, and upper classes. A few days short of the elections, journalist Qamar Zaman aptly described Imran's limitations in an editorial published in the *Express Tribune*:

And in the heart of rural Punjab, you can't win elections based on slogans and pretty manifestos. When it comes to constituency politics in these areas, it's all about who can better negotiate the local *thana* and *katcheri* (local court) and provide people jobs. Party policies, if they matter at all, are not a priority and the ability of local notables to get the job done is what's of importance. That's why these local 'fixers', be they the Chaudhrys or the Maliks, become so important for political parties that when time comes to awarding tickets, they are given preference over life-long party workers.

The lack of Imran appeal in the sloppy rural dung heaps of the country was a household subject in the lead up to the elections. The 2013 election excitement is etched in my memory. It was, after all, the first time I had ever voted. I remember how my politically astute, paunchy looking paternal uncles would go about group thinking the elections, occasionally scratching their barren skulls and sharing with each other their well-estimated prophecies. However, come March–April 2013, many of us had overlooked Imran's lack of appeal in the remote shabby wilderness of the country, and we were actually upbeat about his prospects. It was no illusion to me; the mood did favour Imran's cabin as he had been running his campaigns on pure adrenaline, but an upset was very much on the cards. After all, when it comes to an election, the outcome depends on how many voters actually turn up to vote. We were all ecstatic. Stalls were erected in all major commercial areas around the country selling caps, hats, t-shirts, flags, badges, sleek posters bearing party catchphrases, multicoloured scarves, anthem DVDs, and other eye-catching party souvenirs. It was a festive affair and visibly more pronounced in key urban centres around the country. Being in Islamabad at the time was great fun. Loud speakers were played at full blast, and I personally witnessed many late night roaring PTI processions. My parents told me that they have never seen such pre-election buzz before. I remember how the city's skyline was torched with fireworks every second evening. The frenzy assumed Himalayan proportions. I credit Imran for this. He and Nawaz Sharif were the two most sought-after crowd pullers. PPP, thanks to some bizarre performance in the centre, would be restricted to Sindh only.

By early April, all major political parties had advanced to what would be the final round of carping at each other. All parties had taken a good measure of their formulas for the fledgling country, stated rousingly in their manifestos, which were discussed in the media and sharpened, and the speeches were rehearsed. The Election Commission of Pakistan had already taken notice of all 'would-be' party candidates contesting the elections. The scrutiny of the nomination papers was complete. The election match would be played in 272 constituencies for a place in the National Assembly, the lower house of the parliament. Another sixty seats were reserved for the women and ten seats were for the minority community. Concurrently, regional elections were also staged to form the provincial governments. Looking at the size of the electoral force, the elections were globally dubbed to be the world's fifth largest. Additionally, these were the first ever 'transgender sensitive' elections of Pakistan. The scene was set and the whistle was blown as all parties went ahead, locking horns for the last mile. The key to winning the throne would be determined by the outcome in Punjab as the province accounted for more than half of the National Assembly seats. Punjab, being the traditional fortress of Nawaz Sharif, promised a close contest between Sharif's N-league and Imran's PTI. The only concern holding back PTI was its lack of control over the rural structures in Punjab. However, Imran boasted of a unique 'never-used-before' marketing strategy for the competition: his party had been experimenting with short documentaries and films that highlighted the performances of rival parties, raising awareness on social injustice and reinforcing the importance of voting in an election. Through these videos, the party would attempt to shed light on the perils of *patwari-ism* (land accountants), a thug police culture, and the issue of nepotism in politics. To top it all off, there would be a ten-minute video discussing the evolution of Imran's party from being an underdog of the past to one of the most intriguingly tempting political forces in recent times. Imran tirelessly went about rallying across the country. His most impressive and recurring theme was his own personal tale of perpetual struggle:

At the age of nine, I dreamt to represent Pakistan Cricket Team which I did. Then I dreamt of captaining the team and winning the world cup, which I did. Next dream was to build Shaukat Khanum Cancer Hospital and it was also materialized. Now, I have dreamt that PTI will sweep elections and we are on our way to build a new Pakistan.[1]

Given the backdrop of anti-US sentiments in the country, his vows of not prostrating to the US for aid money and promises of breaking the begging bowl had also hit a chord. Another populist gimmick he experimented with came to the fore in his Faisalabad address: 'We pledge that after coming into power, we will protect the life and property of all minorities including Christians, Hindus, Sikhs and uphold all their other rights in consonance with the teachings of the holy prophet (PBUH)'.

The barbs were also in full swing. At Nowshera, a small town in KP and a traditional hashing zone of the religious parties and ANP, Imran howled a heap of disdain at Maulana Fazlur Rehman, admonishing the religious looney for not putting his foot down when the Americans were raining the drones on their hamlets and ravaging the security condition. The Maulana went into a repelling mode, once again exploiting Imran's

Jewish connections—by now, a predictable taunt for Imran. Addressing his supporters in DI Khan, the orange-turbaned, grey-whiskered *mullah* ruled out any possibility of Imran bringing about a change in the country. 'Imran,' he jeered, 'has kept his own children out of Pakistan, who are not even Muslims and speaks of establishing a seventh-century Islamic welfare state?' The cranky Maulana issued a fiat after a joint deliberation of a coterie of heavy stubbled, loin-scratching *mullahs*, calling it *haram* (forbidden) to vote for Imran. Imran retorted to this slandering by calling Maulana as the third member of the faithless, debauched triumvirate that also included Zardari and Sharif. A few months earlier, Imran had accused the trio of a fleecing worth 3.1 trillion rupees. He also went about gleefully boasting his chances against the Maulana and considered him easy pickings, as Imran never believed the religious parties had the legs to cover much ground in Pakistan—that is true. Going by the records, religious parties have never gained much public attention at the voting counters. With Imran's rallies mounting the charts, Sharif was also determined to up the ante. His dry glossy scalp makes it convenient for his supporters to keep him in sight, and his voracious appetite for unhealthy cuisines is public knowledge. He recently had his head cultivated through a transplant, drawing gossip lovers in the country to gut-busting banter. Unperturbed by Imran's incessant mud-slinging, Sharif fired his own version of protest. He had already been through the mill when his last government was sent packing by a sulking dictator, and desperate for a comeback, Sharif addressed a crampy convergence of his supporters in Sheikhupura—a Mughal hamlet right outside Sharif's home town in Lahore—cautioning the crowd against falling for Imran. Waggling his head at the prospects of an Imran run administration, he called Imran's team a bunch of newcomers, with no real wisdom of governance. 'Please vote for a party that understands the problems of the people, instead of voting for a bunch of newcomers,' cried Sharif to a sea of devoted heads at Sheikhupura.

The election campaign continued on a high throughout April, but it was also not without its lows. April proved to be one of the deadliest months that year. The TTP was fully active, planning attacks on political personalities in an attempt to sabotage the election process. A source close to Imran's party had opened up to me and declared that Imran was on the hit list as well. Slaying Imran would have been a child's play, given the ease with which he presented himself to the flood of people around him. In his dauntlessly revealing prose for UK's *Daily Mail*, Imran wrote: 'I had been told I was on the number one hit-list, although who the terrorists would be was anybody's guess. There are perhaps twenty-five militant groups which now call themselves "Taliban" and any one of them could have been hired by my political opponents'.

By certain accounts, the election-related death toll had risen to 110, with as many as 723 people brutally injured. Together with the assertive election campaigns in April, the terrorist attacks proved another dominant feature of the month. In what proved to be a scary month for the campaigners, Imran got his fair share of scare as well. On 8 May, just three days short of the fate sealing Election Day, Imran was scheduled to hold a rally in Lahore. The crowds had already assembled in great numbers and awaited him with cheerful enthusiasm. Once Imran arrived at the site, close to sunset, a makeshift stage, with a height of around 14 feet, was erected for his address. Imran was being raised on a forklift, flanked by two men holding him by his shoulder. However, just as Imran reached the top and attempted to whisk his way off the forklift, his balance was disturbed by a sudden confusion in the camp, and he, along with his two guards, tumbled off. Imran's feet faced the heavens and his head crash-landed on the ground, brushing off a metal rod during his descent. 'What a tumble!' I intoned, hooked to my television. For a moment, we went into a shock. 'As everything is so controversial in this country, this must be a plot to strike him out,' I mumbled to myself, absolutely flabbergasted, with a biting chill slithering down my spine. Interestingly, it turned out to be a genuine accident. One of Imran's vast supplies of photographers, choosing to be unnamed for this account, gladly shared the ground picture with me:

> The forklift was not designed to handle a lot of people. I could sense that it was senile and off-balanced. Once Imran was in the plunge, my first reaction was that we have lost him. When he crashed on the floor, he was knocked out. People there began to whimper. It was a horrible moment.

An unconscious Imran, with a wide cut on his forehead, was quickly bundled off to Shaukat Khanum hospital for treatment. Several hours later, PTI's vice-chairman emerged from inside the hospital, calming the supporters with the news of Imran's survival. Relieved by the news, Jemima, mother of Imran's two children, wasted no time in flicking out a tweet: 'He is safe ... he is safe'. Imran had a brief tryst with the afterlife, narrowly escaping with two fractures in his spinal column. The angels had refused to take him. His tiring election campaign was already drawing to an end, with only one more address left to be delivered the next evening at Islamabad's D-chowk—Pakistan's Lincoln Memorial. While most of us thought that PTI would cancel its final election rally in Islamabad, Imran thought otherwise; he had more in store, and his best was kept for the last. He gathered whatever was left of him—a fractured back, a senile rib, and a gashed-up head—and got his technicians to plug in the cameras, airing himself live from his inclined hospital bed in Lahore. The speech comes fresh to me as I was there with my wife. Once again, the same theme, but with a greater impact. In his stuttering voice, he took the crowd down his memory lane. A refresher course of his seventeen-year struggle in politics was in the offing, repeating his reasons of venturing into politics, with all the bounties of God already at his door step. That was nothing new, but it still got the youth listening. Imran was at his enterprising best. Two days later, when most of us were making our historic journey to the ballot booths, Imran was lying restlessly in the hospital, jolting out of his sleep in brief intervals, obsessed with the election outcomes.

6

The Rebel in Parliament

In truth, I care little about any party's politics—the man behind it is the important thing.

Mark Twain

The Election Day opened on a feverish note. Imran proved a restless old patient, hobbling in and out of the restroom fitfully. He was not very cooperative with the hospital staff. Being a disturbed soul, his nursing proved a difficult labour as he robbed himself of the hours he needed to fully recuperate. The tumble a few days earlier interrupted his regular workout routine, and the sedatives failed to fully sedate him. That great fall, that constant throbbing of the head and a body that had him considerably jaded was perhaps the closest Imran had ever gotten to embracing death. He had never felt that much knackered. Even bowling a couple of dozen overs on juiceless Caribbean tracks to a raging, misbehaving, West Indian middle order of the 1980s, in comparison, seemed much less disturbing for the soul. Following a strict recovery regimen, which, among other things, included staying away from his inane political gossip and other frivolous party *gup shup* (chit chat), Imran must have felt completely ostracised. After all, Pakistani politics has become irresistibly entertaining as of late. He kept his television screen running and allowed important members of his party to obstruct his sleep in restrained succession. Being drawn to his television was obviously not healthy as reports that come out of a Pakistani election could be horribly unnerving.

The run up to the elections had already proved a bloody affair. Scores of people were wounded and a few were killed. Reports of sporadic violence persisted even on the Election Day. The Baluchistan and KP provinces were the worst hit. The southern part of Baluchistan was particularly difficult to contain. These are the rugged gorges heavily subjected by the displeased Baloch rebels and other separatist elements. The Baloch Liberation Army, the Baloch Liberation Front, and the Baloch Republican Party had called for widespread strikes and boycott, barring people from approaching the voting booths. As a result, the turnout in most of the Baloch dominant districts in the south was far from promising. Things appeared relatively calm in the northern part of Baluchistan, in the area predominantly occupied by the Pashtun tribes. Decent voter turnout was reported in the north. Female participation was also encouraging. The situation in KP was relatively better, with a few scattered incidents of violence. The attendance of women in a conservative province like KP was a sign of maturity. Traditionally, men in KP are known to disenfranchise their women by confining them to the house, scorning at the prospects of them going out unaccompanied. However, in a refreshing development, long queues of *burka*-clad women were spotted in various districts of the province.

Clashes between political parties were also widely reported. In Punjab and Sindh, armed clashes between PTI and the N-leaguers came to notice. In Gujranwala, an old town along the ancient GT road in Punjab and famous for its mouth-watering beef-laden cuisine, one PTI worker was killed in a rumble with PML-N supporters. In Lahore, an armed PTI activist was detained by the police for shooting bullets in the air. In south Punjab, two PML-N activists were shot dead. Reports of rigging allegations in various constituencies of Punjab and Sindh were rife. In Karachi, a bomb explosion rocked the election cell office of ANP, killing eleven people that also included a two-year-old boy, although nearly fifty escaped with fatal injuries. In Quetta, unknown assailants reportedly rained the polling stations in the Killi Shabo area with hand grenades, killing one child and maiming eight people. In Peshawar, one child was killed and nine people were injured in a similar bomb detonation in the outer skirts. Imran, despite his unsettled, out-of-whack spine and his recurring headaches, heavy heartedly absorbed the situation from his hospital room in Lahore. His discomfort was perfectly comprehensible, after all, this was the first time that he and his progressive apostles had thrown all their weight behind their election campaigns, and they were desperate for some cheery news. In the grip of the election fever myself, I, along with a gang of cousins in Lahore, went to vote—my first ever encounter with a polling station in Pakistan. Years of dictatorial rule and lack of faith in democratic governments had undermined the sanctity of voting. Scores of people of a varying age and gender had lined up outside. I overheard two men, seemingly in their thirties: 'What is Sharif going to do for us, build roads again? What will a poor man do of those roads when he is hungry? Stroll on them perhaps'.

The urban sentiments clearly went in Imran's favour, and his earlier hospital campaigns were coming in handy. One poor construction worker said that he was a long-time N-league voter until Mr Khan rescued his mother who was dying of cancer. Another labourer had flown in from Nigeria to cast his vote, saying that he did not want old faces to call the shots anymore. Youngsters hooting for Imran stormed to the polling stations in their cars, chirping and yelling PTI ballads, with their arms and faces decorated with stickers of cricket bats. The tooting of the horns and the fluttering of the flags reassured Imran that it was all hunky dory. However, isolated episodes of rigging kept Imran on the edge of his bed.

As the day unfolded, more disturbing news was in store for Imran's cabin. Few of the well-known media outfits around played their part by providing on-the-ground coverage to rigging complaints coming from various parts of the country. A sudden rage swept across Imran's party. The ace leadership fumed into Imran's room and fed his insatiable appetite for facts and rumour. It appeared that some polling stations in Islamabad and Rawalpindi had no details of the voters' lists, which was highly alarming. It was also highlighted that some polling stations in the capital were established in remote areas, making it hard for families to cast their votes. One PTI supporter, Atika Afzal, accused the N-leaguers of ripping off the chits that had their electoral numbers on them. Another female PTI voter reported that they were stopped from going inside the polling station. The Election Commission of Pakistan (ECP) was also accused of mismanagement. By the standard procedures, the ECP can only establish a polling station to accommodate no more than 1,000 voters, however in violation of the procedures, one polling station set up in the outer skirts of the capital city accommodated 6,000 voters. The staff at some polling stations had also reported not having the possession of voting lists until late in the evening. Surprisingly, the police deployed outside the polling centres to ensure nothing goes wrong took no measures. Worse, the Human Rights Commission of Pakistan (HRCP) had declared that the elections were grossly mishandled by the ECP. By the HRCP observation, the polling stations were not organised enough to accommodate all the voters. The site selection of the polling stations also invited heaps of criticism. The participation of women was also undermined. The HRCP therefore advised a permanent year-long scrutiny of the electoral rolls to ensure mismanagement of a similar scale was evaded in future elections.

A day later, unofficial election results began flashing on the media screens. It became obvious that the argument of Imran's lack of appeal in the rural dung heaps of the country had some credibility, and Nawaz Sharif sensed victory. His goosebumps began to disappear. Overwhelmed by the news, Sharif's supporters had already kicked off their merry making outside his residence in Lahore. Sharif's adversaries, however, viewed this humming on the streets as a premature celebration. Later in the evening, Sharif made a public appearance in his richly decorated and ornate veranda, amid a loud thundering of the crowd, thanking them for the support and reminding them that the results were still unofficial and that they should pray that PML-N secured an absolute majority. Sharif stood there for a few moments, facing the crowd with his flabby palms stretched open and his arms soaring high above his skull. Allah was there to help, and if Allah did not come for his aid, he would rely on his retinue of party flunkeys. Several hours later, as more constituencies hatched their verdict, it became obvious that Punjab, the country's largest province, was firmly in the hands of Sharif. Since Punjab holds the key to the top slot, a majority there seals the fate of the elections. In the centre, off the 272 national assembly seats, 136 were required to form the government. Sharif had already secured 130, implying that he would not have to worry much to achieve the magic number as the independent candidates will soon be flocking towards him.

While Imran's ambition of a clean sweep was too farfetched, his party still registered an impressive showing and proved a roaring new force on the bloc. PTI emerged as the second largest political party in the country, filling the gulf left wide open by PPP. By some analysts, PTI was an underdog, buoyed by an urban-driven social media activism, and for them to dash the prospects of PPP and ANP was a splendid achievement. Nail-biting, riveting contests were witnessed between Imran's candidates and Sharif's bidders in some of the important hashing zones. Imran himself won his native seat from Mianwali, defeating his trailing opponent by a huge margin of 60,000 votes. ANP was robbed of its traditional fortress of KP. The voters in KP had once again proved their democratic disposition by out-right rejecting the nationalist ANP and all the religious parties in favour of Imran's PTI. In KP, Imran had made huge gains, defeating his adversaries by overwhelming margins—winning the majority of his seats from the districts of Peshawar, Mardan, and Nowshera, while also making glaring inroads into other smaller districts of the province. Imran's success in KP, however, was not only a result of his punch lines. The KP electorate rides on a reputation of voting in a new party in every election: in 2002, they had backed the religious parties into power; in 2008, they supported the nationalist ANP; and in 2013, they banked on Imran. Imran had fielded a new team of young politicians who he rewarded handsomely by uprooting the vote banks of long-time power brokers and influential politicians of the province. PTI was well in sight of crossing the fifty-seat threshold required to form the provincial government. The biggest challenge for Imran in KP was living up to his promissory notes as people in KP did not subscribe to false claims and they expected their representatives to deliver on their promises. The electorate in KP had never been the abiding flag-wavers or loyalists, the kind that one usually encounters in Punjab and Sindh. Winning KP was both good and bad news for Imran.

As for PPP, Zardari's flunkeys received a drubbing throughout the country, being shoved back to Sindh. However, PPP was not even expected to reclaim Sindh, courtesy its unpopular policies in the previous regime. Writer and analyst, Zulfiqar Halepoto claims that PPP suspected its prospects in Sindh, and decided to court the local tribal leaders, peers, and other long-time power brokers to secure its hold in the province.

As the election fever subsided and the final verdicts were absorbed by the public, Sharif attempted to bury the hatchet with Imran by visiting the fractured leader at the hospital. Imran had earlier turned down the offer of Sharif's bridge making. The two had been exhausting themselves through a heavy exchange of barbs for the past month. In a bid to keep the government in functional form, it was imperative that the two drew closer and learned to tolerate each other's company. Finally, at the insistence of the Saudi ambassador, Imran responded to Sharif's overtures and had a brief trysting with him in the hospital. Later, Naeem-ul-Haq, a senior PTI leader and a lookalike of Sharif (except for his bushy, heavy moustache, totally concealing his upper lip), ruled out any interference of the Saudi ambassador in facilitation of the meeting. Imran's apprehension towards the meeting was perfectly normal. A peace-making encounter with Sharif would not go down well with his supporters, who had long since been pumped by him against the fleecing of Sharifs, stoutly damning Sharif for his corruption and accusing him of robbing the people's mandate through a nationwide trumping up of votes. Nevertheless, etiquette demanded that Imran showed some poise, ensuring that a brief hosting of Sharif ended on a lighter note. Sharif was escorted to Imran's room: a chaplet of flowers was delivered and *salams* (greetings) were exchanged. Sharif perceived the short meeting as a success and wandered out of the hospital with a relieved expression, delightfully informing the reporters that all differences between him and Imran were history and that they both pledged to work together and serve the *janta* (people). He further added that he respected the mandate of PTI in KP and likewise expected them to respect his. Dodging the plodding reporters as soon as they attempted to quiz the rigging accusations, Sharif hurriedly made his way out of the scene.

While Imran had conceded defeat and accepted Sharif's mandate, he had also made it clear that his party would be one of the strongest oppositions the country had ever witnessed. He vowed to keep the government on its toes. On the issue of rigging, he was unforgiving. A day after the elections, Imran was quoted by every major press in the country:

> We will issue a white paper against the alleged rigging in some of the major constituencies in Punjab and Karachi. We will also show everyone that the biggest power of democracy lies with the opposition. We will show everyone what a strong opposition means. The defeat has not affected me as I have witnessed the unprecedented zeal and fervour of the youth and women in this country.[1]

Demands of recounting swept across the avenues of Karachi, Lahore, and Islamabad. PTI activists thronged the streets to stage peaceful sit-in processions. In Karachi, thousands of displeased protestors assembled on Shahrah-e-Faisal, the nerve centre of the city, in the presence of armed security. A similar turnout was observed in Lahore, where one female PTI activist expressed disbelief over the outcome in her constituency. She told the reports that, in her estimate, over 60 per cent of the people voted for the PTI candidate: 'We reject the result, want Election Commission to intervene'. In Islamabad, over 500 people bickered near the diplomatic enclave, carrying placards that sent a clear message to the ECP. People were seen shaming the Election Commission, expounding that dictatorships were better than a fake democratic system that robbed them of their mandate. A few female activists in Islamabad also informed that PML-N workers were trying to take control over the polling stations and manipulate the whole process. A senior leader of the PTI and a close aide of Imran also turned up for the protest, calling for a recount in the affected constituencies. The hypothesis of Imran's following being restricted to the urban sections of the country was also commonly rejected. One particular extract from the 'Letters to the Editor' section of *The Nation*, a well-known local tabloid strikes an important note:

> It's a propaganda jointly sanctioned by all traditional political parties in the country. They say that majority of the PTI supporters belong to the hyper active cyber generation: people of the urban upper middle class or the Facebooking gentry. In truth, anyone with the ability to think rationally voted for PTI. My own tailor, mechanic and barber voted for PTI, and they do not belong to the upper crust of our society. One of my friends had told me that her driver and all her maidservants had voted for PTI. In fact, during my eight-hour pottering at a polling station, I met with a number of people in their 30s and 40s, who were first time voters and had never subscribed to Facebook or twitter in their life.

FAFEN, an election watchdog operating out of Islamabad, came out with its own revelations. The findings were editorialised in the *Express Tribune* as follows: 'Among many anomalies on the Election Day, there is one that stands out: There was more than 100% voter turnout in many polling stations for national and provincial constituencies across the country'.

The survey revealed that nearly forty-nine polling stations had more than a 100 per cent turnout, and 65 per cent of those polling stations were in Punjab. FAFEN had requested the commission against including numbers from these polling stations into their official estimates. The watchdog also suggested that manipulation was more conveniently handled in female polling stations. Imran, still bedridden, but looking fresher than before, decided to announce his take on the matter through a recorded video message:

We have decided to work together with Nawaz Sharif on all matters of state importance. The country has gone through a tumultuous phase. Terrorism has been our biggest concern and all political parties have a common stance on the issue. We feel that Pakistan will go nowhere if terrorism is not addressed immediately. Secondly, I appeal to the Election Commission of Pakistan to address the grievances of the electorate. I may draw to your attention that this is perhaps the only time in the country's history that people feverishly turned out to vote in an election. I know there are a lot of people out on the streets protesting the results of some constituencies. We feel that reports of rigging are genuine. And if the Election Commission buries the matter here, people will never come out to vote again and will lose faith in the electoral process. I therefore appeal to the commission to look into the matter through recounting of votes, by matching the finger prints of the voters with their finger prints on the national ID cards. Although I suspect manipulation in over twenty-five constituencies but for a start I request you to have a recount in only four of them. This shall only take you two days. Lastly, we will ensure that we bring about serious reforms in KP and show everyone what our version of Naya Pakistan really means. A model government in KP and a watchful opposition is our promise to the nation.[2]

In what turned out to be an encouraging development, the ECP's Secretary Ishtiaque Ahmed confirmed that, in total, 110 rigging-related complaints had been registered with them. The secretary gave his assurances that a proper investigation would be held, stating that they would also take note of Imran's charges of rigging. Meanwhile, a re-poll in forty-three polling stations of Karachi's NA-250 were ordered by the commission under the strict surveillance of the armed forces. The re-poll was scheduled to take place on 19 May. The decision was disputed by the MQM as they wanted a recount of the entire constituency, comprising a total of 180 polling booths. The ECP, however, did not react to MQM's protest and reaffirmed its decision for a recount on only forty-three polling stations. Resenting ECP's rigidity, MQM decided to boycott the contest. Later, PPP also protested and ruled out their participation in the match. Sadly, the lead up to the contest took an ugly turn as PTI's Senior Vice President Zahra Shahid Hussain, a resident of Karachi's upscale Defence Housing Authority, was gunned down by three unknown assailants in front of her house. A howl of protest gripped the city. PTI activists were terribly incensed. Imran was quick to register his objection, rapidly concluding that the Chairman of MQM Mr Altaf Hussain had a hand in the killing, as the London-based politician had been openly threatening PTI activists and leaders, and also expressed his disturbance over the way British authorities pay their lip service to anything that implicated Altaf. The murder was met with a nationwide backlash from all major political parties. Imran had revived his long-time bickering with Altaf. Sorely maddened by Imran's finger pointing, Altaf's *badmash* (rowdy and unruly) supporters vowed to file a defamation suit against Imran. However, 19 May brought some respite for the PTI expounders when Imran clinched another seat in the much-discussed rematch played in NA-250 of Karachi, and by a sizeable margin. With MQM and PPP out of the game, the stage was set for PTI to go for an easy kill. The voter turnout, however, was on the lower side as the killing of a senior PTI leader the night before had petrified the city.

Meanwhile, Sharif was officially nominated by his party as the next Prime Minister of Pakistan. Sharif's tally of seats in the centre had risen to an imposing 180, courtesy the independent candidates, fleeing towards like iron filings drawn to a magnet. Sharif was now busy organising his cabinet and allotting ministerial portfolios. In addition to being the prime minister, Sharif planned on retaining the foreign affairs and defence portfolios. As for Imran, he was finally discharged from the hospital after two long weeks of confinement. During his hospital rehabilitation, Imran had hardly remained detached from his party affairs, never allowing his physical incapacity to obstruct his political dealings. A specially designed spinal brace was wrapped around his neck to ensure he redeemed his ramrod stance. Rest was prescribed by the doctors for another three weeks, before Imran could finally resume taking a crack at his routine workouts. Being shuffled from the hospital to his house in Lahore, he had to dispense with a few important matters, chief among which was governing KP. A lot of point proving awaited him. He would have to translate all his compulsive talking into visible results. A day later, he called a meeting of his party's parliamentary committee to discuss potential candidates for slots in the KP's provincial assembly. Pervez Khattak, the frail-looking, grey haired, and seasoned politician of KP, was appointed as the chief minister. KP was a mountain of mess, dampened by a decade-long War on Terror, where frequent bombings had uprooted families and devastated generations. Thousands of people were in flight, reduced to refugee status in their own courtyards. The extremists prowled the far stretches of the region in search of soft targets. Ancient Sufi shrines and mosques bearing heritage value also went up in flames. US drones breached all boundaries of sovereignty. Cities and villages lived in perpetual fear. The local economy was in tatters. A committed leadership was required to purge the province of all its troubles. Imran knew full well that this was a tough province and failure to bring any change would spell disaster for his political career. He spared himself the physical rest that he sorely needed to get his groove back. During this time, he gave much thought to his priorities for the province. Imran was finally sworn in as a parliamentary representative a few weeks later in Islamabad. Until Imran made his first parliamentary appearance in over five years, the assembly had already been in session for a near two weeks, sifting through the national budget and the security concerns infesting the state. A healthier-looking Imran, gradually retrieving his athletic agility and draped in his traditional white *shalwar kameez*, made his maiden parliamentary speech amid a loud clatter of the house. He intoned '*Bismillah*'—in the name of Allah, the most beneficent, the most merciful. As the clatter of the house abated, Imran announced his arrival. He began with a request to pardon him should he fail to deliver an extensive speech, as he was still not at the top of his fitness. Amusingly, as the speech progressed, Imran lost himself completely and lingered on for nearly an hour. The extract of his unpolished Urdu, laced with a baritone Punjabi accent, went as follows:

I wish not to speak as a leader of the opposition party but as an ordinary Pakistani. I grew up in a country which had stronger institutions. My parents fed me on the privileges of living in a free country. Pakistan was a country whose economic model inspired the likes of South Korea and Malaysia. But now, lack of justice and corruption has buried our economic potential. I fail to comprehend that why a country, whose people, so compassionately dole out charity, have no faith in the sanctity of paying taxes? I disagree with the parliament's decision to impose indirect taxes as that shall spell disaster for the poor, who are already losing the battle to inflation. We must take measures to cultivate a culture of tax compliance. I ask; how does the ruling elite justify its lavish living in a poor country, tainted with never ending piles of foreign debt? There has also been a flight of human capital from the country. Our

biggest asset are the overseas Pakistanis and we must incentivize their
return. Our institutions have collapsed and they can only be rescued by
technocrats and not by the bureaucracy. On terrorism, I strongly abhor
this US ravaging of our tribal regions. This is a breach of all international
charters of peace and security. These Pashtuns will always fight back and
there will be no end to this crusade. The only way to get our feet out of
this war is through a peaceful dialogue. I assure the ruling party that
we will prove to be a constructive opposition and develop a working
consensus on all central matters.[3]

Just as it seemed that Imran had skipped the subject, he pulled the rabbit
out of his hat by making a fleeting reference to the recent elections
and the grievances of the electorate—people who felt that they have
been robbed through rigging. A few sighs erupted sporadically in the
Sharif section of the house. A few mumbles and a few giggles rented
the atmosphere in the parliament as Imran concluded. His speech had
set the tone for what may prove to be a painfully unsettling opposition
for the Sharifs. To them, Imran's opening speech of the season sounded
more like a sermon on the principles of leadership and nation building.
Imran's health was not as concerning anymore, but it demanded regular
inspection. He was exhausted and departed to London for a few days
to recuperate in the company of his sons and fully unwind himself—
months of dogged campaigns, nonstop mud-slinging, and that ugly
crash in Lahore had taken a toll on him. Some strolling with his kids in
the company of Richmond Park's exotic and stunning gardens was just
the right recipe.

KP was Imran's new-found obsession, and he knew that he would
have to hit the ground running on his return from London. A desirably
fitter-looking Imran on his return from London surveyed through all
major departments, and he got down to holding extensive party meetings.
'Reforms is what we want,' exclaimed Imran, with an 'I mean business'
look on his face. Although Imran had fought his way into the government,
he still had to push through the same rotten and shirking bureaucracy
in the province, knowing full well that the politicians could not do their
paper pushing without a powerful civil administration. The civil service of
Pakistan unfortunately has been politicised and mutilated beyond repair.
This makes implementation of any major reforms rather cumbersome. In
my excavation through a local national library, I got hold of an imposing
Jinnah speech, informally delivered on April 1948 to a batch of civil
servants in Peshawar. What the contents of his address attempted to
preach is a stark departure from what the civil administration has now
become. Here is the extract:

The first thing I wish you to know is that you should never be influenced by any political party or individual politicians. You must at any cost, discharge your duties by the state's constitution. Governments come and go but you stay on. You should not support any political party as that is not your business. Putting pressure on the civil administration is a common fault of politicians. You may find yourselves in trouble not for doing something wrong but for doing something that is right.[4]

Imran had long since been battling with the civil service puzzle, often vilifying top-of-the-pile civil officers for their unbounded malfeasance and fouling the whole administration. Weeks before his official entry into the parliament, he was quoted by the *Express Tribune*: 'Civil service in Pakistan has been destroyed through constant politicization with leaders treating government officials as their personal servants'. Imran had never been in the government before, so it was natural to assume that it would not be an easy ruling. It was learning by doing. He had to rely on the same compelling instinct that he deployed so effectively as a social activist. The first three months of his provincial rule was marked by serious brainstorming sessions. A spate of new developments was in the works. Imran had announced his plans of holding the local bodies' elections in the province by the winter of 2013. This was his idea of delegating the authority to the grass roots and ensure that people at the bottom become active participants in economic decision making. 'We want you to take your own decisions,' lectured Imran at one of his many rallies in Peshawar. His provincial minister of labour and industries, Bakht Baidar Khan, was also quick to sanction the new minimum wage policy. The minister had announced that the new wage would be 10,000 rupees, up from a previous 8,000 rupees, and that all private institutions in the province were law bound to follow. Riding on the strength of a reformist agenda, Imran advised the elementary and secondary education department of his government to leave no stone unturned in executing education reforms. In a meeting held at his residence in Bani Gala, Imran directed the authorities concerned to devise a strategy that would bring down the school dropout rate in the province—wanting no child wastefully loitering out of the school. A financial package aimed at improving the quality of the public institutions was being put together. 'There are close to 25 million children currently out of school. Did we ever think about their future?' protested Imran cutting a determined note. Also on his 'to do list' was a makeover of the degenerated police administration. Another refreshing development came to pass; by early August 2013, PTI government had set up women complaint centres in fifty-six police stations of the province. These centres were staffed by over 100 policewomen, tasked to register complaints honourably. 'Honour' is a word one usually does not tie with police stations in Pakistan. They are terror dens; police, much like the civil authorities, have been subjected to the worst form of nepotism. Those who can bribe, can be easily let off scot free. A police station is not a good company to keep. Their public dealings have always been a matter of worry. With a little dose of bribery, police officials can convert facts into fantasy. Innocent victims often complain of harassment by the police staff. Aware of these lewd transgressions, Imran sent a clear message to the police that they must abandon the practice of seeking favours from politicians.

Similar revamping was envisaged for the health sector of KP, a sector in serious need of a repair. By September 2013, Imran had established thirty-five mother and child health care centres across eight districts of the province. Ensuring rapid visible results was not easy and Imran's first ever crack at policy formulation was no less than an ordeal.

The trials of KP were not the only contents on Imran's plate. Throughout the second half of 2013, he had made fitful attempts to court the Supreme Court and the ECP to take note of the rigging complaints. He finally unveiled the white paper that he had promised soon after the elections. In late August 2013, Imran held a press conference at Bani Gala. 'We were caught off guard at the elections,' expressed Imran with a dismissive shrug, highlighting that there were 400 rigging-related complaints, with sixty-four of them coming from his party. With a permanent scowl plastered on his face, and seemingly fed up to his teeth, Imran exposed the fat 2,000-page document, hoisting it by his veiny forearms. 'We wish to strengthen the democratic process and had we wanted we would have announced nationwide protests right after the elections,' said Imran. He pleaded the ECP to have a recount on only four constituencies, so those involved in the gerrymandering can be called to account. Alluding to Sharif's victory speech, Imran stressed that the Prime Minister reacted prematurely by declaring himself the winner with less than a quarter of the vote count completed. In another brazen declaration that came a week later, Imran seemed genuinely distraught:

> We do not have any faith in the current members and officials of the ECP as they are PML-N's 'B' team. We contested the elections because for the first time in Pakistan there was an independent judiciary. And as the judiciary under Iftikhar Chaudhry refused to open the four constituencies, it became clear to us that everyone was involved in the scheme.[5]

Imran's riling was not only limited to the election authorities and the government in the centre. He had been a long-time opponent of the US drone campaigns in the tribal areas. In November 2013, Hakimullah Mehsud, the front man of Pakistani faction of Taliban, was killed when a drone was fired on his on his car near the Afghan border in north Waziristan. A worked-up Imran, already absorbed with KP's dodgy socio-economic challenges, saw this as a disaster for his attempts at restoring peace in his province. Rescuing his province from unsolicited bombings was one of his chief election promises and delivering peace was part of his agenda. Donning an ebony black *shalwar kameez*, at a full house parliamentary session in Islamabad, Imran vehemently threatened to block all NATO supplies to Afghanistan. 'A peaceful dialogue with the aggrieved tribes is what we need. Whenever there is some progress, a fresh pounding of drones rattles the whole bridge making initiative,' blasted Imran, cutting a riotous note. He then told the house that KP has been the worst casualty of these drones: nearly 70 per cent of the local industry, in Imran's words, had been devastated. Furthermore, the tourism industry that was once the cash cow for the province is in complete disarray as people are too petrified to visit the area. Interestingly, the Western press found Imran's fulminations in bad taste. Dulcan Walsh of the *New York Times* reacted:

Partly, it is a product of Pakistan's failure to counter a stubborn insurgency. After years of Taliban—induced humiliations and bloodshed, and of heavy American pressure to step up military action against the Taliban, Pakistan's political and security establishments still agree that starting peace talks with the Taliban is the best course. Such talks may have had slim chances of success—previous negotiations quickly foundered—but Mr Mehsud's death appears to have thoroughly derailed them, at least for now. Beyond that, analysts say, Pakistanis have a consistent, if relatively recent, history of rooting for people the West has deemed villains, and against people the West has praised.

Meanwhile, Imran's maiden experimentation with governance invited an unfavourable response from analysts. His six-month-long indulgence in reviving KP's shrinking fortunes had proved challenging. Six months are too short to deserve any verdict anyway, yet political thinkers and analysts in KP began panning Imran's coalition government, stating that it was not easy for his team to deliver given the peculiar nature of KP's problems. Some of the short-term promises he had made—the local bodies' elections, for example—were yet to see the light of day. The year 2013 nevertheless ended on an auspicious note for Imran: he now controlled a full province and had a wonderful opportunity to present himself as a leader who could deliver; he had shaken the old electoral arrangements of the country by side-lining mainstream political parties like PPP and ANP; and he had managed to drive millions to the voting booths. As promised, he indeed proved a pain in the bum opposition, leaving no margin for error for the ruling government. Imran's biggest challenge from this point was to ensure he followed through with the lofty pledges he made during his clamorous, headline-hitting election rallies. With an unruly province like KP to handle, an uncompromising squabbling with the election tribunal, and an unpopular hostility towards Obama's priceless drones, Imran was fighting on too many fronts, and a little too early. However, as a famous English proverb goes: 'A full cup must be carried steadily'.

7

126 Days

The path to our destination is not always a straight one. We go down the wrong road, we get lost, we turn back. Maybe it doesn't matter which road we embark on. Maybe what matters is that we embark.

Barbara Hall

A journalist, hosting a local television show in Lahore, usually invites well-known personalities as guests for some trivial talking. The idea is to have a lot of banter, while riffling through front-page news items. It is a hit with television viewers across the country. During the spring of 2014, the channel had invited Imran for a light-hearted dialogue. Together they scanned through a series of topics: Imran's favourite pastime; his biggest regrets in life; some recollections from his days as a teenager; and his motivation for politics. Knowing Imran and his erratic temper, the more penetrative question was reserved for the last. 'Sir! Have you never thought of your kids taking over the lead from you later in life?' Imran was abrupt. 'I have never compromised on discipline. My whole struggle is for a genuine democratic culture to take root. I never go out of my way to favour relatives. Even as a cricketer, I only favoured those whom I knew can win us matches'. That was a pretty controlled response from someone who was now embroiled in a variety of conflicts within his party.

By March 2014, Imran was having troubles managing his party. Save for the external rifts, his internal bickering was also growing by the day. He had served a show cause notice to the president of his party's Kohat chapter—Humayun Pehlwan. Humayun was allegedly denouncing PTI's policies in the media and sparked an internal wrangling within the party. Worse, Imran's attempt at his cabinet's reshuffling was also met with discontent as the number of disgruntled party members was on the surge. It all began when Imran started awarding ministries to the MPAs who had become part of PTI after winning the elections as independent candidates. This incensed many within the party, as they felt that they have been robbed of their party rights. Imran saw this as a plot to blackmail him and protested:

> I would prefer to dissolve the provincial assembly and call for fresh elections instead of submitting to their blackmailing. It is their democratic right to convey their concerns to me but if they are under the impression that they can easily blackmail me than they clearly do not know me.[1]

Opposition parties in KP took this 'not care a hoot' response as a threat to the parliamentary process, retaliating through the submission of a privilege motion against Imran. All the opposition parties rendered their signatures to the motion, calling Imran's statement undemocratic and stating that they felt his declaration was a shocking surprise. PTI was also accused of not delivering in tandem with its promises made during their election rallies. Imran decided to respond to all the riling his party was subjected to by holding a meeting at his residence in Islamabad. The meeting buried the hatchet and proved a success. One of his party's leaders, Abdul Qayyum Kundi, reportedly summed the whole episode as follows:

> Yes, it is true that some key positions are being filled by people nominated by the chairman. But these decisions were made after a resolution was passed in a central executive committee meeting that empowered the chairman to appoint officials. This is a temporary arrangement. PTI workers are true democrats and they believe that all party officials should be elected. They are demanding that the chairman announce elections for these posts soon. The elections are likely after the local government polls. Another thought that is gaining traction is that since last intra-party election had legitimacy issues, there might be new elections across the country. Things will become clearer when the process of amendments to the party constitution is completed.[2]

To restore his party's sinking political appeal, Imran made an important move. He was made aware of the misuse of tax funds by some of his party members, allegedly wiring such funds into their personal accounts, which was a clear attack on his party's reputation that rested on cries of anti-corruption and justice. Red with rage and reacting hastily to the charge, Imran urged his provincial chief minister to take an immediate note of this practice, stressing that every penny spent by the government must be thoroughly scrutinised. He re-notified every party ranker that the reason they ventured into politics was to blot out corruption and that they must remain faithful to their word, while also assuring that no parliamentarian would be spared a margin to evade taxes. This was no wonder an important development. The message that went out was rip-roaring: if those in the government set an example by paying their taxes, people would finally see the urgency of having a tax culture. The move in KP had also set a precedent for their counterparts in Punjab and Sindh. A good practice after all has its roots in a bad practice. Pakistan's constrained fiscal hodgepodge is largely a result of poor tax compliance.

Imran's anti-rigging drive never went out of fashion as he pursued it demagogically. His protests against rigging were birthed the day after the election results were announced, and since then, they have remained his constant battle cry. He had been repeatedly demanding a recount of the four constituencies as a specimen exercise, believing that if he fails to address the grievances of the electorate, they will lose faith in the system and will never turn out to vote again. Imran was now openly defaming the election tribunal and the former Chief Justice of Pakistan, the weird-looking Chaudhry, by accusing them of playing a hand in rigging. At a press conference recorded from Islamabad in early May, Imran was threatening:

We accepted the outcome of the 2013 elections because we did not want to derail the democratic process in the country. People involved in the rigging will not be spared. We resolve to expose everyone who was involved in robbing the people's mandate. The former Chief Justice of Pakistan was always reluctant to take any action against rigging. The Chief Justice had been taking *suo motu* notices on insignificant matters but never entertained the issue of rigging. A massive nationwide movement will now be launched against the government from 11 May.[3]

Imran was also sceptical of the role of one leading news channel in the country, GEO Network, declaring the prospects of this channel being funded by foreign agencies and deciding against giving interviews to them unless they put a squeeze on their scheming and registered an apology. He also proclaimed that one of his party's election candidates, who lost the contest, had paid in excess of 5 million rupees to verify the thumb prints from NADRA (National Database Registration Authority). The investigation yielded some hanky-panky by the returning officers, who were assigned to monitor the voting process. Express News, a private TV channel in the country, recorded Imran's statement:

My party has exhausted all legal options and has no choice but to protest on streets. I believe that Article 6 of the constitution should be invoked against the former Chief Justice of the country who played a major hand in manipulating the people's mandate. We waited for one year but were denied justice. We are not calling for mid-term elections. We are also not luring the military to fling its troops and topple the government. We only demand a correction in the system so no ballot tampering is repeated in the future.

So, 11 May it was, the day when the first of a series of rallies was going on the floors. Imran's sanctioning of the movement against rigging did not go down well with the government. Temperatures in the parliament went soaring. A few days short of 11 May, Saad Rafique, Sharif's eloquent Minister of Railways, while addressing a full parliamentary session, needled Imran and his party. While most within Sharif's retinue of cabinet members caved in to Imran's onslaught, Rafique was not the one to surrender, retorting with chutzpah: 'They accuse me of rigging—yet they produce no evidence of it. They have soiled the minds of their supporters. I do not blame the supporters but their leader who have led them towards anarchy. "*Janab*—Mr," the language Khan *sahib* chose during his election campaigns determines the moral standards he subscribes to. They say that the judges don't entertain their petitions, but how would they if they are not provided with satisfactory evidence?' By this time, Rafique was at his full pelt, completely buried in the debate. Imran, sitting a few yards apart along with his vice-chairman, Qasuri, appeared to be losing his poise; the grin on his face disappeared rapidly. Qasuri donned a scowl as Rafique delivered his punchline amid a loud chorus of 'shame, shame' hurled at Imran's corner:

> They have no evidence and conceal the truth because their motives are ulterior and do not favour the prosperity of our democracy. When they win, it's the people's verdict, when we win, its rigging. I suggest that we establish a parliamentary fact finding committee that would determine the truth in their rigging whimpers. But, should the opposition endorse the idea of a parliamentary investigation then no protests should be allowed.[4]

Many in the PML-N feared that Imran's commitment towards a nationwide movement spelt disaster for them. Although not because a transparent investigation would yield a poor verdict for them, but because Imran's new found courage was derived from some 'behind-the-scene deal making' with the third force—the military. Rafique's refusal to pull his punches and his slurring of Imran was basically an attempt to send him a loud message that he must give up on his ambition of bringing down the government. Sharif's honeymoon with the 'Army Generals' had long since rankled him and his party. That was the most sought after conclusion that PML-N derived from Imran's rancour. Imran retorted to this conclusion by ruling out any possibility of aligning with the military dictatorship, also turning down the offer of a fact-finding committee. Having trouble in absorbing the barbs fired at him by Rafique, Imran attempted to lighten himself outside the parliament. Speaking to the reporters, he gave his two cents:

> Rafique's speech was pure bunkum. I am not playing the blame game here. All we ask for is a fair process. If we feel we have been cheated in an election contest, then there should be a process to address our grievances. We are not plotting to hurt the democratic system. We are instead trying to improve it. The government is fearful that on 11 May, people will turn out in droves against them.[5]

Public protests in such quick succession had been a recent theme in Pakistan, and Imran can be singly imputed for this development, engineering a number of protests both large and small during the course of his career. It is unsettling for the ruling government charged with a rigging allegation, if people actually turn out in huge numbers and publicly denounce the electoral system. That would be a statement. Imran would threaten to activate his street power, which he knew full well was his biggest weapon. This reminds me of a quote by Chester Bowles: 'Government is too big and too important to be left to the politicians'.

If Imran's white paper on rigging lacked spine, then another white paper from one of the leading lawyers in the country, Aitzaz Ahsan—a long-time cohort of Benazir Bhutto and a name-dropping Cambridge alumni—surely came as a reaffirmation. This white paper was only an inspection of one of the two constituencies of Lahore, NA 124, and was not an attempt to suspect that the entire mandate was robbed:

> There was massive destruction of the record. Many polling bags were stuffed with garbage and waste material, for which there can be no lawful explanation whatsoever. The returning officer removed and destroyed vital polling material from these bags before sealing them under his seal. He thus made the result unverifiable at any time in the future. The scale of negligence was so large that it cannot be ascribed to mere neglect and innocent oversight. As PML-N wished to announce the results in a hurry, the de-sealing of the polling bags, destruction and re-sealing of the bags was done in a rush, resulting in 38 bags being found without any seal.[6]

The weather on 11 May was as threatening as the protest. It was a weekend and an eventful one. I was drawn to my television. As we lived few miles south of the site marked for the protest, my wife pursued for my consent to attend. I was reluctant as these rallies often turned into an ocean of perspiring human limbs and can get sorely ugly. The sound of the celebrations can be deafening. For someone like me, who is more interested in the contents of the speech than losing my ears in the loud buzz of humans, packed like sardines, being in the company of my television serves me better. The city since early morning was in the grip of strong winds that uprooted the entire decoration of the rally: banners went soaring into the heavens; containers were placed to stage Imran and the media came down with a waggle; and the billowing dust obstructed the vision. 'No point my dear,' I told my wife. Imran was everywhere in the media anyway. A quick survey through a series of channels only yielded Imran. The Interior Minister Chaudry Nisar had ordered a strong police force of over 3,000 to monitor the rally. PTI supporters started descending on the capital from early in the morning. Loud speakers were playing PTI anthems at full blast. Virtually every supporter carried a PTI flag. More fired-up followers had the details of the flag painted on their faces. By afternoon, thousands of them had poured into Islamabad from various parts of the country and waited for their leader with rousing enthusiasm. The proceedings kicked off with a series of anti-government speeches delivered by Imran's coterie of political workers. Finally, after they all had their turns, Imran—donning one of his usual black *shalwar kameez*, with a dupatta bearing his party's colours and hanging down his shoulders—took control of the rostrum. He intoned: '*Bismillah* [In the name of Allah],' his recitation lost in the huge roaring of the crowd, so he went again, this time louder, '*Bismillah—IR—Rahman—IR—Rahim* [In the name of Allah, most gracious, most merciful]'. Commencing his note for the evening with a bang. Rafique's pestering in the parliament was fresh in his mind and he had his own punchline on display:

> I know there have been attempts to sabotage this rally and the protestors have been dissuaded from taking part. I thank all of you for guarding my honour and turning up for this session. People who have nurtured their political careers under the nursery of military dictatorships will never understand our passion for change.[7]

The crowd exploded into laughter as Imran got off the mark handsomely. He took a casual jibe at Zardari before diverting to PML-N:

> Looking at the hypocrisy of N-league, I am forced to praise Zardari. Whatever Zardari was, he never subscribed to hypocrisy. He never

said that he will bring back all the loot to the country. Nawaz Sharif is different. Nawaz Sharif! We want a fair match. We don't want any more match fixing. We wish to build a new Pakistan. A rigged election can never let that happen.

The crowd by now was under the spell. Imran carried on with his barbing for a few moments before launching an offence:

We demand a quick resolution. The four constituencies identified by us must be verified within two weeks. In case our grievances are not entertained this time, we will hold a rally in front of the ECP every Friday. We also demand that election related appeals must be addressed in accordance with the law within 120 days of the Election Day.

He called for all the opposition parties who believe in electoral reforms to form a committee with PTI and draft an electoral reform package for the parliament's approval. Additionally, he declared his plans of staging his next rally in Faisalabad two weeks later. In Faisalabad, the rally went through the same motions, with people fully pumped with resentment over rigging descending from remote areas. Imran was fully charged and threatening, with his chin up, his tongue on a rampage, making yet another statement: there, in Faisalabad, Imran went a step further, calling for a trial of the prime minister, former Chief Justice and Mir Shakil-ur-Rehman—the pioneer of GEO network. Both the rallies in Islamabad and Faisalabad proved overwhelmingly successful. The print media backed Imran. One columnist, S. Tariq of *The Nation*, was fearless:

The ruling party was perhaps concerned that if PTI allegations were proved correct then some big names would take a tumble. One of these was now a sitting minister accused of bulldozing his way into polling stations and carrying out gross violations of the electoral code. The entire country saw proof of this on television and social media, but those mandated to take note of such acts were perhaps suffering from cataract or a cognizance disorder.

The sitting minister Tariq alludes to in his article was the impudent Rafique. The Lahore-born, high-tone politician had been a long-time ranker within PML-N, jockeying for better positions and religiously throwing in his lot with the Sharifs. There is ample videographic evidence of Rafique storming the polling station with his gang of police constables and locking the doors so he could tamper with the election data. Rafique was also the most formidable defence mechanism of PML-N because it was he who would be on his way out of the parliament windows should an independent election inquiry ever takes place.

Imran's movement against rigging provided a platform for another leader, who has been hobbling in an out of the political scene for decades. This man is the bearded Dr Tahir-ul-Qadri, a religious scholar of the Sufi lineage. Often spotted with a wide Turkish cap covering his skull, he enjoyed a revered following in the country. Qadri's real motives aroused suspicion. He is a gifted orator and an acclaimed authority on Islamic jurisprudence. Occasionally, in his sleep, he claims to have been in the company of Prophet Muhammad (PBUH). Fabrications like these soared his South Asian popularity to greater heights. The fishy cleric emerged in the early 1980s, establishing a Muslim charity organisation with political ambitions. Back then, he worked as a scholar in the family mosque of the Sharifs in Lahore. The Sharifs, being his chief benefactors, supported his charity work. Supposedly, he is one of the early voices in Pakistan who rallied around the idea of electoral reforms and pure democracy, giving fiery religious sermons on state television; in no time at all, he secured a significant viewership throughout the country. As his followers grew, so too did his ambition to launch his political career. He established Pakistan Awami Tehrik (PAT)—his political party—in 1989. The sermoniser eventually had a bitter fall out with the Sharifs and even contested national elections in the '90s without much gain. People often refer him as the pawn of the security establishment, installed at irregular intervals to undermine a weak political government. Since 2005, he has been conducting his affairs from the outer wilderness of Toronto, Canada. He held a massive sit-in procession in Islamabad against the corruption of the Zardari establishment in January 2013. He comes, creates a fuss or two, and slips away with a bargain. Taking a stock of Imran's growing anti-rigging crusading, he thought it best to return to Pakistan, use the platform, and pitch himself against the government once again—in what may turn out to be the biggest street movement the country has ever seen.

By the middle of summer, the ruling government was already unsettled by the noises coming out of Imran's quarters. On learning that Qadri was also hashing out a plan to stage a demonstration, the government brooded over prospects of having him arrested on his return from Canada. Qadri was expected to arrive on 23 June. Speculations of his arrest went public through the electronic media. The government's reaction sparked disturbances among Qadri's supporters as they retaliated by placing barricades in an attempt to guard his residence in Lahore. In the early hours of 17 June, a fifteen-member police squad attempted to remove the barriers. The activists saw this as a threat and responded with hostility, forcing the policemen to use force. Soon, the site turned into a battleground as eight PAT workers, including

Above: Imran was never a gifted orator, it was a skill he came to develop over the years.

Right: Finally relieved and posing after a draining few months of round-the-clock book writing—Imran's autobiography, entitled *Pakistan: A Personal History*.

Above: Imran clustered around by an elated gathering of supporters in the 2013 National Elections.

Below: Speaking at a convocation of NAMAL College in Mianwali—a well-endowed institution built on western patterns.

Above: '*Tabdeeli aa nahin rahi, tabdeeli aa gayi hai* [change is not just approaching, it is already here],' chants Imran, cutting a triumphant note at the much hyped 126-day-long campaigning in 2014.

Below: Imran, dubbed as the fashion icon of Pakistani politics, always attracted a sizeable tally of female following.

Above: Selling party souvenirs at the General Elections in 2013.

Below: A jumbo-sized stage erected for Imran's address in 2014.

Above: The year 2013 saw Pakistan's most dramatic elections. The Imran frenzy had reached its summit.

Below: 'I think the Pakistani people have taken a stand. What have the Sharifs done for them?' exclaimed Imran while speaking to the press.

Above: One of Imran's many extensive party meetings held at the KP House in Islamabad.

Below: Diehard followers of Imran camping outside his Bani Gala residence on the eve of 2 November 2016.

Above: They came in throngs, like a roaring ocean invading the shore.

Below left: 'I am thrilled to declare that after seven months of rigid persistence, the apex court of Pakistan has agreed to probe the Panama allegations against Sharif's family. This is our VICTORY'.

Below right: In solidarity with the drone-battered tribes of Waziristan.

Above left: Reviving the near-moribund tourism industry in the Karakoram gorges of KP.

Above right: Unwinding himself at his breezy veranda in Bani Gala.

Below: Unbothered for his safety, Imran was known to present himself to the milling crowds. At one of his election rallies in 2013.

Above left: Imran at the inauguration of his second cancer hospital in the Shaukat Khanum franchise, Peshawar, December 2015.

Above right: At one of his many ear-splitting fulminations, slandering the House of Sharifs for their incessant fleecing of the national vault.

Below: 'Not even a goat will be allowed to graze on the territory,' warned Imran at the launch of his Billion Tree Tsunami Campaign in KP

Above: Scaling up the container for another defiant speech, the long march in 2014.

Below: Responding to the clamour with a winsome glee on his face.

Above: 'I will show Sharif how to respond to the Indian Prime Minister Narendra Modi,' says Imran in a lecturing mood, Lahore, September 2016.

Below: An unsparing Imran protesting for Sharif's resignation.

Above: 'If we do not fix our corruption, we will never fly as a nation'.

Below: 'Twenty-five million children are out of the school, and all that the government cares about is building more motorways'.

Above: Soliciting investment from the Chinese, Islamabad, 2016.

Below: 'They told me that having a cancer hospital in Pakistan was next to impossible. But, I never stopped dreaming'.

Above left: Anarchic scenes in Islamabad in early November 2016, when the police rained Imran's supporters with intermittent gas shelling.

Above right: To liven up his supporters, Imran performed fifty consecutive press-ups, putting to shame the young men that were half his age, with the women around him ogling—their eyes popping and tongues hanging out.

Below: Imran's dream of a knowledge city in Mianwali gradually coming to life.

Above: Imran attempting to keep the crowds on their feet, as the 2014 long march began to fizzle out following Qadri's exit from the campaign.

Below: At another party meeting in Islamabad.

Above: In a jaunty mood at a packed rally in Azad Kashmir, February 2016.

Below: At another ear-popping rally in Lahore, May 2016, threatening to bring down Sharif's government. 'Hold an independent inquiry into your money trails Sharif *sahib*, or prepare for my army to besiege your palace in Lahore,' asserts Imran, cutting a mutinous note.

two women, lost their lives and eighty-five others sustained critical injuries. A day later, the papers showed a picture of a policeman pounding a female PAT activist. The news scattered like wildfire, with the Punjab police turning unpopular virtually overnight. People called them *Goondaas*—a bunch of hoodlums. Imran was quick to register his disapproval. *The Express Tribune* reported Imran's statement under the caption 'Heads Need to Roll':

> The Punjab Chief Minister Shehbaz Sharif and his law maker Rana Sanaullah, must immediately tender their resignations. This is a breach of human rights. We will visit the innocent PAT workers in the hospitals and inquire after them. The treatment of the PAT supporters exposes the mindset of the Prime Minister and his brother—the Chief Minister of Punjab. The government must prepare for serious consequences if they do not open the four constituencies for an investigation. We plan another rally in Bahawalpur on the 27th of June. In Bahawalpur, our party will declare a serious line of action for the future.

To make matters uglier, the Punjab police filed an FIR against PAT supporters. Qadri made an emotionally stimulating tweet before getting on his plane to Pakistan: 'If they assassinate me upon my return to Pakistan, I urge you not to do my *Janaza* [funeral], until you bring the revolution'. The cleric had a dramatic homecoming. His plane was expected to land in Islamabad, but as there were reports of clashes between PAT supporters and the Islamabad police, the plane was instead diverted to Lahore. Meanwhile, Imran braced for another rousing speech in Bahawalpur on 27 June. Bahawalpur, a small town located in south Punjab, on the fringes of the Cholistan desert that stretches into the heart of India, saw a significant turn out. Summer had reached its summit and so did the feverish Imran supporters. Bahawalpur was as dry as a bone. The skies deserted of clouds was suggestive of a dull monsoon ahead. The baked heat, however, did little to keep the supporters away. I captured the scenes live on my television, munching through an evening meal. Imran was eloquent and elaborate, gearing up for an important announcement:

> We demand answers to four question; 1) Who drafted the victory speech for Nawaz Sharif on May 11 2013? 2) What part did the caretaker Chief Minister of Punjab Najam Sethi play in the elections? 3) What was the role of Chaudary—former Chief Justice of Pakistan? And 4) Why were the returning officers not present at the polling stations? If we did not manage to find answers till the 27th of July, then I promise that we will storm into Islamabad with a million men and camp there till our demands are met.[8]

A few days later, while speaking to the press, Imran proclaimed that he was willing to call off the long march should the incumbent chief justice hold an inquiry within two weeks. His calls fell on deaf ears as no word came from the apex court.

Ramadan had arrived, and the festivities were in full bloom; the political fever seen earlier in the year had finally subsided. The parliamentary wrangling, however, continued fitfully. The military operation against terrorist hideouts was in full swing, and the operation uprooted nearly a million people out of their homes from North Waziristan as they scattered across KP for survival, with the figure swelling by the day. Imran, who had long since expressed solidarity with the tribal region, toured various pockets of IDPs to examine their needs, appealing to the federal government to release a grant of 5 billion rupees and rescue the impaired from taking a further plunge.

In an interesting development, the former Chief Justice of Pakistan retaliated by breaking out of his silence to what he believed was Imran's 'wild slogging'. Chaudhry, through a family spokesperson, had informed that he had no business with the elections as that was the role of the ECP, and he threatened to drag Imran to courts. There was more arm twisting in store for Imran as the PML-N declared that Imran must render an apology to the nation for his plans to turn 14 August—the country's Independence Day—into a day of violence. Imran's team protested with a 'tit for tat' strategy should any legal course be taken against their leader. They brooded over the prospects of having the prime minister disqualified through a constitutional impeachment as they had enough evidence of the premier's moral misconduct. This mutual pestering between Imran and the status quo persisted throughout Ramadan. By August, and with the institutions suspected of rigging still unwilling to budge from their position, Imran ruled out all possibilities of talks with the government and officially sealed his plans of sweeping across the capital with a 'never seen before,' long march on 14 August. In a recorded interview, while *en route* to Banu from Kohat, Imran spared no room for any doubts on his marching schedule:

> Come hell or high water, nothing can stop the long march now. The government has threatened us with the invocation of 'Article 245' of the constitution. Basically, they are trying to elicit military support because they feel my protest will jeopardize law and order. Why don't they invoke this clause in Karachi, which is genuinely threatened by extremism, extra judicial killings and sectarian violence?[9]

Imran smirked before striking another discordant note:

There is no way we are backing off now. The government has started to push me for a dialogue. For the past 14 months, we have been denied justice. The time for a dialogue is over. No force in the country can now come in the way of this march, not even the armed forces, as it is not their mandate to obstruct a peaceful protest.

The journalist attempted to extract the real meat from Imran's narrative: 'So you mean that the long march will demand for Prime Minister's resignation, termination of the parliament and call for fresh elections?' Imran was plain and undiplomatic:

Anything we demand will not be a breach of the constitution. You see! If they scrutinise the four constituencies we have been asking them to consider, then the entire election result becomes suspicious. A fair investigation into rigging will prove that the government has been riding on a fake mandate and have been playing games with me in the parliament; they are trying to elude a fair trial.

While Imran welcomed PAT to lump together with his marching parade, he also stressed that the agenda for his demonstration differed from Qadri's. While Imran quibbled for the flaws in the democratic organs of the state, Qadri's protests were on a much larger canvas, demanding a complete repair of the system. Qadri's revamping calls, however, had always been obscure. He always managed to resurface whenever the government found itself on a loose footing, just to stimulate the temperatures further and upgrade the dramatic appeal of the whole mutiny. Yet surely the stage was cut out for a major confrontation? 'What will happen now?' my colleagues at work erupted in a chorus—the '*Azadi* March' ('freedom march') (was the word appropriated for the occasion). There was widespread panic not only within the parliament, but also across the country, with no idea how the government would handle the marchers and where it was heading. For Imran, it was a do or die condition, hanging his career on the line and throwing all his weight behind the campaign. Locking himself and his pack of followers in the avenues of Islamabad, and for an uncertain duration, spelled disaster for his reputation had he failed to justify his outdoor musing. Speculations of another military takeover were rife, yet the military denied such temptations. It was now 12 August, two days short of the '*magnum eventus*'. The analysts in the press hatched their prophesies—some bashed Imran, others extolled him. 'Great Scott! What has he done?' said one journalist friend of mine. The government had sealed the diplomatic enclave, which meant that our offices were shut until further notice. Qadri's followers revved up in Model Town Lahore; Imran, with his apostles, descended on Zaman Park, marking his run-up with a permanent scowl now plastered on his face—the one he had when the great Vivian Richards dispatched his whiff of a bouncer without a trace of bother. Together, they both slogged through the dung heaps of Punjab, along the historic Grand Trunk (GT) road, finally laying siege to the capital on 14 August.

Sharif, now finally robbed off his winsome smile, tested Imran with a few bridge-making offers: 'Talks in the parliament? Ok, judicial inquiry? Hmmm! I can visit your house and let's have a chat there?' Imran only had one response: 'I can consider the offer of a judicial inquiry but only if you step down as the Prime Minister.'

'Oh boy!' pronounced Sharif. Things were getting awkward. Imran was bent on showing Sharif his street power, and Sharif was trying hard to somehow retrieve his grin. The media was having a ball: more riffraff in the parliament meant more sponsors and billing for them. The press captured the drama by the second. Every person in my town with some superficial knowledge of politics rallied with an opinion. From the upper nobility to the down trodden, from landlords to rag pickers, everyone had a bloody fair idea that something was not right. The media in UK, as usual, has never deserted any aspect of Imran's life. The press in London was pushed. Suspecting Imran's moves, Dean Nelson of *The Guardian* wrote:

> The former chief of Pakistan's ISI intelligence agency is guiding Imran Khan's march on Islamabad to topple Nawaz Sharif's government, a senior minister has claimed. The allegation that Lt-General Ahmed Shuja Pasha is serving as 'strategic advisor' for the demonstrations reflects growing tension in the capital as Mr. Khan's planned march from Lahore to Islamabad on Thursday draws nearer. Soldiers have been deployed outside the National Assembly, the president's house and other sensitive sites to stop the marchers entering the capital's central 'red zone'.

As the clock ticked, more drama ensued. Fine speeches peppered with hope and a Pakistan modelled on South Korea left the lips of politicians. Sharif, unnerved and without a glee on his rounded Kashmiri cheeks, made a last-ditch effort to court Imran and Qadri. He reminded the nation that the only way to progress was to provide political stability. His speech was well-scripted, coated with aristocratic Urdu and classic Persian, describing his pipeline of projects to the nation, which he feared would get smothered should the marchers have their own way: Basha dam; Dasu dam; Karachi Lahore motorway; and the China Pakistan Economic Corridor were the major whimpers in his speech. The final verdict from the government was to have the march and bid farewell to democracy. A growling response from Imran followed. His script was unpenned and rode on impulse, perched on his sun-facing Zaman Park rooftop in Lahore; he got off the mark with his usual '*Bismillah*' before cutting into a revolt:

> This is not a personal rift between Imran Khan and Nawaz Sharif. What is it that Allah has not already bestowed upon me? It is an ideological war. It is up to you mere *Pakistanio*—my fellow Pakistanis, to decide whether you wish to elect corrupt governments such as the one that now exists or want a fair system to blossom.

He then gave his audience a refresher course on the incumbent's jobbery: the elections were rigged; the police officials were a bunch of rabbles; they came into power to multiply their wealth; justice was only for the rich and for the poor it is a privilege. 'What democracy are we discussing here?' Imran explodes, 'in which one family swells its fortunes without measure? When you have your brother as the Chief Minister of Punjab, his son as the Deputy Chief Minister, in law as the Finance Minister and some close flunkeys as heads of important state institutions; what democracy are we talking about?' The rebel in Imran was at its full bloom and his aggression slipped out of control. The verdict was obvious: marching orders were shortly issued and there was no budging.

In another part of the city, Qadri was in full motion. Standing at an elevation, blessing his cavalcade with a title—*inqilab*, or revolution march. His supporters were fully buried in his speech—ready to die for him. His fists were waggling, and his lungs were pumped with rage, occasionally emitting saliva from his mouth that landed like a drizzle of bliss on his supporters. He then disclosed the contents of his revolution: free healthcare, free education, shelter for the poor, no hunger, no load shedding, no pounding of women, a dignified society, a welfare state, and a paradise right on our door step. Roars of '*Allah o Akbar*' rented the heavens. The next morning, Imran's *Azadi* March and Qadri's *inqilab* blended into a splendid chorus in the heart of Lahore. By 13 August, the political temperature in the country had crossed its threshold.

I surveyed through the history of our political movements, but none of them generated as much excitement as this one. The news was selling like hot cake. Imran must have slept fitfully through the night. In the morning, he announced his schedule: afternoon prayers to be offered at his residence; team PTI to hold a take-off rally in the outer plains of Lahore, and, by evening, hit the ground running for Islamabad. Rules of the journey were also disclosed: no harm shall befall anything, living or dead, assuring that his marching would remain peaceful. The government suspected Imran's confidence. Interior Minister Chaudry Nisar declared that protestors would not be safe as foreign agencies would exploit the civil unrest in the country. Imran, as non-comital as ever, kept assuring the government that his party did not intend to take the law in their hands. The scenes felt like a replay of Imran's aggressive election rallies a year before. Those who did not buy into his plans said that he had become accustomed to this style of populism and that he relished demonstrating his street power and struggles with an untamed, overinflated ego. His followers, however, considered him the best thing that could have ever happened to their country. 'We have been robbed off our mandate,' they said, knowing full well that justice delayed is justice denied, and were convinced that Pakistan hungers for a person like Imran. He was someone who had an inextinguishable passion in his heart that would light up the nation and purge it of all its blemishes. In a state where people lose faith in the government, where the sanctity of a ballot box is ripped asunder, where the police, courts, and other important state functionaries succumb to the personal gains of a select few, where the rulers evade taxes with impunity and the poor struggle for basic social services, people must eventually come out on the streets to be heard loud and clear. On the eve of 14 August, such were the sentiments that rattled the country, as Imran's evening speech went through the same genuflections: his head bobbing above a sea of crowd, his trademark waggling of the fists, his head-on collision with the Sharif brothers, some compulsive talking, another refresher course on election rigging, and a quick survey of his street power. He was well behind his schedule, but took his time to mobilise the crowd so no force under the sun could impede his avalanche of supporters. The police had placed containers on every major road and roundabout in Lahore as Imran advised the authorities to have these barriers removed or his party workers would gladly pull them out. The cavalcade finally took off from Lahore in the dead of the night, proceeding towards Islamabad at a snail's pace and allowing enough time for the procession to grow to staggering figures. The numbers grew by the hour. The media followed the trail, incessantly trying to buttonhole Imran for a statement or two. Emotionally on a high, Imran spoke to the reporters in Gujranwala:

I think the Pakistani *awam* [people] have taken a stand. What has the Sharifs done for them? They evade taxes and leave the poor to bear the trials of poverty. People are fed up of their narcissist attitude. You can't free the country sitting in the comfort of your house—it entails some struggling. I am so pleased looking at the passion and verve of the people who stayed up all night prepping for the days ahead. I promise you all that we will assemble one million people in the heart of Islamabad. Nawaz Sharif must tender his resignation now. His own government admits that approximately 50,000 to 60,000 votes in every constituency are unverifiable. Constitutionally a rigged election bears no credibility; so the incumbent government must be dissolved; the Prime Minister must resign and fresh elections must be held.[10]

The media also surveyed through the population that was now advancing rapidly towards the capital: there were old men, old women, young men, young women, university students, school children, young girls, labour class, working class, business community, and peasants all stewed together in splendid harmony, intoxicated with promises of a new world. The pain of the journey failed to dampen their spirits. Celebrations were in full motion. Roars of the crowd went soaring to the heavens. Qadri's cavalcade was a few miles ahead. In an interesting episode, just as Imran went into his lustrous jet-black SUV, about to drift out of Gujranwala, a few unfamiliar, well-compensated snipers emerged from somewhere in the crowds and fired more than one bullet straight into the front windscreen. The vehicle's bulletproof features came in handy as the gunmen rapidly slipped out of the scene.

By the night of 15 August, after nearly forty hours of cramming through GT road, Imran and his party of believers came within easy reach of Islamabad. There was no sleeping that night. Offices were shut, and shops closed early as PTI and PAT supporters braced to lay siege to the capital. Islamabad presented the scene of a dry port, with containers scattered across the city. The incoming storm of people sorted that out as all barriers were uprooted and slogged out of the way. At the heart of the cavalcade entering the capital was Imran, sorely in need of sleep but high in spirits. Not a trace of fatigue escaped his eyes. The crowd from afar seemed meandering through the city, steadily approaching the site of Imran's address. Dramatic scenes followed: the city was torched; the crowds were rumbling; people were strolling out of their homes; the monsoon night was cloudless; the gust of winds indicated an approaching shower; music was played at deafening volumes; and celebrations kicked off in abundance. I was trying to capture the scenes from my rooftop. '*Bhainchod* [sister fucker]!' I mumbled within, like a typical thrilled Punjabi, obviously ensuring my cussing wisdom does not fall on my wife's ears. Lights were dancing over the skyline of downtown Islamabad. 'We should be a part of this,' proclaimed my elated spouse. I gave her proposal some thought before slothfulness took the better of me. A series of anthems peppered with a revolutionary spin were played in quick succession. One of my favourites was a heavy metal, fast-paced, adrenaline booster that reminded me of Sylvester Stallone, revving up before a boxing brawl in *Rocky* (1976). However, one of the ballads, sloppily translated by me, particularly stood out; it enjoys a household status and has been a regular feature in all of Imran's rallies:

Dil Naik ho Neeyat Saaf to ho Insaf Kahe 'Imran Khan' [*A pure heart and a sturdy faith must yield justice says 'Imran Khan'*]

Jo Chali hai ab tehreek k Hoga Theak ye Pyara Pakistan [*This movement of ours will purge all the blemishes of Pakistan*]

Quaid ka tha Farmaan Hai Pakistan Falahi mumliqat [*Declared Quaid e Azam Muhammad Ali Jinnah: This state was destined to become the centre of welfare*]

Huwe Leader jab Be-Emaan Kiya Nuqsaan Bhula kr Aaqibat [*Its faithless rulers pillaged and plundered without a scare*]

Ab Log nahi Naadan gaye sab Jaan Kahen 'Imran Khan' [*No more are its people clumsy, enlightened they are, says 'Imran Khan'*]

Ab hogi jo Nigraan, ye Nasal Jawaan Barhe ga Pakistan [*Its youth will govern; boasting of a new Pakistan*]

Insaf jo ho Bunyad ho Mulk-o-Qoum Hamesha Shaad rahen [*When fair treatment becomes the state character, nations stand to thrive*]

Ho Pak zameen mazboot, Bohat mazboot tu hum Azaad Rahen [*May this land of the pure strengthens; may our sovereignty never rive*]

Ab hoga har Insaaf, Bara Shafaf Kahe 'Imran Khan' [*Justice will now be dispensed fairly says 'Imran Khan'*]

Ab Aayen ge Hamdard, wo Sache Mard, K jin ka hai Emaan [*Honest will be those men; in faith they subscribe*]

Tere Sath hain tere Jawaan, Sabhi Imran, Tu hoga Kamyaab [*The youth stands by you Imran, you are bound to fly*]

Maon Behno ka maan, Tu rakh Imran, hon Sache tere Khuwab [*You are the guardian of our women, may your dreams never die*]

Wo din bhi hai Nazdeek, k ye Tehreek bane gi Ik Toofan.... [*Soon this movement will mature into a storm....*]

Dil Naik ho Neeyat Saaf ho Insaf Kahe 'Imran Khan' [*A pure heart and a sturdy faith must yield justice says 'Imran Khan'*]

Jo Chali hai ab tehreek k Hoga Theak ye Pyara Pakistan [*This movement of ours will purge all the blemishes of Pakistan*]

Imran's motorcade, caged around by an exuberant group of party workers, finally stilled before the platform erected for his address. The gusty winds managed to pluck some clouds from afar and thrusted them over the city, delivering showers and rescuing the city from an otherwise humid weekend. Imran fought out of his car, with the prodding cameras hooked on him. Maintaining his ramrod stance and his head protruding above a formidable tally of supporters, he stretched out his arms to scale

up the platform and presented himself by the rostrum. A full glimpse of
their leader caused a huge uproar. The crowds went berserk. Holding the
mic firmly in the cup of his palms, Imran intoned, '*Bismillah Ir Rehman
Ir Rahim.*' The crowd missed out on his opening words, so he went again
loudly, '*Bismillah Ir Rehman Ir Rahim, Iya kana budu wa iya kanas tayeen*
[Oh Allah, you alone do we worship and you alone do we call for help]'.
Imran took control of the procession. The roaring crowd began to calm,
expecting an important announcement. Imran's speechmaking was at its
career best, as he cut a hysterical note: 'I have not slept for the past 40
hours; I had a light breakfast and have not eaten anything since then. But
let me tell you all, that looking at your passion tonight, I can stay awake
for another 40 hours'. The crowd exploded. It was just the perfect opening
to keep them bustling. Just the right recipe to revive them after a long,
arduous journey. It was an assembly of nearly half a million resting entirely
on Imran's prerogative, his allegations, his ambitions, and his hard-nose
approach towards the government. After a brief pause and some poor
dancing moves, only restricted to some air punching, Imran resumed: 'The
determination I have witnessed over the past 40 hours was unprecedented.
It only goes to show that Pakistan has changed. Not every day do we get
an opportunity like this. This is your moment—my fellow countrymen.
Seize it and let it not go to waste'. The shower was now pounding the city,
but it was not heavy enough to dampen the spirits of the audience. Imran
rolled back his soaked hair with his fingers, dabbed raindrops from his
face, rustled up his memory, and returned to the most regular monotones
of his speech: barbing at the Sharifs for the kind of Pakistan they had
given us; tax evasion; pillaging and plundering; load shedding; dwindling
economic prospects; boot polishing the Americans; the shame that comes
by holding a green passport; policemen as thugs; judges with questionable
characters; and finally, to top it all off, another refresher course on the
tactics employed to ravage the 2013 elections. Once the crowd was ready,
Imran dropped his bombshell:

> Tomorrow you all return to this site at 3 p.m. I will also freshen up and
> join you. And, I resolve to stay here with you all for as long as we must.
> We will not leave this place until Nawaz Sharif tenders his resignation.[11]

Amid a thunderous round of applause, Imran switched off for the night. It
was already 3 a.m. of 16 August, and the rain was torrential. A few miles
south of the city was the venting ground of Qadri and his disciples. Qadri
was as vehement and unforgiving, if not more so, as Imran. His devotees
were also worked up, clearly out of their wits, as he gave the government
a forty-eight-hour ultimatum. Borrowing some notes from Imran's speech,

Qadri called for the dissolution of the federal and provincial governments and the resignation of the prime minister. He hardly made an impact on his last similar binge in the country in January 2013, but on that occasion, joining forces with Imran yielded some useful clatter. 'What's in store for the country?' I muttered to myself. No serious reaction came from the government. A few stray comments and that was all. The president of the PPP in KP, Khanzada Khan, was quoted in the press the next morning: 'In the name of rigging, Imran is damaging the current democratic system in the country'.

It rained without pause, occasionally heavy, but mostly mild. The next afternoon, supporters began reviving their energies and charging their slogans of change. They had to make it a routine. No one except Allah and maybe the generals knew the duration of their stay in the capital. Loud speakers were plugged again and the festivities for the day kicked off. A few party workers of Imran, roped in to warm up the crowds, delivered a couple of steamy lectures. By the evening, a fresh-looking Imran pulled up in his SUV. The rustiness of the journey had disappeared from his face. He scaled up the stage and took over the proceedings, desperate for a wicket as they say in cricket. On learning of Imran's arrival, the crowds removed themselves from unworthy engagements and rushed to join the procession. Imran was more threatening that night: 'Where are you Nawaz Sharif? You see I can only stop my tsunami for a couple of days. After that I will cease to have control over my team as they will blow through the walls of your lodge'. Following this, the crowd exploded into rambunctious laughter. The speech progressed through the same motions. I knew full well that if there was no imminent breakthrough, Imran's dictionary of absorbing speechmaking would run out of steam. Soon, there would be nothing innovative left in his mind to share with his zealots. Although Imran had been a crowd pleaser and had repeatedly enthralled his audiences, the festival in Islamabad asked for the impossible—the unremitting noise. It could not have gone forever. The government reacted with an overture of talks; they proposed a dialogue with Imran and Qadri, although they ruled out any prospects of Sharif's resignation. The camping resolutions of Imran were so uncompromising that any government proposal that failed to comply with his demands would be considered unworthy of any deliberation. Anyway, the music persisted well past midnight—another day gone without much action.

The forty-eight-hour deadline did not yield much dividends save for the reshuffling of the procession from a safe distance to within easy reach of the parliament house. Moving any further down from that position would be a breach and the government would order its gang of pot-bellied policemen to retaliate with shelling and some calculated jerking of their bamboo sticks. An occasional clubbing of supporters did come to pass as a few trespassers had their heads oozing with blood. Some media reporters were manhandled and female activists were also assaulted. The scenes of policemen beating the reporters flashed on the screens. PTI and PAT activists did not recede, fetching slingshots crafted out of tree branches and retaliating by shooting stones. Sharif remained tight-lipped and bummed out. His parting with his grin seemed permanent. Imran was running out of options. A few more dry spells and the march would come down crashing.

By September, the march had begun to lose its lustre. It had certainly lost its threatening appeal. The monsoon was coming to an early end as torrential rains were not as regular as they were in August. People in the city had become somewhat used to the sight of marchers. One evening in September, I decided to take a stroll down to the site and examine the area. It had turned into a litter field: the rag pickers abode and a pile of garbage donned the constitutional avenue. The marchers were in camping mood, occupying empty spaces on road sides for an afternoon siesta. By the evening, the crowds began ramming in, although not with the same fervour. They were mostly women, both young and old, shining under layers of cosmetics and their well-tailored skin-tight suits. Sensing their arrival, stray rabbles slipped into the crowds for a good look at female bottoms—effortlessly fleeing with a stroke or two. Such salacious episodes became routine. Imran would emerge somewhere from behind the containers, strolling on them for a while, surveying the attendees, and delivering a note for the evening. This was the schedule that was followed every evening with military procession. Every day, Imran would slip out a piece of paper from his pockets and lecture the audience on the fundamentals of rigging, on the politics of corruption, or on the principles of macroeconomics. He was quite professorial, and well informed, sufficiently endowed with enough wisdom in the art of governance. His voracious repertoire of insult vocabulary, however, was fast running out of stock. He would appear, fire shafts of sarcasm at Sharif, go over his lessons for the day, and doze off for the evening. By early November, the frantic Qadri, Imran's stomping partner, withdrew his share from government shaming and wrapped up his fund of supporters, fleeing the capital citing health reasons—or reasons that we may never come to know. That meant a solo ride ahead for Imran. Imran and his party associates had already relinquished their parliamentary offices and had started calling for a plan 'B'—an independent judicial commission for an inquiry into the 2013 elections. By the middle of November, he had also withdrawn his demand for the prime minister's resignation, but insisted on the continuation of the *dharna* (sit in) until an independent judicial commission sanctioned an inquiry. I felt sorry both for Imran and his disciples, many of whom had come from afar and genuinely believed in the sanctity of their life-changing journey to the capital. A vast section of supporters denounced their worshipping of Imran as they began to suspect his mental condition. A good number of unworthy rational thinkers in the press speculated that Imran was showing symptoms of dope addiction—regarding his ready impulsiveness to be a literal case of hashish obsession. The suspicion hardly made any sense to me, given Imran's formidable fitness regimen and his athletic, fat-free midriff at this age. There was also little evidence to officially sanction such slandering, but every third person I met during Imran's endless outdoor parade seemed to have subscribed to the grapevine. His adversaries even suggested him to have his vitals examined. Few of the notable media giants in the country panned Imran for his narcotic behaviour. A particularly displeased Kantawala from the *Friday Times* vented:

> Speaking of damp squibs, the *dharna* is still raging while I write this, and Imran Khan is all up in the news cycle (only in Pak, btw. The rest of the world doesn't really care about Naya Pakistan, what with Gaza and the Kardashians having stolen its thunder). Through the week I saw all of the PTI leadership on that 'container' (if only it could contain their craziness) while having confident, open-air tactical discussions. I could see, from the way they genuflected and frowned and mouthed angry nothings, that they were trying to work out their position, just 'coz, you know, that's something you always do after you've mounted your remove-the-government/bring-on-the-coup campaign.[12]

The government sensed the stuttering and fizzling of Imran's movement and went about its routine business with renewed confidence. With no response forthcoming from the government's quarters, a resolute Imran, amid a rejuvenated crowd, howled his plan 'C': 'If our demands are not met, I will shut down Lahore on 4 December; shut down Faisalabad on 8 December; Karachi on 12 December and the entire country on 16 December'. I am a first-hand witness of that speech; it was a spectacle, an exhibition of Imran's ability to plug life into his audience, who had for months lain dormant, like rejected son-in-laws in the pathways of the capital city. Just as I thought that it was curtains for Imran's camping ambitions, I was dumbfounded to see another ocean of people flooding their way through the capital. Imran never stopped fighting.

As Imran gambled with his options to revive his fading movement, and before he could brainstorm his plan 'D', Peshawar (the seat of PTI's authority in KP) was rocked by one of the bloodiest terrorist attacks on the morning of 16 December. Nearly 132 families, as per routine, dispatched their kids, hardly teenagers, to the army public school in the cantonment town of Peshawar. Little did they know that a few hours later, the school would go up in smoke and its halls would become a scatter of decaying corpses. Close to a dozen armed terrorists brazenly hurried into the building and opened fire, shooting kids point blank who were in the middle of their coursework. Soon, the army arrived and flushed out the terrorists from the scene. The news sent waves across the world. TTP claimed responsibility for the attacks, calling it a reaction to what the Pakistan Army had been doing in the tribal areas. The entire nation drowned in a state of shock. It was more than just an ordeal. Parents, sending their children to school, became wary, and fear took complete charge over all matters. I buried myself in solitude. It was by all measures the darkest moment in our recent history. As for Imran, there was no longer a plan 'D', only a press conference calling off the rally. 'In view of the present security condition of the state, and in our expression of solidarity to the children who lost their lives in Peshawar, I am afraid we will have to call off this procession,' a droopy looking Imran confessed. It was a good decision. His demands for an independent judiciary commission, however, remained unheeded, but more pressing issues drew his attention. He could not have dragged the sit-in any further, knowing that KP, where he promised a terror-free world, was emotionally shattered and shedding tears in abundance. A *Naya* KP was no longer a small piece in the *Naya* Pakistan puzzle.

8

Smallest Coffins are
the Heaviest

Fighting corruption is not just good governance. It's self-defence. Its patriotism.

Joe Biden

'Morons!' I exploded restlessly in protest; my mind was set aflame with rage. Pictures of the deceased kids in Peshawar began flashing on the TV screens; they laid indistinctively in piles, riddled with bullets, cleansing the parched earth with streams of their blood flowing profusely—answers were demanded. What was their fault? The episode had sent ripples of silence across the country. Never had we witnessed such a brutal massacre in the country's recent or distant history. The whole nation stood muted in a moment of shock. I saw scenes of parents on their knees pounding the earth in a trauma. I saw mothers collapsing in disbelief, their eyes turning into a pond of tears. We had once again let the *fundoos* have their way. A howl of protest went up. Reactions started gushing in. Imran readied himself for a press conference. The winter blossomed with trademark intensity. Unaffected by the falling temperatures, Imran, with a red scarf muffled up round his neck and donning a scowl on his face, turned up to face the reporters. The press circled around him, desperate to record his take on the matter. 'Being a father myself, it is unfathomable for me that something like this can even happen,' cut a mournful-looking Imran; he concluded with on a decisive note:

I call the entire nation to come together and also advise the politicians not to use this tragedy as a point scoring tool over their opponents. For a moment think about the parents who sent their children to school without having the foggiest of idea that their schedule for the evening would be to carry heaps off coffins to the cemetery. This is our collective failure. There have been bloody massacres in the years past, but nothing as unsettling as the one in Peshawar. We, as a political party are now willing to cooperate with all state institutions and provide a blueprint to counter terrorism.[1]

He had long since been one of the few voices rallying against the invasion of the tribal areas, but that evening, he looked genuinely distraught. A couple of days later, Imran surveyed the school in Peshawar. There at the main entrance of the school, he placed a wreath of flowers and said his prayers before embracing the parents who had been robbed of their progeny. The parents shed tears in abundance, beating their chests, and overflowing with grief. The bereaved fathers still managed to recover their poise, but the mothers seemed to have lost track of their existence. Imran knew full well that he would not be able to deliver on all the pledges he committed to the people of KP, considering the profusion of issues that afflicted the province. The incident in Peshawar was no doubt the failure of the entire state machinery, but it also hurled Imran at the forefront of accountability.

Imran and his coterie of party devotees were bent on declaring their resolution on counter terrorism, citing FATA as the hot bed of all the tumult that scattered across the country. Imran had always claimed his long-time association with the tribal areas and his grounding in their local customs. To him, a full-scale war would only invite more radicalisation to Pakistan proper. That was a sanely proposition. These tribes as we know are impossible to contain once driven to war. They ride on a war resistance history that spans hundreds of years. Here, puberty for boys is traditionally seen as their birth right to embrace the gun culture. For girls, a different lifestyle is sanctioned; as soon as they reach sexual maturity, they are shut away, disappearing from view behind closed quarters, draped in claustrophobic layers of textile. The incident in Peshawar, however, demanded a response, but only on credible intelligence. You cannot go on ravaging the whole FATA region with bombs, and sucking them into a ceaseless crusade with the Pakistani state. After giving considerable thought to the matter, Imran gave his two cents:

KP is unfortunately seeing the fallout of whatever hash that we all have created in the FATA region. Incessant bombings and militancy in the tribal areas has rattled the province. There has been an influx of nearly 1.7 million Afghan refugees and a close to 2 million internally displaced population due to these battles. The brunt is now borne out of KP's budget. These refugees have troubles blending into our mainstream

society. We need to integrate them fully otherwise we dread scores of
youth drawing towards radicalization and digging more innocent graves
in our courtyards. We appeal to the federal government to spare us
more resources so we can mitigate the socio-economic massacre of these
refugees and hatch a permanent solution to the problems of terrorism. I
also feel that we must station and restore the old Frontier Constabulary
force along the border of FATA and KP, to monitor uncalled for
movement into our province. Our police establishment is also in need of
a revamp to defend the cities. Presently, they do not have the backing of
a strong intelligence that could well be an aid to pre-empt terror strikes
on major public centres. It is also time that we regulate our borders with
Afghanistan. Every year, we issue not more than 500 hundred visas to
Afghan citizens but are recipients of nearly 20,000 of them; and we have
not the foggiest of idea on what these people do and where they go. The
sealing of borders with Afghanistan; the guarding of borders with FATA
and economic replenishment of millions of refugees is our short-term
solution. And, the only long term measure to restore peace as it once
were, is to expend resources and amalgamate them into our mainstream
society and put a permanent end to their marginalization.[2]

As we moved into the new year, gossip mills began tossing up stories of
Imran's alleged involvement with a local diva, Reham Khan, an anchor
of passable prospects. Soon, the affair was discarded on grounds that it
was not just a man–woman hunch up, but there was more to it. Imran
supposedly had roving eyes for the lady; irresistibly drawn to her like a
moth driven to a flame. The couple had secretly married. The nation was
stunned. 'Why did he have to marry at this age?' protested my sister-in-
law, a long-time Imran diehard. As the nation pumped more curiosity,
growing restless on eliciting more inside scoop into the scandal; Imran
decided not to keep the adventure under wraps and spilled the beans.
'Second marriage is not a crime anywhere,' declared a riotous Imran while
speaking to the reporters from his residence in Bani Gala. That much was
enough for us all to know that Imran was under the charms of the forty-
or-so-year-old damsel. 'Clearly not a crime,' I muttered to myself. A soft
whispering campaign in the neighbourhood of Bani Gala even suggested
Reham's ill-timed trips to Imran's chamber. Such malicious talk over the
duo's carnal exploits was hardly surprising given Imran's yesteryear image
of being the ideal ladies' man. All that suspicious chattering over Imran's
love life proved that he still retained his celebrity appeal—and the kind
that is usually relished by young movie stars. A local super model, Nadia
Hussain dubbed him the fashion icon of Pakistani politics. Imran still
gathers a hefty tally of female fandom, a statistical fact that plummets

any good-looking thirty-year-old into envy. So, who really was this lady Khan who managed to intrigue and convince Imran out of a decade-old retirement into bachelor life? Reham was reared by her parents abroad. Interestingly, like Imran, it was her second marriage. Her maiden merger was with her first cousin, a British psychiatrist in 1993; this was an arrangement that ended in a divorce twelve years later. Her first marriage yielded three children. She debuted as a television presenter in England in 2006, later joining the BBC as a weather forecaster. There, at the BBC, she had the freedom to dazzle under the cover of her mini-skirts—a privilege she lost once she decided to pursue a journalism career outside of Pakistan. Her looks were her most redeeming feature, an attractive woman by all standards. She had almond-shaped smoky eyes, often ringed and darkened with *kohl*, a milky white complexion, without a trace of scar or a sprout of wrinkles, and hair that rolled down to her slender waist. A gifted linguist, she speaks English, Urdu, Pashto, and Punjabi with aplomb. As soon as the news of the couple's pairing up made the headlines, Imran's political competitors began scoffing at Reham's mini-skirting and thigh baring in London. *The Telegraph* chronicled:

> Imran's opponents have seized on Miss Khan's high profile and television career as a sign that she was ill-suited to marry the politician, and launched vicious attacks against her character. On Facebook, photographs of her smiling in the company of a female friend were captioned: 'Reham Khan drunk at a private party, rubbing a woman's back. Is she a lesbian now?' Photos of her attending a horse race in a knee-length dress were criticised, as were shots of her dancing a tango on a BBC show. In one image, she is shown striding through a boutique in a skimpy pink negligee and suspenders while carrying a whip—critics said that she was in a sex shop.

The bootless controversy over marriage dragged on for a few more days before Imran stepped out to end the gossip. 'I would have made a public declaration of my marriage few weeks later but the way this affair has drawn a lot of flak from the press forced me into an early announcement,' a disconcerted-looking Imran calmed the reporters. Once all the details of the undercover marriage had been made public and no further spice was spared for the media, Imran now had to resume focusing his energies on propounding reforms in KP. 'Reforms, reforms and more reforms,' said Imran cutting a tutorial note. His inexhaustible 126-day procession in the open-air avenues of Islamabad were constantly panned by his critics. An oversupply of Imran's protests made analysts sceptical about his commitment towards addressing the real issues of KP. The homicide in

Peshawar proved reputation damaging. If not a wholly *Naya* KP, at least a foretaste of it should have been very much in the works. Sharif decided to strike when the iron was hot by holding a massive rally in KP, trying to win back the province to his side. He began to butter up the audience by pattering down on them a series of pipeline infrastructure projects envisaged for the province. 'KP will have express ways and motorways and we will build them for you and your generations to follow,' nailed Sharif, crowned with a Pashtun turban, amid a jammed assembly of fired up supporters.

Imran was down to business. His economic model was at variance with Sharif's flood of infrastructure schemes. He wanted reforms, knowing full well that the country would not go anywhere without a serious makeover of the system. He cherry-picked health, police, education, tourism, and environment and swore to make an example out of them. He also made himself reachable by regularly turning up at a live radio show in Peshawar in his attempt to network and ingratiate with the public. In his maiden crack at building bridges with the people he ruled, Imran seemed to be in an enlightening mood:

> I had no idea that KP has such a well-established radio network. I will make it a point to take these live sessions at regular intervals as that should fill me in with the real problems of the people. I know my party is yet to deliver on all the commitments made, but we will get there. Unlike PML-N, who favours investing in big ticket infrastructure projects, we, unfortunately do not have that much money to burn and aim to spend our resources on the people as only a strong human capital force can provide the platform for a robust economy. We need better hospitals, medical facilities, better quality of education and a political free judiciary and police system—and that is our game plan for the province.[3]

A working group on health, tasked to evaluate the problems in the health sector of the province, had already been in the hopper. The working group exposed the sorry state of the provincial health sector- rates of maternal mortality, infant mortality, and child mortality, which had skyrocketed to depressing levels. Imran wanted a reconstitution of all major health institutions in the province, demanding a sector that scored high on efficiency. He wanted one that was free from all political meddling; had a merit-based appointment of all medical staff; and one that ensured regular training to conduct their business faithfully. The health institutions in KP had been battered by years of incompetence and politicisation. I personally vouch for the condition, based on my many official UN-sanctioned travels to the region. The job came in handy as it kept my purse contended and provided me with an opportunity to travel through the far stretches of the province. The health quarters were a roughhouse, with scores of patients battling for the scarce hospital beds. The medical staff on duty fled work scot free. The condition of hospital rooms soiled my paunch, often inducing me into a vomit. Ponds of phlegm scattered the floor, cigarette butts sprawled in the corridors, and the smell of rustic bottoms made the atmosphere toxic. The walls were laden with juice of chewed up betel leaves. Rats and cockroaches crawled with honeymoon enthusiasm. Nothing in my view suggested that any conscious effort had ever been made to clean the structure. Toilets were a disaster, with stool lying unattended and unflushed in commodes since only God knows when. Nurses were seen foul-mouthing the patients, reclining on their seats, cross-legged, lighting cigarettes, and sending rings of smoke down their nostrils. To me, they looked more like harlots going about soliciting a paramour for the evening. This is the picture of a typical public sector health facility completely ignored by the powers that be—rotting its own death. If Imran's mind was set aflame with pity, then clearly he was thinking in the right areas. To implement an overhaul of the system, he would first require a legislative cover. For that, Imran relentlessly pushed for a health reforms act. His breakthrough came in February 2015, when the KP Medical Teaching Institutions Reform Act went on the floors. As per the law, every medical facility in the province had to be governed by an independent board of directors, hiring medical staff on pure merit. The board of governors were entrusted with the responsibility of prescribing procedures for hiring, approving annual budgets, and approving annual business plans. External help was sought from Dr Nausherwan Burki, Imran's cousin and godfather of the Shaukat Khanum enterprise. Burki would fly down from the US for a few days every month to ensure no brakes were hit during the implementation of the law. Unfortunately, the implementation was not snag free, as a small group of doctors who favored the old system raised a howl of protest and began filing petitions against the law at the Peshawar High Court. The stay of the court kept the law from being fully transformed into practice. This proved a stumbling block for Imran's ambition towards a remodelled health sector. A repulsed Imran began digging the facts to heave scorn at the old health mafia:

> These doctors who are coming in our way hardly conduct their duties as per the law. Nearly 33% of them work for five hours a day, 27% work for four hours, 22% for three hours, 17% for two hours, and 7% work for one hour every day. Almost 100 million patients come to hospitals in KP annually. How can doctors with this work ethic and timings treat them?[4]

The mafia, as Imran's rebuffing suggested, certainly had their way, and they managed to drag the matters into oblivion. In another interesting move and in a bid to lift the lives of the beggarly and the fortuneless civilians of the province, Imran ordered to launch health insurance cards. Terms of these cards were bountiful: those identified as worthy would be issued the permits, making their access to public and private health facilities free of charge. Help for the project was solicited from foreign agencies. Imran's health minister Shahram Tarakai was upbeat, calling this a first of its kind venture in the country's history.

Policing was another area that had rankled Imran for a long time. The corruption in the police departments had been pervasive and people had completely lost faith in the system. You would curse your stars if, God forbid, you got hitched up in a police station. The staff at the police stations not only had poor interpersonal skills, but were also robbed of any compassion towards the community they were sanctioned to serve. Those in top positions were usually found ingratiating themselves with the politicians, and as a consequence, they become recipients of huge favours that came in the form of money and better positions. The politicians hijacked all discipline in the police and solicited their services to oppress their opponents. Worse, what made police more vulnerable to overtures of corruption were the poor welfare benefits that they had at their clearance. One reason for the religious *fundoos*, who managed to slog through the plains of KP with self-granted exemption, was the incompetence of the local police. The *fundoos* found havens within the local communities and went about bombing with grace. The spill over impact in KP, of a war-ravaged FATA, was unprecedented, with nearly 900 policemen and over 3,000 civilians killed since 2007. Imran knew full well that a strong police force was essential to fortify KP's internal defense mechanisms. He took a range of important measures, and by the summer of 2015, significant changes saw the light of day. To me, this was Imran's work of the season: a point-scoring initiative. He held long, closed-door brainstorming sessions with the IG Police of KP—Nassir Durrani, a man of stern authority, sporting snow-coloured whiskers. Together, they hashed out a series of constraints that included a lack of skilled human force, uncalled-for political nosiness in the conduct of business, absence of specialised units, poor welfare benefits for the staff, and a civilian stripped of his faith in the system—a system dampened by a poor résumé and many years of malfunctioning. Imran's treatise on police reforms kicked off with a complete retreat of politicians from the system. A disunion between the police and political forces created operational autonomy. Durrani, a man with an impressive record already, was pleased to be left to his own devices.

Much like Imran, he hated sycophancy and the idea of being a doormat to the politicians. 'We are grateful to the provincial government for granting us the operational freedom, now I am unconstrained in making appointments and approving transfers,' proclaimed Durrani, with a convincing expression on his face. Imran envisaged a police force that was equipped to counter militancy in all its forms. A legal coverage had to be provisioned for the police to operate glitch free. Imran was quick to have counter terrorism bills passed by the provincial assembly. The legal cover was extensive:

> All hotels in the province were obligated to register with the local police station, and supply a list of all the guests booking in on a daily basis. The penalty in case of a breach carried a one-year sentence. Landlords of all rented structures, were law bound to conduct an in-depth scrutiny of the potential tenant before signing off on any deal. Again, a one-year confinement in case the landlord fumbles. All other sensitive structures for example educational institutions, hospitals, wedding halls, public parks and market areas, etc., were required to follow strict security instructions sanctioned by the police. The implementation of the law was safeguarded by a strong scientifically armed counter terrorism department and a rapid response force. These ready forces were bolstered by the intelligence, operations and investigation wings. The forces were also schooled in the use modern warfare equipment. The Pakistan Army was invited to toughen up the officers and guarantee that they are battle ready.[5]

The corruption that long since blossomed within the police ranks had fouled the atmosphere. Bribes both petty and hefty were commonplace. Imran also wanted an internal cleansing of the department. This meant that the IG police had Imran's unwavering endorsement to hire men of calibre and merit, and get a handle on any hanky-panky in operations. A directorate of police complaint and accountability was established, endowed with the duty to monitor all internal procedures of the department. In case, any mischief was detected, a formal inquiry was commissioned. Ever since Imran pulled his reform trigger in the fall of 2013, nearly 600 shady police staff had been removed from service. A triumphant-looking Imran exuded a sense of accomplishment in one of his regular tours to Peshawar: 'We are improving the police force to make it an example for the rest of the country. In KP, the police are completely neutral and making all out efforts to improve law and order'. In one of my field expeditions to the region, a female acquaintance serving the media circles in Peshawar validated this development:

The police system surely scores high on transparency. Bribes which were once drawn under the open skies, without a hint of remorse are not as daring. Things are still far from perfect but there is a marked improvement in the transactions of the police administration. IG Police of KP displays his personal cell number on advertising hoardings across the province. As a test, I personally dialed that number and was pleased to learn that it was not just a publicity stunt. The element of fear that had stilled all commercial and personal life in the province is also tapering off. The tourism industry that was on clutches is showing signs of revival. Things are getting better.

Imran has always been a lover of forests and a passionate nature watcher. Unsettled by a draining schedule of everyday life, he would often escape to the stream laden valleys in the north to recover himself, confiding in the lowlands and the wildlife that flourished in them. The bustling of Lahore and Islamabad runs him down. That is why he was particularly unforgiving towards the timber mafia in KP, who had reportedly axed nearly 40,000 trees in a local valley in the province. KP, divested off its wildlife appeal, was like a virgin forcibly robbed of their purity. 'At this rate the country runs a risk of turning into a barren desert over the next forty years,' fulminated Imran while speaking to the press. It occurred that the forest department had teamed up with the local timber mafia— an unpardonable sin in Imran's dictionary, as he began booting out a good number of officials from the forest department. He then launched a billion-tree tsunami operation, giving his province a facelift and aiming to increase the forest cover by 22 per cent over a five-year period. 'Not even a goat will be permitted to graze on the territory,' warned Imran during the launch of the campaign.

Imran was particularly keen on reforming the education sector as it had been his most vital electoral battle cry in 2013. He was sold to the idea that without increasing access to quality education, there was no way Pakistan would be able to meet its development goals. Public sector education in KP had been in perpetual decay and in serious want of a revamp. The public schools were teemed with incompetence and corruption. Teachers hardly turned up to teach, and as a consequence, enrolment of children was also on the retreat. I have personally visited number of public schools in 2011 across the tentacles of the province and found them in need of furniture, water, bathrooms for the children, and playing areas. The condition of the infrastructure had been appalling. Furthermore, the gap between the quality of the public schools and their counterpart private ones was colossal. As private education was a drag on the poor man's purse, millions of children were confined to state education that unfortunately was good for nothing. Imran was fully absorbed with the task. In a sermon he gave to a party of teachers in Peshawar, he sounded idealistic and reassuring:

> I recall when I was young, all the best crop in the country used to churn out of public schools. Then, gradually the state of public education went into a decay and private schools took their place. Although private education had all the privileges, it came with a higher cost. Soon, children who milled though the public system began struggling for better jobs and disappeared from view, reducing into menial wage earners and seized up in a vicious cycle. Their generations were destroyed. Having good quality state education should be the fundamental goal of a government. In Germany and France; the best intellectual output comes from state schools and those who struggle to perform there, end up in the private medium. We will also ensure that in years to follow, teaching will become the most highly paid profession in the country. I do realise that one reason for low teachers' attendance is the lack of welfare incentives rationed to them—we will change that.[6]

Compulsive chatter to a jammed audience had become Imran's chief qualification. He used his wide global exposure and knowledge of the first world history to great effect—yet reforms require more than just ceaseless babbling, and a lot of work had to be done. Imran started off with the appointment of a *bona fide* young man, Mohammad Atif, as the minister for education—a lookalike of Imran, seemingly Mongol-eyed and with locks that curled down his neck. Physique wise, he cuts a striking departure from Imran's shredded exterior, hardened by decades of drilling in the gym. Muhammad Atif kicked off his tenure with a purpose; he meant business, announcing a spate of uplift measures: merit-based teacher recruitment policy, introduction of uniform curriculum, training of existing teachers, biometric system installed at a select specimen of schools to monitor teachers' attendance, a monitoring and evaluation wing established to ensure that reforms permeate into action, and a widespread children enrolment drive to guarantee school attendance. In addition, thousands of public schools in more remote districts were given a new look through infrastructure restoration. Towards the close of 2015, a London-based development consultancy firm was solicited to conduct a sample survey of schools in ten KP districts and the findings were surprising; nearly 34,000 private school students had fled for public education. This development came to pass because state education was far lighter on the wallet and had an elevated standard of instruction—though it was still not at the level of private schools, but it was showing a marked improvement. I made a personal inquiry to ratify this sudden up-tick in

quality and spoke to a friend, a Kohat-born educationist and former head
of IUCN in Baluchistan, Zabardast Khan Bangash. He sounded convinced:
'A lot of teachers I know are taking their jobs seriously. They were made to
take courses during the summer vacations and their welfare packages have
also been given a revision. Reforms in education are obviously something
that take a while to transform into visible change and there is no overnight
success. The good part is that Imran's men are strong-minded'. Sharif's
nit-picking continued as he saw no substantial changes in the fortunes of
KP. 'Reform' was a jargon that never penetrated his thoughts. His model
of development had always failed to transcend short-term infrastructure
projects—schemes that are sufficient to bid for his next re-election. In his
more than two decades of brushing with politics, he has remained tight-
lipped on giving a facelift to education, health, police, and courts. In fact,
he, along with his flunkeys, are the cause that state institutions have now
hit rock bottom. On the contrary, Imran was more of a farsighted dreamer,
one who imported his wheels of ambition from the forward-thinking
Europe. Through his speeches, he often gave his nuts and bolts of an ideal
Pakistan, a state that empties its resources on the sharpening of the human
mind, endowing its people with all the faculties to liberate themselves
from an insecure life. This reminds me of the lines from Epictetus, a Greek
philosopher of the Roman Empire: 'Only the educated are free'.

Given the energy constraints of the province, Imran made a point
to exploit the multitude of free-flowing streams that decorated the
landscapes of KP. A list of micro hydel projects was sanctioned soon after
Imran formed the provincial government. Most of these projects were
dubbed to be functional by the close of 2016 or 2017. Remote villages
of the province, which were completely detached from the technology of
grid energy, were brought under the supply through off-grid solar rooftop
solutions. Imran also took a crack at saving some foreign exchange for the
federal treasury by extracting indigenous resources of oil and gas. Soon,
his party began rallying around claims that KP had become the largest oil-
producing province in the country. Unfortunately, the media in Pakistan
remained zipped in providing ground coverage to these developments in
the province. However, no passable effort on judicial reforms came into
view—an area where Imran and his disciples have remained mum and
often found groping, despite their calls for justice and fair play. I also
believe that several of Imran's henchmen are in the sport simply because
they want themselves to be printed in non-fiction texts and benefit from
being in the same frame as Imran the celebrity; if this was the purpose,
then they have been hugely successful. One particular gentleman, Imran's
lanky cohort and a former corporate success story, turned out to be as
dishevelled a politician as I have ever come across in recent times. After

getting elected as a member of the nation's bungled-up parliament, he worked as hard as the rag pickers in town, evidenced by a growing pile of garbage close to his quarters in Islamabad. His chief contribution was to appear in late night political shows, where he was seen squabbling around with his opponents on issues not even remotely linked with his constituency. The MNA's insistence on being a reachable politician lured me towards slipping a note under his apartment a near dozen times. No word ever came from him. I heard similar complaints from other men who, like me, wanted to discuss petty municipal issues with Imran's irresponsive public servant. The truth is that PTI bears a small uncommitted minority in its ranks, people who may not share the same vision as Imran, but have serious hang-ups about Imran's illustrious celebrity résumé and just want to be close to him. Being close to Imran fetches them decent publicity and serves the purpose.

The year 2015 also culminated with a *coup de théâtre* in Imran's private life as he retreated to his bachelor ways, ending his conjugal vows with Reham. Tragically, the marriage could only sustain for ten months. The media dropped in for some political mileage. Reports that came had made a botch of the couple's split. One version was particularly amusing: the pair was under the spell of witchcraft. Another version suggested that Reham had sold her soul to the devil, as she attempted to poison Imran and spy on his party's secret congregations. All of that was garbage. The marriage from day one was deprived of lasting prospects. Imran's plate was full of politics, and he was buried in his schedule up to his eyeballs. He was not even remotely responsive to his partner's domestic skills and was terribly untamed to play his part of a family loving devotee. Long years of living as a hermit, divesting himself of all ready family duties, had made him too rusty in the art of matrimony. Reham, in her interview with *The Sunday Times* in November 2015, provided a saner account of her separation with Imran:

Soon after our marriage, things were sloping downwards. We both turned out to be strikingly opposite to each other. I am a little loose-lipped whereas Imran is too restrained and inward for my taste. With Imran you must talk politics all the time, whereas I like to discuss the shades of the curtains and the latest Bollywood gossip, subjects that turned him off. I also did not find him very romantic and he never bought me anything after marriage. He abstained from an organised domestic life. His closet was bungled up—consumed by a good number of moths that found a permanent home inside. His kitchen was in need of food. He also did not like having my children causing any clamour in the house.

With such austerity measures in place, foreboding the pair's break up was simple guess work. In fact, many of us believed that it came as a relief for Imran. He was no longer cut out for matchmaking given his political life, which was always on the move. The only break he periodically afforded himself was a reunion with his two children. Qasim and Suleiman are big boys now, old enough to be granted permission to fly down to Islamabad unguarded and entice their old man into a camping sojourn in the company of snow-laden peaks of the Karakorum Range. Being with his kids reconditions Imran, shedding his years and making him young again as he girds up his rejuvenated loins to resume his clattering in politics. On 29 December 2015, Imran inaugurated in Peshawar his second cancer hospital in the Shaukat Khanum franchise. An eight-storied red-brick structure, erected at a cost of 4 billion rupees and supplied with the same inventory of facilities as the hospital in Lahore—a staggering feat. The media thronged the grand opening ceremony hosted by Imran's party. His guest list for the occasion was endless. His old cricket chums, including the likes of Wasim Akram and Javed Miandad, had also bobbed up in the crowd. 'Every Pakistani has pitched in; this is a joint effort of the entire nation,' exclaimed Wasim, cutting a gleeful note. Highlight of the afternoon was a seven-year-old cancer patient chosen to perform the ribbon clipping. Imran was in fine feather that evening as he headed out to Islamabad, where Sharif, on the rebound, had announced his scheme of free medical treatment for the poor: an insurance-based program covering fifteen districts across the country. The news had us on the edge of our sofas. Sharif's paperwork is usually note-perfect, however, his credentials in social service delivery have been disputable. Will Rogers once stated: 'I don't make jokes. I just watch the government and report the facts'.

The Panama Plague

Loyalty to country ALWAYS. Loyalty to government, when it deserves it.

Mark Twain

Sometime in the late spring of 2015, a sudden pinging of the phone belonging to a nerdy looking journalist of German origin yielded revelations that sent shockwaves across the planet. Little did he know that with that 'never do wrong' look on him, he would be drafted into a serpentine schedule of investigative journalism: a project of unheard of dimensions in recent journalism history. Yes, I am alluding to the intriguing Panama leaks. The poor Obermayers sadly found themselves consumed in one of the biggest data dumps of our times. Through anonymous encrypted messages, the German reporter retrieved approximately 11.5 million shady pages exposing stark naked the global armies of corruption. The paper trail led them to a rogue industry, a world of disguise, a crowd of decent characters who have piled up a lot of indecent wealth in offshore shell companies. The scoop was irresistible. The list of suspects was teemed with politicians, military dictators, leading bankers, lawyers, industrialists, oligarchs, people traffickers, drug dealers, arms smugglers, diamond pinchers, thug mafias, sports stars, and many other scumbags glutted with ceaseless ill-gotten fortune. A Sherlock Holmes-style gumshoeing was activated as major international networks of devoted journalists began sifting through the documents to excavate sellable stories that would send many heads rolling and many kingdoms tumbling.

So how does it all work? Panama is a smallish belt sandwiched between North and South America, and bounded on either side by the Atlantic and Pacific Oceans. For over 100 years, its economy has been under the nursing care of the States. US President Theodore Roosevelt is accredited for rescuing a disaffected Panama, then a province of Columbia. In 1903, at the urging of leading US bankers and industrialists, Roosevelt sent his military missionaries to liberate Panama from the fleecing of Columbia. Thereafter, Panama remained a US outpost as it transformed from a literal nothing into a big-time tax haven. Panamanian tax laws, dating back to 1927, sanction large money inflows without the questioning need to examine their moral source. This granting of safe passage to unauthorised treasures triggered the growth of the Panamanian economy. Notable law firms registered their plush offices in the heart of Panama City, with the abiding passion to solicit both first and third world clients, guaranteeing their hoardings a fool proof security. The usual list of clients lured to the privileges Panama offered included the long list of dirt bags I previously mentioned—people who have something to hide. The law firms were well-skilled in the art of setting up unidentified, camouflaged, and, as the world of espionage goes, 'John Doe shell companies'. So, if you have something to hide, say taxpayers loot, turn to these expert and savvy law firms who know their onions well and will have it all arranged for you in a matter of hours. Sadly, there is nothing goof-proof and unerring in this world. One of these law firms apparently spilled to what it believed was guarded and well-fortified information. Its files were hacked and its reputation was sorely impaired. On 3 April 2016, the Obermayers' published accounts of a yearlong data scrutiny sprawled in the book stores the world over. There was panic. To many, it was an act of fine journalism—to others, it was blasphemy. The revelations spared no one. Big names implicated in offshore concealing included the head of Russia, Iceland, Malta, the United Kingdom, Spain, Argentina, Saudi Arabia, and Pakistan. High-ranking banks and law firms also came under the radar for their unbounded malfeasance. A wave of objection went up. Former US President Barack Obama was forced to make a public address, citing tax evasion and undercover corruption as a serious issue. Similar reactions erupted in Europe and Latin America. For the purpose of my account, Pakistan was totally jolted. Prime Minister Mian Muhammad Nawaz Sharif, already notorious for his stripping of the national vault, had his head in the noose. As per the latest data cracking, Sharif's three children—the milky white heiress of the Pakistan empire, Mariam Nawaz, and her two shapeless-looking brothers, Hussain and Hasan—allegedly owned upscale real estate possessions in London's exclusive Mayfair *ilaka* (area). The flats, supposedly four in count, were bought over two decades ago through the auspices of their two offshore companies, namely Neilson Enterprise Limited and Nescoll Limited—planted incognito in the British Virgin Islands. The pet-lawyers and other flatterers of the House of Sharif began scampering for cover-ups in their attempt to keep the story under wraps.

Everyone except the Sharif flunkeys knew that the writing was clearly on the wall. No sleuthing of the knighted Conan Doyle was required.

For Imran, this was the moment; striking while the iron was hot. His reward for the 126 days' wait in the whiffy parks of Islamabad and his undying disputes over Sharif's gerrymandering had finally fallen from the stars. In his typical fast bowler's stride, he searched for the bloopers in the convoluted official statements that now popped up from Sharif's progeny. Various versions surfaced. One particular version that left me with cramps in my paunch was the procurement of the Mayfair holdings in the early 1990s at a time when the children were hardly a couple of decades old, yet they had such a strong DNA in the trade of fortune building that they managed to pick up inordinately valuable properties in the ornate neighbourhood of central London. Another slip-up suggested that the much probed-off spring had only lapped up the assets in 2006 contrasting declarations. Imran was not the one to spare such goof-ups. After a few days of his own digging and shuffling through statistics and timelines, he came out simplifying the matter. It turned out that no serious study of Sharif's prior business transactions was needed as it was hardly a brainteaser. A superficial glance through Google yielded the Hudaibiya Paper Mills case, heard and settled in London during Sharif's second tenure as prime minister. Nawaz Sharif and his two brothers, Shehbaz and Abbas, sometime in the early to mid-1990s raised a debt from a London-based investment fund, managed by the Al Towfeek Company. Abiding by the trend in Pakistan, the Sharif brothers never paid back their borrowings, forcing Al Towfeek to move the courts for a trial. On 4 September 1998, a notice was served upon the brothers demanding a settlement. On their rebound, the Sharifs filed an application, pleading the court to set aside their proceedings. The plea was heard by Justice Buckley of the Queen's division bench. Puzzled by the petition, Mr Buckley, through a one pager notification, refused the solicitation and subsequently commanded the defendants (the Sharifs) to repay the investment fund. The Sharifs remained mum over the court's ruling, dragging the scene for another six months before the court decided to grab the underlying properties used as collateral. When things came to a tipping point, the brothers recompensed and rescued their four Mayfair properties from being raided and snatched. These were the same properties looked down with suspicion following the Panama leaking eighteen years later. No profound auditing was required. The journalists began their curious prying, flooding the three Sharif children with a surplus of questions. The kids retorted with stutters, stammers, and more baffling responses. Under the heat-belching sun on the evening of 4 April, a triumphant-looking Imran—decked with his chic jet black goggles, well-shaven, scrubbed, and devoured of all traces of stubble, gleaming under the receding sunlight—fought his way through a large assembly of snoopy journalists and took control of his microphone. He quickly surveyed through the reporters and disapproved the fluttering of their outstretched forearms and the clamour they were causing. With a roaring shush and an invisible magic wand, Imran plunged the throng into graveyard silence. 'Listen to me now very carefully,' cut Imran, with an interesting blend of repulsive and triumphant glee on his face. In the offing was his usual professorial, fact-emitting sermonising: Imran's routine soapbox pontification and extracts from global affairs—a complete contrast to what other leaders in the country do while addressing the unschooled, unwise fellow countrymen. Trashing reactions emerged from the Sharif squad, censuring Imran for spreading canards against them. The sixty-four-year-old object of lust rebuked all the attacks made on him:

> Let me be very clear that this is a global leak. This has nothing to do with Imran Khan. As I speak, investigations have already started in several countries. Government heads of Iceland and United Kingdom are already under pressure to respond to allegations of concealing their wealth in off shore accounts. Iceland is a small country with less than half a million population and nearly 20,000 of them are already out of their roofs demanding an explanation. So, my dear Pakistanis, it seems as if Allah has taken a *suo motu* on Pakistan. This is your opportunity to speak out. I have now been fighting against our notorious elite for nearly twenty years and the Panama revelations clearly proves that I was not goofing up all this while. Nawaz Sharif only paid Rupees five thousand as tax few years back, yet his offshore companies own assets that run into billions of rupees.[1]

'But what about you Khan *Sahib*?' interrupted a teasing reporter, messing-up Imran's eloquence, 'There are reports that your cancer hospital in Lahore made a whopping investment of $3 million in an offshore company and has incurred a painful loss.'

Imran was not the one to talk himself out of it: 'I say on record that there was an investment made by the endowment fund of my hospital. But, what you do not know is that the investment has been recovered and you are most welcome to flip through our official balance sheets for details'. After hushing the probe-eyed reporter, Imran resumed his bashing of the Sharifs:

> This is an obvious case of money laundering. All these state institutions including ECP, NAB, FIA and our courts, seemingly planted to improve accountability standards, must do their part. The ECP is the Election

Commission of Pakistan, not the Election Commission of Nawaz Sharif. And if these institutions are robbed of their honour and are simply there to do the emperor's bidding then what use do we have of these establishments?

'Pakistanis!' roared Imran with his forefinger marking in the direction of the flickering cameras, 'If you want a *Naya* Pakistan then now is your moment.'

Pakistan was yet again panic-stricken. What will happen? Will the PM go? Will the government resign? These were the wringers, the press people mulled over. Sadly, the old-school thinkers and other men of declining age were pretty frigid about the whole Panama fuss. A retired brigadier of some acquaintance told me. 'Pakistan's politics is very amusing. You will see all this noise over the leaks will gradually fizzle. Sharif and his cute looking baggy children will wade their way through the storm and soon Panama will be a textbook thing.' Dismally, this Panama thing was not only about how comical Pakistan's politics is, it's a global thing. It is also about those thousands of millions of displeased and disgusted voters in Iceland who heaved empty fizzy drink bottles, banana coverings, rolls of toilet paper, and whatever else was humanly possible to hurl at their country's parliamentary compounds. In Malta, similar sentiments came to light as thousands of demonstrators lamented their leader Joseph Muscat for being one of the Panama boys. After all, as Ayaz Amir, a well-known columnist in Pakistan, wrote: 'These offshore ghost companies are not into philosophy or charity. Every babe in the woods know this full well'. What amused me the most was a spoof imprinted in the interior pages of *The Nation*—Pakistan's veteran English publication—bearing a caption that read: 'The royal cutlery'. It showcased Sharif's two male scions, Hussain and Hasan, satirically pointing their guns on Imran: 'This is pure *Imraniyat* [Imran's marketing], there is no blame on Sharifs'. More entertaining was the prime minister's first public appearance on state television following the Panama *bazar* (exhibition) and Imran's ventilation. The premier made fleeting remarks aimed at his political adversaries for tampering his reputation with pointless conspiracy theories before giving a PowerPoint-style refresher course on how from being an ordinary nobody, his forbearers amassed a business empire. There was no citation of Panama, and no clarifications were provided. A shameless attempt to trick out of the issue. 'No dodging us this time Sharif *Sahib*,' scoffed Imran.

Imran Khan, Pakistan's lone, noisiest, anti-corruption missionary of late, was in full repelling mode. One of his zippy party helpers, often ramming in and out of his leader's palatial chateau in Bani Gala, recently told me: 'Ever this Panama scandal happened, Khan *Sahib* has been losing sleep like an insomniac'. His evening diet, he told, was limited to a bowlful of roasted peanuts, enough to stock his ripped belly. His nights, however, had been awfully boring. No romping of kids, no television watching, and certainly no past hang-ups, just sifting through party documents or holding dry runs of his ear-splitting fulminations at press conferences. 'Now that you are fully consumed by politics, how do you cope with such a restless life?' quizzed a fellow Cantab and former English test cricketer Michael Atherton.

'You see my present life is far more interesting and promising than any other phase of my life. But, it has come with a heavy price.'

'Your family?' intercepted Atherton.

'Yes,' says Imran, 'My biggest discomfort is that I do not have my kids with me.' Imran's schedule was full. His next safari was the parliament house on 7 April. Pulling up in his lustrous black four-wheeler, numbered LEE-01, he emerged out of the front seat with his eyes down, dodged the prodding reporters, and steamed into the parliament. Moments later, he was seen reciting passages from his knowledge of first world politics, occasionally letting out the foulest of temper aimed at the ruling benches to suppress their censorious whispers:

> You must all know by now that Iceland's Prime Minister yielded to public clamour and has tendered his resignation. I do not think the honourable Nawaz Sharif has any moral authority left to lead the country. If he feels he is innocent, he must prove himself through an independent judicial inquiry.[2]

There was some back talking in the N-league corner, disturbing Imran's winding lecture. Overcome by his raging tantrums, Imran turned around facing Sharif's pavilion and blurted '*Hosla rakho* [have patience]' as the entire hall plummeted into an eerie calm. Troubled by the ranting Imran, N-league partisans started giving out erratic statements. Various versions surfaced: Sharif's children are innocent; Sharifs pay their taxes; Sharif's children are very religious. Yet no description of the Panama accused money trails ever left their lips. The evasions were clearly not working out. The 'Sharifovs', as my favourite Pakistani wordsmith and critic Ayaz Amir calls them, had no way of escaping this time. The days of wine and roses for the Sharifs, writes Ayaz, were over because the queries of the Panama leaks were too unavoidable and the Sharifs, with all their skull scratching, were unable to provide convincing answers. So right was Ayaz, the whiskered, long-standing evaluator of Pakistan's enthralling and unfortunate political soil. A week later, Panama had become the most enterprising feature of the planet: a front-page news item. It had become the most tweeted, the most ridiculed, and the most common buzzword. Cartoonists around the globe sharpened their pencils and turned their bantering wit towards the naked wealth of dirty capitalism. One that I am particularly fond of contains three inflated-looking obese and heavily loaded cheats, scorching themselves on an unknown island. One of them placatingly stated: 'You may call us refugees! We escaped the oppressive tax regimes'. There was another one showing a shirtless Putin with a bandana knotted around his skull, digging a trench to conceal a treasure box filled with $2 billion worth of bullion and notes.

In Pakistan, Imran mused over the Panama trails with Obermayer enthusiasm. Activating his team of sycophants, he excavated proof-worthy documents so that no clear passage was spared to the Sharifovs. Then, more mud-slinging followed. 'Oh my God! This "Im" has shoved in to their bums,' expounded one of the opposition supporters as Imran plunged into the nitty-gritties. 'It is not only the children of Pakistan's Prime Minister who own a shell company. The Prime Minister himself owns one,' waggling a curious piece of document:

> The name of the offshore concern is Shamrock. Then, his Finance Minister, Mr Ishaq Dar and his children own two multistore skyscrapers in the ritzy corner of Dubai. Each structure costs a whopping $100 million. I ask, where are they getting all this cash from? If we do not fix our corruption, our economy will never fly.[3]

Imran then gushed out with astronomical statistics, stating that, as per NAB, daily corruption amounted to an eye-popping $100 million or more. In a Punjabi-laced accent, Imran stated:

> The British Prime Minister David Cameron was one of the Panama recruits and has even confessed to have profited less than fifty thousand dollars and that too before his signing up as Britain's leading political man. But, as soon as the word of his bonding with the ghost company slipped out, there were noticeable demonstrations in the Westminster. And here in Pakistan, these ravagers have rinsed away the national purse and we are still unbothered.

Imran, with a damning streak on his face, even produced a coloured illustration of the Mayfair flats printed on A4 paper and gripped firmly in his longish Pashtun fingers, giving the accursed, fortuneless, and broke Pakistanis a feel of the fruits of laundering taxpayers' loot into tax havens abroad. 'This is their lifestyle, yet sixty million people in this country are on the breadline,' yawps a maddened-looking Imran, hinting at an unforgiving rallying schedule in the days and months to come, additionally threatening to fence around Sharif's gilded, grand country home on the outer edges of southern Lahore. Timelines were not announced, but Imran made his mutinous intentions loud and clear. 'He is a compulsive talker and lures young loins like iron fillings drawn to a magnet,' remarked a decrepit, weather-beaten old lady who, despite my many evasions, frequently stumbled into my path at Islamabad club. During my writing of this tale, she was my biggest distraction. 'Don't you find Imran too monotonous? I think he has become a bit of a bore with his pointless tattling. He is always crying,' she exclaimed. I always ignored her until one day she spilled the rub herself. 'When Imran was young, we virgins would just drool at his Tarzan-like shirtless, shredded six-pack midriff, there at the Lahore Gymkhana Cricket Ground. He the Greek God of our dreams, we the star gazing youthful fantasizers.'

'Then why all this talk about him being a crashing bore now?' I protested. She was silent and totally bemused. The truth is that Imran's incessant revolting has earned him a bad name among the out-of-mileage, grey-haired population. It is mostly the young or the young hearted who find him and his revolutionary alarms attractive. His unsparing, relentless punchlines aimed at the misruling elite is a renaissance in Pakistan. It is he who repeatedly goes around drumming into our heads that politics should be a responsible career taken up by responsible men. Going by these standards, concealing of assets was a sin and laundering money was an even a bigger transgression.

In the meantime, there was widespread panic in the Sharif circles following the prime minister's sudden flight to London. Fortune-tellers, well-versed in Pakistan's eventful politics, suggested that Sharif had fled the country to benefit from Zardari's vulpine counselling. Others felt that this was it, and that Sharif was not coming back. However, N-leaguers quickly triggered the social media buttons to mitigate all grapevines by making it clear that the premier had gone to London for a regular medical examination and would soon be returning. In an experiment to dodge out of the Panama crap, Sharif's partisans prescribed drafting of a retired judge to conduct an inquiry into the case. This scheme was abruptly rejected by most opposition leaders, citing that similar arrangements in past years had hardly yielded anything worthwhile. Furthermore, all the retired judges reaching out for the game plan disapproved of the overture. Sadly, the Sharifs had always been a regular feature in the country's maligned judicial system. Nearly twenty years ago, when the Supreme Court of Pakistan was pressing similar Panama-style charges against the then-second time Prime Minister Sharif, a mob of N-leaguers assaulted the Supreme Court in a shameless trampling of the apex courts law giving sanctity. Then, attempts were made by the Supreme Court to identify the soldiers waging *jihad* against the judges who had the nerve to question Sharif's trespassing. Videographic evidence was also produced, showing leading N-league party workers and cabinet ministers exhorting the mob. Court hearings had become a window dressing affair as no serious verdict ever came out of the trial. The probing lingered for nearly two years, until Musharraf overthrew the government in October 1999.

Returning to Panama, hours after Sharif's London departure, Imran also headed for the British Isles. The former plausibly for a medical inspection, the latter to solicit funds for Shaukat Khanum and to meet with credible audit firms. At an impressive rally held in Birmingham, Imran revealed what this audit firm musing was all about. 'We once again reject the option of a retired judge. How can a judge of the premier's own choosing give an unbiased ruling? We demand an independent judicial commission, aided by international audit firms to examine the money trail,' expounded Imran. There was also some small talk about Imran's offshore companies established back in his cricketing days in England in the 1980s. Mariam Nawaz was quick to cling on the word and dispatched a tweet: 'Meet Mr Khan, Pakistan's pioneer of offshore companies. The trail blazer award goes to him'. Sharif's long-time backscratcher and chairman of the Privatization Commission, Mohammad Zubair, bashed Imran for disguising his offshore romance at a well-known private channel. As the buzz began to assume threatening dimensions, Imran retorted with an elaborate response:

> Yes, I had an offshore once but I was not violating any law. I was a Pakistani citizen, playing county cricket for Sussex. I was already paying 35 per cent taxes in England and wanted to evade further taxes, which was my right. I was not liable to fund the English tax schemes.[4]

Back in Pakistan, Imran, after extensive internal meetings with his party, declared his list of things to do, and a spate of nationwide crusades against the Panama-stricken Sharifovs was on the cards. Sweeping rallies were planned. The summer heat was in the ascending gears, with deep blue skies ruling out prophecies of seasonal rainfall. This meant that the rallies were to be even more taxing and sweaty. The itinerary of the prelude was out: starting from Islamabad in late April, mass demonstrations would be held in Lahore, Faisalabad, Sindh, and KP, packing the entire month of May. The atmosphere of the rallies had a typical Imran touch to it. Hooting, chirping, howling, and an occasional booing at the ruling party, and, yes, some great dancing moves too. Of course, the usual soundtracks, save for a couple of additional numbers on the playlist, were used. Young men were dressed in lousy casuals with PTI colours smeared over their faces. Women, however, were more tastefully decked to sweeten up the concerts. A synopsis of a near dozen outings yielded an interesting mixture of mud-slinging and sermons on how great nations are built. The mainstay of the preaching, however, was Panama, and the bottom line was as follows: 'Hold an independent inquiry of your money trails Sharif *Sahib*, or else prepare for my army to besiege your palace in Lahore'. Imran stated this, knocking the air with his heavy duty Pashtun fists. By June, the nation plunged into the Ramadan slumber, and Imran finally took a break from his grumbling. For Sharif, the lull of Ramadan and much of the remaining summer laid signs of an impending storm. If Panama was upsetting enough at home, then having India howling on the eastern borders was a bigger nightmare. Imran was a little dim throughout the summer, but it was only a matter of time before he discovered his voice. On 18 September, four unknown assailants allegedly hopped over the Kashmir boundaries of India and robbed eighteen Indian soldiers of their lives. Indian authorities and nationalists flooded Pakistan with the foulest of flak. Without much probing, cross-border firing commenced with patriotic zeal. Regrettably, cultural exchange between the two countries came down cracking as Pakistani artists, swaggering away in India, were unapologetically kicked out. Likewise, Pakistani filmmakers vowed to ban importing of all Indian content. Right in the middle of this latest India–Pakistan bickering, Imran announced his million-man marching plans for Lahore—the promised besieging of the Sharif palace. Few of us wondered that Imran perhaps could have waited until tensions on the eastern front settled, but Imran thought otherwise. The Lahore show would go on as per the schedule, he insisted: 'I will show Sharif how to respond to the Indian Prime Minister Narendra Modi'—another of Imran's crafty schemes to belittle Sharif and turn his head in the noose.

On 30 September, flanked by tens of thousands of gung-ho supporters, Imran resumed his Panama bashing just a few miles short of Sharif's country estate in southern Lahore. Also in stock was some tongue-lashing reserved for the Indian High Minister:

> The last I saw of Modi, I found him to be a man of sane thinking. Sadly, he turned out to be a prejudiced extremist. Modi! We all are united and one. Not all Pakistanis are like Nawaz Sharif. Not all Pakistanis put their honour up for sale. I appeal you to keep your threatening notifications in check. War is not an option. We demand peace in the region. Fix Kashmir and you will fix the region.[5]

Imran blurted all that his heart concealed, sparing no thoughts for late night rumination. Reactions from the Indian media were rattling. 'Imran has no authority in his so called *Naya* Pakistan. Let him rant. He has no value,' protested Zee News from India. For Sharif, it was Mayday, as his heart sank into his boots. 'Hold an independent inquiry and prove yourself guilt free or else this time we will shut the capital till our demands are met,' forewarned Imran, aged sixty-four, proud scion of the Niazi Pashtun tribe in all his senses. '*Yeh toh pagal ho gaya hai* [He has gone bonkers],' gushed out an old World Bank colleague in panic. That was populist politics at its best or worst—the South Asian style. If the Panama criminals were unshaken, so was the opposition under the directorship of an unforgiving Imran. Sharif and his loyalists, by now battle-hardened with Imran's ceaseless onslaughts in recent years, refused to cave in. Imran responded by dropping the curtains, sealing the doors of pardon and blowing the whistle. 'We will lockdown Islamabad on November 2,' said Imran, cutting a riotous note. A lockdown he later clarified would be a peaceful, unharmed protest. The country was yet again in the middle of a nail-biting nowhere. What will happen? Will Nawaz Sharif give up? Will N-league fend off a mutinous Imran by shunting him in jail? Will there be another martial law? Will there be a civil war? Will the religious *fundoos* take advantage of these internal brawls and resume their bomb strikes? These were some of the probabilities that we mulled over.

Sadly, few days short of 2 November, just as Imran's followers began their point-making excursions towards the capital, the government sealed the town. Worse, more counteroffensive moves were sanctioned. First, a federal army of policemen, armed with long, fat wands and tear gas detonators, waited impatiently to pounce on the Imran squad. Second, whale-sized containers were deposited to obstruct all safe passages to Islamabad. Those *Imranites*, crafty enough to dodge their ugly welcoming to the capital, took a detour, sparing themselves a blood-oozing thrashing. Making the arduous undercover journey, they slogged through prickly and unkempt hamlets of Punjab and KP, finally arriving at their headquarters in Bani Gala. Those unskilled in the art of dodging slothfully treaded along the main route, battling downpours of police shelling and on-the-head thumping. Imran was furious: 'What version of democracy does the N-league practice? This is worse than dictatorship. Even Musharraf was better than this. We are being ripped off our right to hold peaceful demonstrations'. Discovering a sudden growth in the number of Imran supporters camping along Bani Gala's garbage laden bumpy boulevards, the police hastened to cordon off the entire area, literally putting Imran under house arrest. A steamed-up Imran, with his hackles rising by the second, told the police to dislodge the barriers or else he would let his men go wild over them. The next morning and just a day short of the appointed 2 November, I witnessed the worst version of state torture. I saw truth-preaching journalists being clubbed profusely and thrown into police vans; I saw young women obscenely handled and locked away; and I saw policemen letting out the foulest of abuse. Nearly 400 PTI workers were arrested. In the middle of this blasphemous sinning, some spirit lifting was provided by Imran as he advertised his physical potency by knocking away fifty consecutive press-ups, putting to shame young men half his age and having women around him ogling, with their eyes and tongues hanging out.

As law and order cascaded to new lows, the Supreme Court of Pakistan baled out the nation from an anarchic freefall, deciding to enrol the Panama problem and take a stock of the allegations pressed against the Sharifs. Elated at the prospects, Imran, indifferent to a cold November evening and with a triumphant glee pasted on his face, told the reporters:

> Listen to me carefully you all. I have made every effort to fight against corruption in this country. I have clamoured for twenty years to strengthen democracy. In a genuine democracy, the head of the state is accountable to its people. I have riled on the streets against election rigging. I have protested ill governance. And now, we objected because our Prime Minister has lost all moral credibility. I am thrilled to declare that after seven months of rigid persistence, the apex court of Pakistan has agreed to probe the Panama allegations against Sharif's family. This is our VICTORY.[6]

Amid a deafening applause of elevated supporters, Imran called off the rally, willing to put a squeeze on his labour of Hercules and willing to eat his words to let the courts play their part. Few of his disputers panned him for leaving the job unfinished. The panning was not out of place. A good literature review of Pakistan's judicial system yields a number of high-profile cases, shelving away for ages and having reduced to nothing more than piles of dusty, moth-eaten pages. I can certainly bet on my bottom's dollar that courts in Pakistan, in all its seventy years of controversial, disorderly existence, have not particularly been fond of the word 'justice'. It will therefore not be a surprise if the Panama case also lingers on and on until the cows came home. Yet Imran Khan Niazi, Pakistan's biggest renaissance man, the country's only statesman who has seen his personal net worth regress through a career in politics, knows well that his wranglings do not end here. He is not going to rest, or will he? He replies. 'I will only rest when I am dead and gone'.

Endnotes

Chapter 1

1. Khan, I., *Imran Khan Pakistan: A Personal History* (London: Bantam Books, 2012).
2. Khan, I., *Imran Khan Pakistan: A Personal History*, (London: Bantam Books, 2012).
3. Lieven, A., *Pakistan: A Hard Country* (London: Penguin Books, 2012).

Chapter 2

1. Constitution of Pakistan Tehreek-e-Insaaf (PTI), www.insaaf.pk.

Chapter 3

1. Musharraf, P., *In the Line of Fire* (London: Simon & Schuster, 2006).
2. Imran Khan speaking to the associated press, www.youtube.com/watch?v=90shS0Y9B-A.
3. Imran Khan in an interview with the PTV News, www.currentaffairspk.com/imran–khan–vs–talat–hussain–old–conversation–in–2002/.
4. Imran Khan demanded 100 National Assembly seats from Pervez Musharraf in 2002 elections YouTube, online video, 2012, www.youtube.com/watch?v=H9v2xibSzA0.
5. 'Khan 'optimistic' about Pakistan elections', BBC News, 21 June 2002, news.bbc.co.uk/2/hi/south_asia/2056431.stm.
6. Imran Khan speech in Hangu | May 2002, online video, 2002, www.youtube.com/watch?v=d1ZCW_5g2ew.
7. Khan, I., *Imran Khan Pakistan: A Personal History* (London: Bantam Books, 2012).

Chapter 4

1. Mohsin, J., *Howzzat?! by Im the Dim* (Lahore: Vanguard Books, 2014).

Chapter 5

1. Ilyas, F., 'Imran Khan delivers his own "I have a dream" speech', *The Express Tribune*, 31 March 2013, tribune.com.pk/story/529130/imran-khan-delivers-his-own-i-have-a-dream-speech/.

Chapter 6

1. Usman, A., and Jafri, O., 'Imran says PTI will sit in opposition', *The Express Tribune*, 13 May 2013, epaper.tribune.com.pk/DisplayDetails.aspx?ENI_ID=11201305130168&EN_ID=11201305130137&EMID=11201305130017.
2. Speech from Shaukat Khanum Hospital in Lahore following the national elections, online video, 15 May 2013, www.youtube.com/watch?v=F0pRDkMrwKM.
3. Imran Khan's oath taking speech at the National Assembly, online video, 19 June 2013, www.youtube.com/watch?v=VQJ6w4aH688.
4. Mujahid, S., and Merchant, L., *Quotes from the Quaid* (Karachi: Oxford University Press, 2007).
5. 'PTI to hold sit-in on October 4 if ECP members do not resign: Imran', *Dawn*, 29 August 2013, www.dawn.com/news/1203646.

Chapter 7

1. Farooq, U., 'K–P political crisis: Imran warns "blackmailing" MPAs he'll dissolve assembly', *The Express Tribune*, 5 April 2014, tribune.com.pk/story/691547/k–p–political–crisis–imran–warns–blackmailing–mpas–hell–dissolve–assembly/.
2. Ur-Rehman, Z., 'We could not keep our promises', *The Friday Times*, 25 April 2014, www.thefridaytimes.com/tft/we–could–not–keep–our–promises/.
3. Imran Khan holding a press conference at his residence in Islamabad, online video, 2 May 2014, www.youtube.com/watch?v=H9l-IpKqg4o.
4. Saad Rafique speech in the National Assembly, online video, 8 May 2014, www.youtube.com/watch?v=IT_euGv5cQw.
5. Imran Khan and Sheikh Rasheed Press Conference outside Parliament, online video, 2014, newsbeat.pk/news/imran–khan–and–sheikh–rasheed–press–conference–outside–parliament–8th–may–2014–video_dc145532f.html.
6. Ahsan, A., *Robbing an Election* (Lahore: Jumhoori Publication, 2015).
7. Imran Khan's speech in Islamabad, online video, 11 May 2014, www.youtube.com/watch?v=_Jv5Liw_lwE.
8. Imran Khan speech at Bahawalpur, online video, 27 June 2014, www.youtube.com/watch?v=v1ovgdm_Dow.
9. Khan, I., interviewed by Javed Chaudhry, 2014, *Express News*, www.youtube.com/watch?v=I6guqJJMyUA.
10. Imran Khan interview in Gujranwala, online video, 15 August 2014, www.youtube.com/watch?v=78bgLKdY8mI.
11. Imran Khan speech in Islamabad, online video, 16 August 2014, www.youtube.com/watch?v=pfM6rVK-nU.
12. Kantawala, F. T., 'Where's my ice bucket?', *The Friday Times*, 29 August 2014, www.thefridaytimes.com/tft/wheres–my–ice–bucket/.

Chapter 8

1. Imran in an interview with ARY News, online video, 16 December 2014, www.youtube.com/watch?v=ZZvQwsq_1rs.
2. Ali, M., 'Pressing the issues: Imran seeks return of FC force to K-P', *The Express Tribune,* 23 December 2014, tribune.com.pk/story/810932/pressing-the-issues-imran-seeks-return-of-fc-force-to-k-p/.
3. Imran Khan Pakhtunkhwa Radio Mardan World Radio Day–13 February 2015, online video, 2015, www.youtube.com/watch?v=zaP8beKBAyY.
4. Imran Khan in a press conference reported by Waqt News, 3 November 2015, nation.com.pk/national/03-Nov-2015/doctors-mafia-impeding-hospital-development-in-kp-imran-khan.
5. Strategic Initiatives and Institutional Reforms in Khyber Pakhtunkhwa Police 2015-16 (Peshawar: Government of KP, 2016).
6. Imran Khan's Speech on World Teachers Day in KPK, online video, 5 October 2016, www.youtube.com/watch?v=1ebtuIHbhbA.

Chapter 9

1. Imran Khan's press conference on the Panama Scandal, online video, 4 April 2016, www.youtube.com/watch?v=Wb9ObrG7ayw.
2. Imran Khan Speech in Parliament on the Panama Leaks, online video, 7 April 2016, www.youtube.com/watch?v=APKB1CfSEtM.
3. Imran Khan's address to the nation, online video, 10 April 2016, www.youtube.com/watch?v=m7F5KqD_WVY.
4. Imran Khan speech in London, online video, 17 April 2016, www.youtube.com/watch?v=xnroX32zyaA.
5. Imran Khan speech in Lahore, online video, 30 September 2016, www.youtube.com/watch?v=cpkIWkDGKWs.
6. Imran Khan's press conference outside Bani Gala Islamabad, online video, 1 November 2016, www.youtube.com/watch?v=hl2C–lOHzec.

138138   *Let There Be Justice*

Bibliography

Books

Ahsan, A., *Robbing an Election* (Lahore: Jumhoori Publication, 2015)
Ali, T., *The Duel Pakistan on the Flight Path of American Power* (New York: Scribner, 2008)
Burki, S. J., *Pakistan: Fifty Years of Nationhood* (Lahore: Vanguard Books, 2004)
Gilani, I. S., *The Voice of the People: Public Opinion in Pakistan 2007–2009* (Karachi: Oxford University Press, 2010)
Jaffrelot, C. (ed.), *Pakistan at the Crossroads: Domestic Dynamics and External Pressures* (Gurgaon: Random House India, 2016)
Khan, I., *Pakistan: A Personal History* (London: Bantam Books, 2012)
Khan, R., *Pakistan: A Dream Gone Sour* (Karachi: Oxford University Press, 1998)
Lieven, A., *Pakistan: A Hard Country* (London: Penguin Books, 2012)
Mohsin, J., *Howzzat?! By Im the Dim* (Lahore: Vanguard Books, 2014)
Mujahid, S., and Merchant, L., *Quotes from the Quaid* (Karachi: Oxford University Press, 2007)
Musharraf, P., *In the Line of Fire* (London: Simon & Schuster, 2006)
Obermayer, B., and Obermaier, F., *The Panama Papers* (London: One World Publications, 2016)
Sanford, C., *Imran Khan: The Cricketer, the Celebrity, the Politician* (London: Harper Collins Publishers, 2009)

Magazines, Journals, and Articles

'All roads lead to Raiwind', *The Express Tribune*, 12 May 2013, epaper.tribune.com.pk/DisplayDetails.aspx?ENI_ID=11201305120635&EN_ID=11201305120501&EMID=11201305120072
'And it begins...: Mark the date: NA session on June 1', *The Express Tribune*, 28 May 2013, tribune.com.pk/story/555389/and–it–begins–mark–the–date–na–session–on–june–1/
'Anti–Islam film: Desperate govt moves to quell simmering protests', *The Express Tribune*, 18 September 2012, epaper.tribune.com.pk/DisplayDetails.aspx?ENI_ID=11201209180275&EN_ID=11201209180190&EMID=11201209180040

'Anti–Islam Film: Protests reverberate across Muslim world', *The Express Tribune*, 15 September 2012, epaper.tribune.com.pk/DisplayDetails.aspx?ENI_ID=11201209150122&EN_ID=11201209150084&EMID=11201209150011

'August 14 faceoff: Too late for talks, Imran tells govt', *The Express Tribune*, 29 July 2014, epaper.tribune.com.pk/DisplayDetails.aspx?ENI_ID=11201407280112&EN_ID=11201407280075&EMID=11201407280014

'August 14 rally: PML–N hits out at Imran for 'tsunami march', *The Express Tribune*, 8 July 2014, epaper.tribune.com.pk/DisplayDetails.aspx?ENI_ID=11201407080051&EN_ID=11201407080027&EMID=11201407080006

'Back in the game: Imran Khan's recovery', *Dawn*, 24 May 2013, www.dawn.com/news/1013371

'Baldia factory fire: PTI, MQM in a war of words', *The Express Tribune*, 10 February 2015, epaper.tribune.com.pk/DisplayDetails.aspx?ENI_ID=11201502100405&EN_ID=11201502100125&EMID=11201502100059

'Beefing up security: Army on standby in volatile', *The Express Tribune*, 23 November 2012, epaper.tribune.com.pk/DisplayDetails.aspx?ENI_ID=11201211150488&EN_ID=11201211150378&EMID=11201211150037

'Blasts, rocket fire and clashes leave dozens dead', *The Express Tribune*, 12 May 2013, epaper.tribune.com.pk/DisplayDetails.aspx?ENI_ID=11201305120644&EN_ID=11201305120510&EMID=11201305120073

'Cartoonists around the world tell the Panama Papers story', *ICIJ*, 5 May 2016, panamapapers.icij.org/blog/20160505–cartoons–panama–papers.html

'Complaint centres for women set up at police stations', *Dawn*, 25 July 2013, www.dawn.com/news/1031729/complaint–centres–for–women–set–up–at–police–stations

"Costliest' and 'grossly mismanaged' polls: HRCP', *The Express Tribune*, 13 May 2013, epaper.tribune.com.pk/DisplayDetails.aspx?ENI_ID=11201305130225&EN_ID=11201305130184&EMID=11201305130022

'Countering terror: Imran renews demand for redeploying FC', *The Express Tribune*, 18 February 2015, epaper.tribune.com.pk/DisplayDetails.aspx?ENI_ID=11201502180304&EN_ID=11201502180100&EMID=11201502180051

'Development work in KP to be refocused, says Imran', *Dawn*, 18 January 2015, www.dawn.com/news/1157813

'Doctors' mafia impeding hospital development in KP: Imran Khan', *The Nation*, 3 November 2015, nation.com.pk/national/03-Nov-2015/doctors-mafia-impeding-hospital-development-in-kp-imran-khan

'E–governance', *Dawn*, 5 August 2013, www.dawn.com/news/1034092/e–governance

'Election rigging: May 11 will mark start of a movement, says Imran', *The Express Tribune*, 5 May 2014, epaper.tribune.com.pk/DisplayDetails.aspx?ENI_ID=11201405050069&EN_ID=11201405050041&EMID=11201405040004

'Electoral prospects: Snap poll likely to affect PTI's parliamentary future', *The Express Tribune*, 18 January 2012, epaper.tribune.com.pk/DisplayDetails.aspx?ENI_ID=11201201180291&EN_ID=11201201180204&EMID=11201201180010

'Ex–wife Jemima wishes Imran best in 'new phase of life'', *Dawn*, 7 January 2015, www.dawn.com/news/1155299

'FAFEN report: Over 100% turnout in 49 polling stations', *The Express Tribune*, 14 May 2013, epaper.tribune.com.pk/DisplayDetails.aspx?ENI_ID=11201305140534&EN_ID=11201305140461&EMID=11201305140044

'Farid Khan's Murder: Seven dead in reprisal over PTI's lawmaker slaying', *The Express Tribune*, 5 June 2013, epaper.tribune.com.pk/DisplayDetails.aspx?ENI_ID=11201306050356&EN_ID=11201306050310&EMID=11201306050035

'FATA polls: Residents in tribal areas vote despite terror threats', *The Express Tribune*, 12 May 2013, epaper.tribune.com.pk/DisplayDetails.aspx?ENI_ID=11201305120537&EN_ID=11201305120429&EMID=11201305120060

'Food for thought: PTI quizzes govt over presence of foreign security firms', *The Express Tribune*, 7 February 2014, tribune.com.pk/story/668683/food–for–thought–pti–quizzes–govt–over–presence–of–foreign–security–firms/

'Free screening for diabetes launched', *Dawn*, 25 July 2013, www.dawn.com/news/1031735/free–screening–for–diabetes–launched

'Future of fast bowlers at risk: Imran', *The Nation*, 20 July 2010, nation.com.pk/sports/20–Jul–2010/Future–of–fast–bowlers–at–risk–Imran

'Gates all praise for Khan's 'Sehat Ka Ittehad' polio campaign', *Dawn*, 25 March 2015, www.dawn.com/news/1171808

'Giant Leak of Offshore Financial Records Exposes Global Array of Crime and Corruption', *ICIJ*, 3 April 2016, panamapapers.icij.org/20160403–panama–papers–global–overview.html

'Hangu suicide blast: Protests hit streets as death toll rises', The Express Tribune, 3 February 2013, tribune.com.pk/story/501938/hangu–suicide–blast–protests–hit–streets–as–death–toll–rises/

'Helpline launched for violence victims', *Dawn*, 10 October 2013, www.dawn.com/news/1048713/helpline–launched–for–violence–victims

'Immunisation drive to begin across province', *The Express Tribune*, 16 February 2015, tribune.com.pk/story/838980/immunisation–drive–to–begin–across–province/

'IMPPA passes resolution to temporarily ban Pakistani artists in India; Twitter reacts', *International Business Times*, 29 September 2016, www.ibtimes.co.in/imppa–passes–resolution–temporarily–ban–pakistani–artists–india–twitter–reacts–695956

'Imran exposes Punjab govt's 'gerrymandering'', *The Nation*, 9 July 2010, nation.com.pk/politics/09–Jul–2010/Imran–exposes–Punjab–govts–gerrymandering

'Imran Khan challenges NAB chief's appointment', *Dawn*, 29 October 2013, www.dawn.com/news/1052667

'Imran Khan featured in Benaud's 'Greatest Test XI'', *Dawn*, 12 April 2015, www.dawn.com/news/1175335

'Imran Khan launches `hope`', *Dawn*, 20 October 2011, www.dawn.com/news/667849/imran–khan–launches–hope

'Imran Khan, Chaudhry Nisar depart for UK', *Dawn*, 14 April 2016, www.dawn.com/news/1252054

'Imran Khan: K–P's hero', *The Express Tribune*, 20 July 2015, tribune.com.pk/story/923302/imran–khan–k–ps–hero/

'Imran Khan's favourite Tehrik–i–Taliban claim deadly UN office blast', *Dawn*, 06 October 2009, letusbuildpakistan.blogspot.com/2009/10/imran–khans–favourite–tehrik–i–taliban.html?m=0

'Imran launches drive for flood affectees', *The Nation*, 19 August 2010, nation.com.pk/national/19–Aug–2010/Imran–launches–drive–for–flood–affectees

'Imran lavishes praise on KP in bid to attract investment', *Dawn*, 25 February 2015, www.dawn.com/news/1165843

'Imran lavishes praise on KP in bid to attract investment', *Dawn*, 25 February 2015, www.dawn.com/news/1165843

'Imran opposes return of Benazir, Nawaz', *Dawn*, 11 August 2002, asianstudies.github.io/area–studies/SouthAsia/SAserials/Dawn/2002/aug172002.html#vows

'Imran praises Iceland, Britain for action on Panama leaks', *Dawn*, 15 April 2016, www.dawn.com/news/1252180/imran–praises–iceland–britain–for–action–on–panama–leaks

'Imran promises 'change' in three months', *Dawn*, 25 May 2014, www.dawn.com/news/1108466

'Imran renews support to centre's welfare programme for IDPs', *Dawn*, 24 February 2015, www.dawn.com/news/1165597

'Imran says would stand by army in case of military operation', *Dawn*, 22 January 2014, www.dawn.com/news/1081968

'Imran unveils 2000–page white paper on poll rigging', *Dawn*, 21 August 2013, www.dawn.com/news/1037385

'Imran visits Army Public School, houses of deceased', *Dawn*, 23 December 2014, www.dawn.com/news/1152642

'Imran warns Nawaz of 'tsunami march' if demands not met', *Dawn*, 28 June 2014, www.dawn.com/news/1115509

'In the aftermath: PTI disputes poll results in up to four cities', *The Express Tribune*, 14 May 2013, epaper.tribune.com.pk/DisplayDetails.aspx?ENI_ID=11201305140490&EN_ID=11201305140421&EMID=11201305140041

'Intra–party polls to uproot undemocratic political culture: Imran', *Dawn*, 17 November 2012, www.dawn.com/news/764795

'Irregularities: Thumbprint verification to begin in two weeks, says ECP', *The Express Tribune*, 17 May 2013, tribune.com.pk/story/550567/irregularities–thumbprint–verification–to–begin–in–two–weeks–says–ecp/

'Journey of progress: No long march can detract us, says Shahbaz', *The Express Tribune*, 2 August 2014, tribune.com.pk/story/743265/journey–of–progress–no–long–march–can–detract–us–says–shahbaz/

'Judicial commission: Imran renews threat of street protests', *The Express Tribune*, 30 January 2015, epaper.tribune.com.pk/DisplayDetails.aspx?ENI_ID=11201501300116&EN_ID=11201501300045&EMID=11201501300017

'Khan 'optimistic' about Pakistan elections', *BBC News*, 21 June 2002, news.bbc.co.uk/2/hi/south_asia/2056431.stm

'KP police given 'free hand'', *Dawn*, 4 October 2013, www.dawn.com/news/1047396/kp–police–given–free–hand

'LRH to be made model health institution: Imran', *Dawn*, 29 April 2015, www.dawn.com/news/1178877

'Making a new Pakistan only possible with youth: Imran Khan', *Dawn*, 4 November 2012, www.dawn.com/news/761520/making–a–new–pakistan–only–possible–with–youth–imran–khan

'Messiah without a message', *The Nation*, 28 November 2010, nation.com.pk/columns/28–Nov–2010/Messiah–without–a–message

'Mianwali constituency: Imran decides to vacate NA–71', *The Express Tribune*, 16 May 2013, tribune.com.pk/story/550048/mianwali–constituency–imran–decides–to–vacate–na–71/

'Militants attack Indian army base in Kashmir 'killing 17'', *BBC*, 18 September 2016, www.bbc.com/news/world–asia–india–37399969

'Mother, child health services in eight districts', Dawn, 10 October 2013, www.dawn.com/news/1048718/mother–child–health–services–in–eight–districts

'MQM files Rs5bn defamation suit against Imran Khan', *Dawn*, 23 July 2013, www.dawn.com/news/1031331

'Nato supplies to be blocked after Nov 20, Imran tells NA', *Dawn*, 4 November 2013, www.dawn.com/news/1054075

'Nawaz vows to deliver 'Naya Khyber Pakhtunkhwa", *Dawn*, 26 March 2015, www.dawn.com/news/1172024

'New Pakistan' not possible without fair polls: Imran', *Dawn*, 26 May 2014, www.dawn.com/news/1108519

'No force can withstand 'youth tsunami': Imran', *Dawn*, 30 April 2013, www.dawn.com/news/794807

'No power can stop me from protesting on Nov 2, claims Imran', *The Express Tribune*, 28 October 2016, tribune.com.pk/story/1213116/confrontation–looms–pti–go–ahead–protests–despite–ban–islamabad/

'No PTI minister involved in corruption: CM', *Dawn*, 20 November 2013, www.dawn.com/news/1057334/no–pti–minister–involved–in–corruption–cm

'Oil up as Opec looks to cut supply again', *Dawn*, 11 May 2003, www.dawn.com/news/101285

'On the sidelines: PTI refutes claims of consultations over caretaker set–up', *The Express Tribune*, 10 September 2012, epaper.tribune.com.pk/DisplayDetails.aspx?ENI_ID=11201209100362&EN_ID=11201209100263&EMID=11201209100046

'Pakistan Floods: The Deluge of Disaster–Facts & Figures as of 15 September 2010', *Reliefweb*, 15 Sep 2010, reliefweb.int/report/pakistan/pakistan–floodsthe–deluge–disaster–facts–figures–15–september–2010

'Pakistan judges refuse oath demanded by Pakistan's rulers', *Waycross Journal–Herald*, 31 January 2000, news.google.com/newspapers?id=8GFaAAAAIBAJ&sjid=70wNAAAAIBAJ&dq=pakistan%20judge%20oath&pg=6907%2C2851269

'Pakistan Tehreek–e–Insaf Chairman Imran Khan', *The Express Tribune*, 8 June 2013, epaper.tribune.com.pk/DisplayDetails.aspx?ENI_ID=11201306090467&EN_ID=11201306090397&EMID=11201306090042

'Pakistan US ambassador offers to resign over 'memogate", *BBC News*, 17 November 2011, www.bbc.com/news/world–asia–15782297

'Pakistan's Corruption Problem', Editorial, *The Express Tribune*, 17 December 2012, tribune.com.pk/story/480473/pakistans–corruption–problem/

'Pakistan's Monsoon 2011 (July & August)', *Wayback Machine Internet Archive*, 2011, web.archive.org/web/20111126104515/http:/www.pakmet.com.pk/cdpc/prg/monsoon2011/monsoon2011progress.htm

'Panama Papers and Pakistan PM Nawaz Sharif', *BBC*, 21 April 2016, www.bbc.com/news/world–asia–36092356

'Peace march: Defying all odds, PTI rally rumbles on', *The Express Tribune*, 7 October 2012, tribune.com.pk/story/448188/peace–march–defying–all–odds–pti–rally–rumbles–on/

'PML–N attains simple majority in NA', *The Nation*, 27 May 2013, nation.com.pk/E–Paper/Lahore/2013–05–27/page–1/detail–3

'PML–N workers protest outside Jemima's residence in London', *Dawn*, 17 April 2016, www.dawn.com/news/1252666

'Policemen told not to seek favours from politicians', *Dawn*, 1 November 2013, www.dawn.com/news/1053372/policemen–told–not–to–seek–favours–from–politicians

'Political 'fatwa': Voting for PTI is haram, says Maulana Fazl', *The Express Tribune*, 6 May 2013, tribune.com.pk/story/544667/political–fatwa–voting–for–pti–is–haram–says–maulana–fazl/

'Poll rigging: Role of ex–CJP, media house be probed, says Imran', *The Express Tribune*, 30 April 2014, tribune.com.pk/story/702159/poll–rigging–role–of–ex–cjp–media–house–be–probed–says–imran/

'Poll: Pakistani youth disenchanted with democracy', *Dawn*, 4 April 2013, www. dawn.com/news/800213

'Predator and prey', *The Economist*, 6 November 2008, www.economist.com/node/12566901

'Pre–poll Violence: Bloody Ballots: 110 killed in April', *The Express Tribune*, April 2013, epaper.tribune.com.pk/DisplayDetails.aspx?ENI_ID=11201305090402&EN_ID=11201305090323&EMID=11201305090034

'Protests in Pakistan: Wrath of Khan', *The Economist*, 11 August 2014, www. economist.com/blogs/banyan/2014/08/protests–pakistan

'PTI announces decision to field candidates for parliamentary positions', *Dawn*, 25 May 2013, www.dawn.com/news/1013726/newspaper/newspaper/column

'PTI can eliminate corruption in 90 days: Imran', *The Nation*, 8 July 2010, nation. com.pk/lahore/08–Jul–2010/PTI–can–eliminate–corruption–in–90–days–Imran

'PTI Chief Imran Khan', *The Express Tribune*, 5 June 2013, epaper.tribune.com. pk/DisplayDetails.aspx?ENI_ID=11201306050352&EN_ID=112013060503 06&EMID=11201306050035

'PTI chief not to attend meeting on national security', *Dawn*, 6 July 2013, www. dawn.com/news/1023114

'PTI puts Google on notice for not removing anti–Islam film', *The Express Tribune*, 23 September 2012, tribune.com.pk/story/441212/pti–puts–google–inc–on–notice–for–not–removing–anti–islam–film/

'PTI to hold sit–in on October 4 if ECP members do not resign: Imran', *Dawn*, 29 August 2015, www.dawn.com/news/1203646

'PTI workers see manipulation in intra–party elections', *Dawn*, 10 December 2012, www.dawn.com/news/770276

'PTI, allies vow to continue drive against drone attacks', *Dawn*, 1 December 2013, www. dawn.com/news/1059785/pti–allies–vow–to–continue–drive–against–drone–attacks

'Raiwind march on Sept 30: Imran Khan', *Dawn*, 18 September 2016, www.dawn. com/news/1284554

'Reham spills the beans on divorce with Imran Khan', *The Express Tribune*, 15 November 2015, tribune.com.pk/story/991792/reham–spills–the–beans–on–divorce–with–imran–khan/

'Religious parties directly involved in terrorism: Imran Khan', *The Express Tribune*, 5 May 2013, tribune.com.pk/story/544640/religious–parties–directly–involved–in–terrorism–imran–khan/

'Re–polling controversy: PTI grabs one NA, two PA seats in Karachi', *The Express Tribune*, 21 May 2013, tribune.com.pk/story/552251/re–polling–controversy–pti–grabs–one–na–two–pa–seats–in–karachi/

'SC quashes contempt case against Imran Khan', *Dawn*, 28 August 2013, www. dawn.com/news/1038933

'Shaukat Khanum cancer hospital inaugurated in Peshawar', *Dawn*, 29 December 2015, www.dawn.com/news/1229420

'Shun politics of the gun, Imran tells Altaf', *The News*, 10 April 2015, www. thenews.com.pk/print/11906–shun–politics–of–the–gun–imran–tells–altaf

'Sit–in outside Imran Khan's residence', *Dawn*, 14 April 2015, www.dawn.com/news/1175820

'Statesman's spirit: Nawaz invites Indian PM to his oath–taking', *The Express Tribune*, 14 May 2013, epaper.tribune.com.pk/DisplayDetails.aspx?ENI_ID=11201305140462&EN_ID=11201305140401&EMID=11201305140014

'Supreme Court issues contempt notice to Imran Khan', *Dawn*, 1 August 2013, www.dawn.com/news/1033227

'Task force set up to regulate arms business', *Dawn*, 7 August 2013, www.dawn.com/news/1034635/task-force-set-up-to-regulate-arms-business

'The after-party PML-N, PTI: The suggestive rhetoric begins', *The Express Tribune*, 1 November 2011, epaper.tribune.com.pk/DisplayDetails.aspx?ENI_ID=11201111010001&EN_ID=11201111010001&EMID=11201111010002

'The tragedy of Sita, heiress entangled in a murky business', *Independent*, 14 August 2004, www.independent.co.uk/news/world/americas/the-tragedy-of-sita-heiress-entangled-in-a-murky-business-51729.html

'Thousands protest against drone strikes in Peshawar', *Dawn*, 20 November 2013, www.dawn.com/news/1058051

'Threat to minorities: Imran condemns hate video', *The Express Tribune*, 15 February 2014, epaper.tribune.com.pk/DisplayDetails.aspx?ENI_ID=11201402150132&EN_ID=11201402150118&EMID=11201402150015

'Three Waziri tribes showed their support to PTI 'peace rally': Imran', *Dawn*, 30 September 2012, www.dawn.com/news/753159/three-waziri-tribes-showed-their-support-to-pti-peace-rally-imran

'Train ride to promote tourism in KP', *Dawn*, 4 October 2013, www.dawn.com/news/1047393/train-ride-to-promote-tourism-in-kp

'Truth about Jemima and Imran's split', *Mail Online*, 10 June 2008, www.dailymail.co.uk/news/article-1025569/Truth-Jemima-Imrans-split.html

'US embassy cables: Imran Khan criticises 'dangerous' US policy', *The Guardian*, 6 February 2010, www.theguardian.com/world/us-embassy-cables-documents/247596

'US official guns down two motorcyclists in Lahore', *Dawn*, 27 January 2011, www.dawn.com/news/601997/us-official-guns-down-two-motorcyclists-in-lahore

'US official guns down two motorcyclists in Lahore', *Dawn*, 27 January 2011, www.dawn.com/news/601997/us-official-guns-down-two-motorcyclists-in-lahore

'Violence leaves dozens dead', *The Express Tribune*, 12 May 2013, epaper.tribune.com.pk/DisplayDetails.aspx?ENI_ID=11201305120640&EN_ID=11201305120506&EMID=11201305120072

'Voicing Opposition: March will expose US terrorism: PTI', *The Express Tribune*, 5 October 2012, epaper.tribune.com.pk/DisplayDetails.aspx?ENI_ID=11201210050231&EN_ID=11201210050181&EMID=11201210050020

'Vote for me and I will bring peace, jobs and electricity: Nawaz', *The Express Tribune*, 1 May 2013, tribune.com.pk/story/542848/vote-for-me-and-i-will-bring-peace-jobs-and-electricity-nawaz/

'Voters transcend any class', *The Nation*, 25 May 2013, nation.com.pk/E-Paper/Lahore/2013-05-25/page-7/detail-2

'We deserved better', *The Nation*, 18 January 2010, nation.com.pk/letters/18-Jan-2010/We-deserved-better

'Wedding bells: Second marriage is not a crime, says Imran', *The Express Tribune*, 7 January 2015, epaper.tribune.com.pk/DisplayDetails.aspx?ENI_ID=11201501070102&EN_ID=11201501070041&EMID=11201501070015

'Who's the real villain?', *The Guardian*, 24 January 2003, www.theguardian.com/sport/2003/jan/24/cricket.iraq

'Will no longer travel with protocol, says Imran Khan', *Dawn*, 15 January 2015, www.dawn.com/news/1157192

'Working group recommendations: K-P government approves health sector reforms', *The Express Tribune*, 6 August 2013, tribune.com.pk/story/587259/working-group-recommendations-k-p-government-approves-health-sector-reforms/

Abid, Z., 'PTI rallies — hazardous for women', *The Express Tribune*, 8 May 2016, tribune.com.pk/story/1098997/pti–rallies–hazardous–for–women/

Abrar, M., 'PTI stands divided as Khan announces Raiwind march on Sept 30', *Pakistan Today*, 19 September 2016, www.pakistantoday.com.pk/2016/09/19/pti–stands–divided–as–khan–announces–raiwind–march–on–sept–30/

Adams, T., 'The path of Khan', *The Guardian*, 2 July 2006, www.theguardian.com/sport/2006/jul/02/cricket.features3

Ahmad, A., 'PPP, 'N' responsible for all chaos: Imran', *The Nation*, 5 February 2010, nation.com.pk/politics/05–Feb–2010/PPP–N–responsible–for–all–chaos–Imran

Ahmad, I., 'Imran Khan targets Modi, says Pakistanis not cowardly like Sharif', *Hindustan Times*, 1 October 2016, www.hindustantimes.com/world–news/imran–khan–targets–modi–says–pakistanis–not–cowardly–like–sharif/story–2ofRh1QDyoZD4RVjuBHuEP.html

Ahmad, R., 'Our Darkest Hour', *The Express Tribune*, 17 December 2014, tribune.com.pk/story/808019/our–darkest–hour/

Ahmadani, A., 'Imran criticises govt for 'poor handling' of flood situation', *The Nation*, 7 August 2010, nation.com.pk/national/07–Aug–2010/Imran–criticises–govt–for–poor–handling–of–flood–situation

Ahmed, R., 'Brazen attack: Taliban blitz Peshawar airport near PAF base', *The Express Tribune*, 16 December 2012, tribune.com.pk/story/480351/brazen–attack–taliban–blitz–peshawar–airport–near–paf–base/

Ali, H., 'Decision pending: Women participation presents conundrum for PTI', *The Express Tribune*, 5 October 2012, epaper.tribune.com.pk/DisplayDetails.aspx?ENI_ID=11201210050232&EN_ID=11201210050182&EMID=11201210050020; 'Policy matters: 25% of tickets to go to young members: Imran Khan', *The Express Tribune*, 21 December 2012, epaper.tribune.com.pk/DisplayDetails.aspx?ENI_ID=11201212210579&EN_ID=1120121221210459&EMID=11201212210053

Ali, H., and Rauf, A., 'Intra–party polls: PTI candidates prepare for elections', *The Express Tribune*, 15 September 2012, epaper.tribune.com.pk/DisplayDetails.aspx?ENI_ID=11201209150162&EN_ID=1120120915011112&EMID=11201209150014

Ali, H., et al., 'PTI proposes Pervez Khattak as K–P Chief Minister', *The Express Tribune*, 14 May 2013, epaper.tribune.com.pk/DisplayDetails.aspx?ENI_ID=11201305140469&EN_ID=11201305140406&EMID=11201305140014

Ali, M., 'After much ado: K–P Assembly passes bill on medical teaching institutes', *The Express Tribune*, 13 January 2015, tribune.com.pk/story/821408/after–much–ado–assembly–passes–bill–on–medical–teaching–institutes/; 'Dues shy: Only 35 K–P legislators paid income tax last year', *The Express Tribune*, 17 February 2014, tribune.com.pk/story/672641/dues–shy–only–35–legislators–paid–income–tax–last–year/; 'Horse–trading in Senate polls: Imran Khan threatens to dissolve K–P Assembly', *The Express Tribune*, 5 March 2015, tribune.com.pk/story/848020/horse–trading–in–senate–polls–imran–khan–threatens–to–dissolve–k–p–assembly/; 'Imran's Tsunami: Khyber–Pakhtunkhwa Lives up to tradition', *The Express Tribune*, 13 May 2013, epaper.tribune.com.pk/DisplayDetails.aspx?ENI_ID=11201305130138&EN_ID=1120130513010109&EMID=11201305130014; 'Preplanned debate: Opposition bemoans 'unfair' allocation of funds', *The Express Tribune*, 25 February 2014, tribune.com.pk/story/675660/preplanned–debate–opposition–bemoans–unfair–allocation–of–funds/; 'Pressing the issues: Imran seeks return of FC force to K–P', *The Express Tribune*, 23 December 2014, tribune.com.pk/story/810932/pressing-the-issues-

imran-seeks-return-of-fc-force-to-k-p/; 'Taking offence: Opposition submits
motion against PTI chief's 'threat", *The Express Tribune*, 8 April 2014, tribune.
com.pk/story/692594/taking–offence–opposition–submits–motion–against–pti–
chiefs–threat/; 'Vertical construction: Official residences limited to one kanal of
land', *The Express Tribune*, 10 January 2015, tribune.com.pk/story/819274/
vertical–construction–official–residences–limited–to–one–kanal–of–land/

Ali, S., et al., 'Govt should stay, PM not: PPP', *The Nation*, 6 April 2016, nation.
com.pk/E–Paper/Lahore/2016–04–06/page–2/detail–1

Ali, Z., 'LG bill sails through KP Assembly', *Dawn*, 1 November 2013, www.dawn.
com/news/1053375/lg–bill–sails–through–kp–assembly

Amin, T., 'Education, law enforcement: PTI–led KP government's reforms
bringing positive changes', *Brecorder*, 25 March 2015, fp.brecorder.
com/2016/03/2016032528809/

Amir, A., 'Endgame Zardari; or goodbye to all of this', *The News*, 13 March 2009,
www.thenews.com.pk/print/87306–endgame–zardari;–or–goodbye–to–all–of–this;
'Kerry–Lugar: bill or document of surrender?', *The News*, 2 October 2009,
www.thenews.com.pk/print/87439–kerry–lugar–bill–or–document–of–surrender;
'Modi victory a wakeup call for Pakistan', *The News*, 20 May 2014, www.
thenews.com.pk/print/88497–modi–victory–a–wakeup–call–for–pakistan; 'Net
tightens...sadly, no escaping Panama leaks', *The News*, 5 May 2016, www.
thenews.com.pk/print/119593–Net–tightenssadly–no–escaping–Panama–leaks;
'Pakistan's velvet marches', *The News*, 26 August 2014, www.thenews.com.pk/
print/88557–pakistan%E2%80%99s–velvet–marches; 'Panama Leaks...Pakistan's
opportunity', *The News*, 8 April 2016, www.thenews.com.pk/print/111102–
Panama–LeaksPakistans–opportunity; 'Sharifovs in Wonderland', *The News*,
10 May 2016, www.thenews.com.pk/print/118762–Sharifovs–in–Wonderland;
'Tracking the marches...reading the tea leaves', *The News*, 15 August 2014, www.
thenews.com.pk/print/88552–tracking–the–marches...reading–the–tea–leaves;
'Triumph of the will...the power of determination', *The News*, 23 September
2014, www.thenews.com.pk/print/88575–triumph–of–the–will%E2%80%A6the–
power–of–determination; 'Well on the road to chaos', *The News*, 23 May 2014,
www.thenews.com.pk/print/88500–well–on–the–road–to–chaos; 'When hype
meets reality: the great climb–down', *The News*, 19 August 2014, www.thenews.
com.pk/print/88553–when–hype–meets–reality–the–great–climb–down

Amir, I., 'KP's real issues succumb to PTI's populist approach', *Dawn*, 25 November
2013, www.dawn.com/news/1058450/kps–real–issues–succumb–to–ptis–populist–
approach

Ansari, M., 'Imran Khan urges new Chief Justice to hold President Asif Zardari to
account', *The Telegraph*, 22 Mar 2009, www.telegraph.co.uk/news/worldnews/
asia/pakistan/5029192/Imran–Khan–urges–new–Chief–Justice–to–hold–President–
Asif–Zardari–to–account.html

Asghar, W., 'PTI's performance in KPK so far–better than the rest', *ARY News*, 23
November 2015, blogs.arynews.tv/ptis–performance–in–kpk–so–far–better–than–
the–rest/

Ashfaq, M., 'Imran okays education reforms', *Dawn*, 5 August 2013, www.
dawn.com/news/1034100/imran–okays–education–reforms; 'KP govt hints at
holding LG elections by end October', *Dawn*, 20 July 2013, www.dawn.com/
news/1030389/kp–govt–hints–at–holding–lg–elections–by–end–october; 'KP has
over 2,500 schools with one teacher only', *Dawn*, 1 December 2013, www.dawn.
com/news/1059787/kp–has–over–2500–schools–with–one–teacher–only; 'Public
vs private schools: KP's fight for educational reform', *Herald*, 15 November 2015,
herald.dawn.com/news/1153590

Bacha, A. H., 'KP to fight terrorism by creating more jobs, industrialisation', *Dawn*, 25 July 2013, www.dawn.com/news/1031734/kp-to-fight-terrorism-by-creating-more-jobs-industrialisation

Bacha, K. R., 'Only PTI can end terrorism, says Imran', *Dawn*, 1 April 2013, www.dawn.com/news/799351/only-pti-can-end-terrorism-says-imran

Bajwa, A., 'Model Town Mayhem: They started it', *The Express Tribune*, 19 June 2014, epaper.tribune.com.pk/DisplayDetails.aspx?ENI_ID=11201406190042&EN_ID=11201406190027&EMID=11201406190005

Bajwa, A., and R. Tanveer, 'Brutalised in Lahore: Descent into mayhem', *The Express Tribune*, 18 June 2014, epaper.tribune.com.pk/DisplayDetails.aspx?ENI_ID=11201406180060&EN_ID=11201406180030&EMID=11201406180008

Bangash, Z., 'Internal politicking: PTI's Kohat president suspended for violating party discipline', *The Express Tribune*, 6 February 2014, tribune.com.pk/story/668075/internal-politicking-ptis-kohat-president-suspended-for-violating-party-discipline/

Batty, D., 'Pakistani president earns fatwa by flirting with Sarah Palin', *The Guardian*, 2 October 2008, www.theguardian.com/world/deadlineusa/2008/oct/02/sarah.palin.pakistan.president.flirting

Bhatti, H., and F. Shah, 'Will head to PM house if supporters harmed: Dr Qadri', *Dawn*, 22 June 2014, www.dawn.com/news/1114417

Brown, A., 'America's New War', *CNN*, 27 September 2001, transcripts.cnn.com/TRANSCRIPTS/0109/27/se.50.html

Burke, J., 'Imran Khan: set to play the innings of his life', *The Guardian*, 1 January 2012, www.theguardian.com/theobserver/2012/jan/01/observer-profile-imran-khan; 'Imran Khan: the man who would be Pakistan's next prime minister', *The Guardian*, 4 March 2012, www.theguardian.com/world/2012/mar/04/imran-khan-pakistan-cricketer-politician

Butt, Q., 'Report says Pakistan reneging on commitments to increase spending on health, education', *The Express Tribune*, 15 November 2012, epaper.tribune.com.pk/DisplayDetails.aspx?ENI_ID=11201211150488&EN_ID=11201211150378&EMID=11201211150037

Chittum, R., 'Iceland Prime Minister Tenders Resignation Following Panama Papers Revelations', *ICIJ*, 5 April 2016, panamapapers.icij.org/20160405-iceland-pm-resignation.html

Cooper, H., 'Obama announces killing of Osama bin Laden', *The Lede*, 1 May 2011, thelede.blogs.nytimes.com/2011/05/01/bin-laden-dead-u-s-official-says/?_r=2

Cowasjee, A., 'A free press', *Dawn*, 25 November 2001, www.dawn.com/news/1072513/a-free-press; 'As white as driven snow', *Dawn*, 3 November 2002, www.dawn.com/news/1072652/as-white-as-driven-snow; 'Brutal fanatics', *Dawn*, 3 March 2002, www.dawn.com/news/1072553; 'Commander of the faithful', *Dawn*, 14 October 2001, www.dawn.com/news/1072495/commander-of-the-faithful; 'Justice-II', *Dawn*, 2 September 2001, www.dawn.com/news/1072477; 'Law and order', *Dawn*, 21 May 2000, www.dawn.com/news/1072293; 'Pakistan first', *Dawn*, 15 June 2003, www.dawn.com/news/1072743/pakistan-first; 'Paucity of Pakistan's Politics', *Dawn*, 25 September 2011, www.dawn.com/news/661607/paucity-of-pakistans-politics; 'Poppycock', *Dawn*, 13 October 2002, www.dawn.com/news/1072644/poppycock; 'Referendum 2002', *Dawn*, 7 April 2002, www.dawn.com/news/1072567/referendum-2002; 'Rights and wrongs', *Dawn*, 1 June 2003, www.dawn.com/news/1072737/rights-and-wrongs; 'Sixty-three and down on our knees', *Dawn*, 15 August 2010, www.dawn.com/news/553070/xty-three-and-down-on-our-knees-by-ardeshir-cowasjee; 'Storming of the Supreme Court I', *Dawn*,

21 November 1999, www.dawn.com/news/1074388; 'The depths to which we sink', *Dawn*, 1 April 2007, www.dawn.com/news/1073289; 'The end of the beginning?', *Dawn*, 4 January 2004, www.dawn.com/news/1072825/the–end–of–the–beginning

Farooq, U., 'Embezzlement or aid?: Enquiry under way over allegations against PTI MPAs', *The Express Tribune*, 23 June 2014, tribune.com.pk/story/725605/embezzlement–or–aid–enquiry–under–way–over–allegations–against–pti–mpas/; 'Green living: Imran announces plans to open Balahisar Fort to public', *The Express Tribune*, 10 February 2014, tribune.com.pk/story/669625/green–living–imran–announces–plans–to–open–balahisar–fort–to–public/; 'In the pipeline: K–P to be the first to issue health insurance cards', *The Express Tribune*, 15 January 2015, epaper.tribune.com.pk/DisplayDetails.aspx?ENI_ID=11201501150088&EN_ID=11201501150034&EMID=11201501150014; 'K–P political crisis: Imran warns 'blackmailing' MPAs he'll dissolve assembly', *The Express Tribune*, 5 April 2014, tribune.com.pk/story/691547/k–p–political–crisis–imran–warns–blackmailing–mpas–hell–dissolve–assembly/

Filkins, D., 'As Pakistani's Popularity Slides, *"Busharraf"*, Is a Figure of Ridicule', *The New York Times*, 5 July 2002

Ghauri, I., 'A double edged sword: Imran inspires the youth', *The Express Tribune*, 4 May 2013, tribune.com.pk/story/544278/a–double–edged–sword–imran–inspires–the–youth/; 'Articles 62 & 63: PTI mounts legal steps to disqualify PM', *The Express Tribune*, 10 July 2014, tribune.com.pk/story/733532/articles–62–63–pti–mounts–legal–steps–to–disqualify–pm/; 'Federal cabinet unveiled: Enter the Ministers', *The Express Tribune*, 7 June 2013, epaper.tribune.com.pk/DisplayDetails.aspx?ENI_ID=11201306080291&EN_ID=11201306080268&EMID=11201306080025; 'Peace dialogue: Nisar takes offence at doublespeak', *The Express Tribune*, 3 May 2014, tribune.com.pk/story/703560/peace–dialogue–nisar–takes–offence–at–doublespeak/; 'PTI gets conditional nod for rally in capital', *The Express Tribune*, 9 May 2014, tribune.com.pk/story/706164/pti–gets–conditional–nod–for–rally–in–capital/

Ghauri, I., and Ali, R., 'Election anomalies: ECP announces re–polling schedule', *The Express Tribune*, 15 May 2013, epaper.tribune.com.pk/DisplayDetails.aspx?ENI_ID=11201305150451&EN_ID=11201305150402&EMID=11201305150042

Ghauri, I., et al., 'Nawaz claims victory; 'tsunami' sweeps K–P; PPP confined to Sindh; Nationalists show strength in Balochistan', *The Express Tribune*, 12 May 2013, epaper.tribune.com.pk/DisplayDetails.aspx?ENI_ID=11201305120642&EN_ID=11201305120508&EMID=11201305120073

Ghori, H. K., 'Imran vows to ensure justice and self–respect', *Dawn*, 11 August 2002, asianstudies.github.io/area–studies/SouthAsia/SAserials/Dawn/2002/aug172002.html#vows

Ghumman, K., 'Corruption allegations: Govt plans to fight 'media campaign'', *Dawn*, 15 December 2012, www.dawn.com/news/770973/corruption–allegations–govt–plans–to–fight–media–campaign; 'Imran and Mengal demand fair election process', *Dawn*, 8 July 2013, www.dawn.com/news/1023528; 'The more things change, the more they stay the same', *Dawn*, 25 April 2016, www.dawn.com/news/1254276; 'What does Imran want?', *Dawn*, 12 May 2014, www.dawn.com/news/1105684

Gishkori, Z., 'Impressive turnout: Seventy–two National Assembly members–elect bag 20% of total votes', *The Express Tribune*, 18 May 2013, tribune.com.pk/story/550995/impressive–turnout–seventy–two–national–assembly–members–elect–bag–20–of–total–votes/; 'New beginning: PTI proves itself a force to reckon with', *The Express Tribune*, 12 May 2013, epaper.tribune.com.pk/

DisplayDetails.aspx?ENI_ID=11201305120631&EN_ID=112013051204
98&EMID=11201305120072; 'South Waziristan rally: Imran vows to go ahead
with anti–drone march', *The Express Tribune*, 5 October 2012, epaper.tribune.
com.pk/DisplayDetails.aspx?ENI_ID=11201210050228&EN_ID=112012100501
80&EMID=11201210050020

Gover, D., 'Pakistan Cricket Legend Imran Khan Shot at by Assassin during Rally in
Gujranwala', *Newsweek*, 15 August 2014, www.ibtimes.co.uk/pakistan–cricket-
legend–imran–khan–shot–by–assassin–during–rally–gujranwala–1461255

Graham, S., 'Zardari has been marked by legal woes and tragedy', *Boston.com*,
7 September 2008, archive.boston.com/news/world/asia/articles/2008/09/07/
zardari_has_been_marked_by_legal_woes_and_tragedy/

Gul, I., 'Now or never', *The Friday Times*, 29 August 2014, www.thefridaytimes.
com/tft/now–or–never–2/

Habib, M., 'Schooling in KP', *Dawn*, 5 October 2015, www.dawn.com/
news/1210916

Haider, S., 'Imran Khan hails commitment of youth at Tank rally', *Dawn*, 7 October
2012, www.dawn.com/news/770973/corruption–allegations–govt–plans–to–fight-
media–campaign

Hamilton, M. M., 'Pakistan's PM Leaves Country, Spanish Minister Resigns',
ICIJ, 8 April 2016, panamapapers.icij.org/20160415–pakistan–pressure–spain-
resignation.html

Hanif, A., 'Imran Khan admits forming offshore company to 'evade British taxes'',
Dawn, 14 May 2016, www.dawn.com/news/1258139

Hussain, Z., 'Asif in Blunderland', *Newsline Magazine*, August Issue, 2008,
newslinemagazine.com/magazine/asif–in–blunderland/

Ilyas, F., 'Imran Khan delivers his own 'I have a dream' speech', *The Express
Tribune*, 31 March 2013,

Islam, S., '2013 election 'rigging': Imran Khan calls for 'trial of troika', *The Express
Tribune*, 26 May 2014, tribune.com.pk/story/713168/2013–election–rigging-
imran–khan–calls–for–trial–of–troika/; 'Imran pledges pluralistic, terror–free
society', *The Express Tribune*, 6 May 2013, tribune.com.pk/story/545018/imran-
pledges–pluralistic–terror–free–society/

Iyengar, R., 'The Panama Papers, One Week Later: What We Know, and What
We Still Don't', *Time*, 8 April 2016, time.com/4286371/panama–papers–leak-
mossack–fonseca/

Javed, N., 'PTI lawmaker's strange, solo flight', *The Express Tribune*, 21 June 2013,
epaper.tribune.com.pk/DisplayDetails.aspx?ENI_ID=11201306210099&EN_
ID=11201306210090&EMID=11201306210009

Kantawala, F. T., 'Where's my ice bucket?', *The Friday Times*, 29 August 2014,
www.thefridaytimes.com/tft/wheres–my–ice–bucket/

Khan, A., 'Austerity measures: Imran asks K–P chief minister to ban discretionary
funds', *The Express Tribune*, 10 April 2014, tribune.com.pk/story/693652/
austerity–measures–imran–asks–k–p–chief–minister–to–ban–discretionary-
funds/; 'Back in action: Imran wants drone issue taken up at UN', *The Express
Tribune*, 20 June 2013, epaper.tribune.com.pk/DisplayDetails.aspx?ENI_
ID=11201306200008&EN_ID=11201306200007&EMID=11201306200001;
'Demands spelled out: 48–hour deadline', *The Express Tribune*, 15 August
2014, tribune.com.pk/story/749809/demands–spelled–out–48–hour–deadline/;
'No law justifies immunity to Zardari, says Imran', *The Nation*, 22 January
2010, nation.com.pk/politics/22–Jan–2010/No–law–justifies–immunity–to-
Zardari–says–Imran; 'Poll rigging chorus: Former CJ to take legal action
against Imran', *The Express Tribune*, 7 July 2014, epaper.tribune.com.pk/

DisplayDetails.aspx?ENI_ID=11201407070155&EN_ID=112014070700
75&EMID=11201407070019; 'PTI announces boycott of Geo, Jang', *The Express Tribune*, 3 May 2014, epaper.tribune.com.pk/DisplayDetails.aspx?ENI_ID=11201105030013&EN_ID=11201105030004&EMID=11201105030004; 'Still bickering: Govt rejects PTI's agreement over rigging dispute', *The Express Tribune*, 10 May 2014, tribune.com.pk/story/706551/still–bickering–govt–rejects–ptis–agreement–over–rigging–dispute/; 'Upper House polls: PTI to take part in Senate polls from K–P', *The Express Tribune*, 31 January 2015, epaper.tribune.com.pk/DisplayDetails.aspx?ENI_ID=11201501310085&EN_ID=112015013100 30&EMID=11201501310012

Khan, H., 'PTI: Promises, Promises', *Newsline Magazine*, October Issue, 2014, newslinemagazine.com/magazine/pti–promises–promises/

Khan, I., 'Article 6', *The Express Tribune*, 5 May 2014, epaper.tribune.com.pk/DisplayDetails.aspx?ENI_ID=11201405050057&EN_ID=112014050500 31&EMID=11201405050007; 'How I cheated death by assassin's bullet... thanks to the fall that nearly killed me', *Mail Online*, 27 July 2013, www.dailymail.co.uk/news/article-2380018/How–I–cheated–death–assassins–bullet—thanks–fall–nearly–killed–me.html; 'Imran Khan Speech at Faisalabad Jalsa', 5 May 2013, www.dailymotion.com/video/xzm4o0_imran–khan–speech–at–faisalabad–jalsa–5th–may–2013_news; 'Imran Khan's speech at PTI Swat Jalsa', 31 March 2013, www.tuneinfo.pk/video/1041298/geonews–imran–khans–speech–at–pti–swat–jalsa

Khan, J. A., 'Imran appreciates KP police role in peace', *The News*, 19 November 2015, www.thenews.com.pk/print/74043–imran–appreciates–kp–police–role–in–peace

Khan, J., 'KP education reforms produce outstanding results: report', *Daily Times*, 21 August 2016, dailytimes.com.pk/khyber–pakhtunkhwa/21–Aug–16/kp–education–reforms–produce–outstanding–results–report

Khan, R., 'Reham Khan: 'Marrying Imran Khan meant everyone in Pakistan got involved in my private affairs', *The Guardian*, 17 November 2015, www.theguardian.com/lifeandstyle/2015/nov/17/reham–khan–imran–khan–pakistan–politics–marriage–divorce

Khan, S., 'Democratic Transition: Transfer of power to new govt by June 2: Nizami', *The Express Tribune*, 14 May 2013, epaper.tribune.com.pk/DisplayDetails.aspx?ENI_ID=11201305140496&EN_ID=112013051404 27&EMID=11201305140041; 'Exclusive: The curious Presidency of Mr Zardari', *Dawn*, 7 March 2016, www.dawn.com/news/1041287

Khan, T., 'Karzai's successor: Millions of Afghans vote in historic polls', *The Express Tribune*, 6 April 2014, tribune.com.pk/story/691974/karzais–successor–millions–of–afghans–vote–in–historic–polls/

Kharal, A., 'Audit report: 'Irregular' payment of Rs74 billion BISP money', *The Express Tribune*, 20 May 2013, epaper.tribune.com.pk/DisplayDetails.aspx?ENI_ID=11201305200234&EN_ID=11201305200183&EMID=11201305200026

Lancaster, J., 'A Pakistani Cricket Star's Political Move', *Washington Post*, 4 July 2005, www.washingtonpost.com/wp–dyn/content/article/2005/07/03/AR2005070301078.html

Malik, H., 'Imran Khan Announces to File Defamation Suit against Altaf Hussain', *Pakistan Tribune*, 9 February 2015, www.pakistantribune.com.pk/imran–khan–announces–file–defamation–suit–altaf–hussain.html

Malik, M., 'Imran announces long march towards Raiwind', *Dawn*, 9 April 2016, www.dawn.com/news/1251031; 'Imran vows to bring plunderers to book', *Dawn*, 3 May 2013, www.dawn.com/news/795294

Manan, A., 'Bouquet diplomacy: Nawaz offers, Imran accepts hatchet–
  burying offer', *The Express Tribune*, 15 May 2013, epaper.tribune.com.
  pk/DisplayDetails.aspx?ENI_ID=11201305150433&EN_ID=11201305
  150386&EMID=11201305150042; 'Grand plan: PM unveils free health
  treatment programme', *The Express Tribune*, 1 January 2016, tribune.com.pk/
  story/1019964/grand–plan–pm–unveils–free–health–treatment–programme/;
  'Lobbying season: PML–N close to finalising cabinet', *The Express
  Tribune*, 16 May 2013, epaper.tribune.com.pk/DisplayDetails.aspx?ENI_
  ID=11201305160411&EN_ID=11201305160352&EMID=11201305160037;
  'PML–N rally: From 'go Zardari' to 'go Imran'', *The Express Tribune*,
  1 January 2012, epaper.tribune.com.pk/DisplayDetails.aspx?ENI_
  ID=11201201010005&EN_ID=11201201010003&EMID=11201201010001;
  'Raiwind revelations: Nawaz picks Ishaq Dar as finance minister', *The Express
  Tribune*, 17 May 2013, tribune.com.pk/story/550558/raiwind–revelations–
  nawaz–picks–ishaq–dar–as–finance–minister/
Manan, A., and Ghauri, I., 'PML–N's game plan', *The Express Tribune*,
  13 May 2013, epaper.tribune.com.pk/Images/Karachi/20130513/
  SubImages/11201305130165.JPG
Mehboob, A. B., 'Whither electoral reforms?', *Dawn*, 24 January 2014, www.dawn.
  com/news/1159028
Modi, N., 'Call for concern', *The Express Tribune*, 9 April 2014, epaper.tribune.
  com.pk/DisplayDetails.aspx?ENI_ID=11201404090104&EN_ID=112014040900
  97&EMID=11201404090013
Mohammad, Z., 'The PPP's terrible economic performance', *The Express Tribune*,
  6 November 2012, tribune.com.pk/story/461671/the–ppps–terrible–economic–
  performance/
Muhammad, P. and Shah, F. A., 'In Islamabad: Voters report harassment by
  PML–N supporters', *The Express Tribune*, 12 May 2013, epaper.tribune.com.
  pk/DisplayDetails.aspx?ENI_ID=11201305120570&EN_ID=112013051204
  58&EMID=11201305120064
Muhammad, P., "Cash–for–chair' remarks: Senators press for apology from
  Imran', *The Express Tribune*, 18 February 2014, tribune.com.pk/story/673134/
  cash–for–chair–remarks–senators–press–for–apology–from–imran/; 'Bracing
  for the worst: PAT warns govt against arrest of their leader', *The Express
  Tribune*, 16 June 2014, epaper.tribune.com.pk/DisplayDetails.aspx?ENI_
  ID=11201406160105&EN_ID=11201406160052&EMID=11201406160013;
  'D–Chowk Day: Federal capital braces for 'tsunami'', *The Express
  Tribune*, 11 May 2014, epaper.tribune.com.pk/DisplayDetails.aspx?ENI_
  ID=11201405110120&EN_ID=11201405110068&EMID=11201405110022;
  'Rigging chorus: Thunder in D–chowk', *The Express Tribune*, 12 May 2014,
  tribune.com.pk/story/707282/rigging–chorus–thunder–in–d–chowk/
Naeem, R., 'Interview: Tariq Ali', *Newsline Magazine*, December Issue, 2008,
  newslinemagazine.com/magazine/interview–tariq–ali/
Naeem, W., 'Spiral of violence: Terror revisits capital', *The Express Tribune*, 10 April
  2014, tribune.com.pk/story/693654/spiral–of–violence–terror–revisits–capital/
Najam, D., 'KP making progress in police reform', *Daily Times*, 25 August 2016,
  dailytimes.com.pk/opinion/26–Aug–16/kp–making–progress–in–police–reform
Nangiana, U., 'Unprecedented Return: He is Back', *The Express Tribune*,
  6 June 2013, epaper.tribune.com.pk/DisplayDetails.aspx?ENI_
  ID=11201306060392&EN_ID=11201306060320&EMID=11201306060043
Nangiana, U., and Q. Zaman, 'Newly elected MNAs take oath in Pakistan's 14th
  National Assembly', *The Express Tribune*, 2 June 2013, epaper.tribune.com.

pk/DisplayDetails.aspx?ENI_ID=11201306020411&EN_ID=112013060203
27&EMID=11201306020043

Nelson, D., 'Imran Khan bowls back onto Pakistan political agenda with mass
Lahore rally', *The Telegraph*, 31 October 2011, www.telegraph.co.uk/news/
worldnews/asia/pakistan/8860135/Imran–Khan–bowls–back–onto–Pakistan–
political–agenda–with–mass–Lahore–rally.html; 'Pakistan foreign minister denies
Bilawal Bhutto affair rumours', *The Telegraph*, 27 September 2012, www.
telegraph.co.uk/news/worldnews/asia/pakistan/9571120/Pakistan–foreign–
minister–denies–Bilawal–Bhutto–affair–rumours.html; 'Pakistan's former spy chief
is behind Imran Khan's revolt, claims minister', *The Telegraph*, 12 Aug 2014,
www.telegraph.co.uk/news/worldnews/asia/pakistan/11028579/Pakistans–former–
spy–chief–is–behind–Imran–Khans–revolt–claims–minister.html

Niazi, I., 'Imran apney Agha Jaan ki nazar mein (Imran in the eyes of his father–
Urdu Article)', 15 December 2013, www.unewstv.com/10589/imran–khan–apney–
agha–jan–father–ki–nazar–mein–by–ikramullah–niazi

O'Toole, M., 'Tahir ul–Qadri: A political 'enigma'', *AlJazeera*, 22 October 2014,
www.aljazeera.com/indepth/features/2014/10/tahir–ul–qadri–political–enigma–
pakistan–2014102271530973245.html

Orakzai, A. M. J., 'Situation in FATA: Causes, Consequences and the Way
Forward' *Institute of Policy Studies*, 2009, www.ips.org.pk/global–issues–and–
politics/1057–situation–in–fata–causes–consequences–and–the–way–forward

Orr, J., 'Civilian rule returns to Pakistan as Zardari becomes president', *The Guardian*, 9
September 2008, www.theguardian.com/world/2008/sep/09/pakistan.benazirbhutto

Ousat, A., and H. Tunio, 'PTI leader shot dead night before NA–250 re–polling', *The
Express Tribune*, 19 May 2013, epaper.tribune.com.pk/DisplayDetails.aspx?ENI_
ID=11201305190835&EN_ID=11201305190691&EMID=11201305190076

Peshimam, G., 'Anti–drones rally: PTI marches to the brink, comes
around', *The Express Tribune*, 8 October 2012, epaper.tribune.com.pk/
DisplayDetails.aspx?ENI_ID=11201210080289&EN_ID=112012100802
10&EMID=11201210080026; 'PTI peace march: Fears dissipate as rally
gathers momentum', *The Express Tribune*, 7 October 2012, tribune.com.pk/
story/448191/pti–peace–march–fears–dissipate–as–rally–gathers–momentum/

Rana, S., 'Economic Survey 2013: Almost all key targets missed', *The Express
Tribune*, 12 June 2013, epaper.tribune.com.pk/DisplayDetails.aspx?ENI_
ID=11201306120601&EN_ID=11201306120507&EMID=11201306120061

Raza, S., 'Suspension of disbelief', *The Friday Times*, 5 December 2014, www.
thefridaytimes.com/tft/suspension–of–disbelief/

Roy, A., 'Imran is Pakistan and Pakistan is Imran', *The Telegraph*, 2 October 2011,
www.telegraphindia.com/1111002/jsp/7days/story_14577884.jsp

Sadaqat, M., 'Deforestation blues: Imran vows to crack down on timber mafia', *The
Express Tribune*, 7 February 2015, tribune.com.pk/story/834369/deforestation–
blues–imran–vows–to–crack–down–on–timber–mafia/; 'Green day: Imran Khan
inaugurates 'Billion Tree Tsunami'', *The Express Tribune*, 21 February 2015,
epaper.tribune.com.pk/DisplayDetails.aspx?ENI_ID=11201502220364&EN_
ID=11201502220114&EMID=11201502220062

Salahuddin, Z., 'The not–so–reluctant fundamentalist', *The Friday Times*, 27 June
2014, www.thefridaytimes.com/tft/the–not–so–reluctant–fundamentalist/

Shaheen, A., 'Aye or nay: Dialogue should be first option, says Imran', *The Express
Tribune*, 27 February 2014, tribune.com.pk/story/676670/aye–or–nay–dialogue–
should–be–first–option–says–imran/

Sherazi, Z. S., 'Explosion kills 20 in Bannu; TTP claims attack', *Dawn*, 19 January
2014, www.dawn.com/news/1081329; 'Pakistani Taliban chief Hakimullah Mehsud

killed in drone attack', *Dawn*, 2 November 2013, www.dawn.com/news/1053410/
pakistani–taliban–chief–hakimullah–mehsud–killed–in–drone–attack

Shinwari, S., 'Pakistan FM Hina Rabbani's love affairs exposed: Rumors', *Khaama
Press*, 25 September 2012, www.khaama.com/pakistan–fm–hina–rabbanis–love–
affairs–exposed–rumors–261

Siddiqi, A. R., 'Chronicles of carnage: US 'war' in Pakistan regains intensity, states
report', *The Express Tribune*, 2 February 2013, tribune.com.pk/story/501578/
chronicles–of–carnage–us–war–in–pakistan–regains–intensity–states–report/

Sirajuddin, 'Nearly 275 schools non–functional in KP: report', *Dawn*, 13 March
2015, www.dawn.com/news/1169334

Sumra, A., 'PTI will eradicate corruption: Imran Khan', *The Express Tribune*, 15
December 2012, tribune.com.pk/story/480009/pti–will–eradicate–corruption–
imran–khan/; 'See for yourself: PTI boasts new strategies for election campaigns',
The Express Tribune, 21 December 2012, tribune.com.pk/story/482336/see–for–
yourself–pti–boasts–new–strategies–for–election–campaigns/

Sumra, A., and Tanveer, R., 'Finally home: Standoff on the runway', *The Express
Tribune*, 24 June 2014, epaper.tribune.com.pk/DisplayDetails.aspx?ENI_
ID=11201406240003&EN_ID=11201406240003&EMID=11201406240001

Tariq, S., 'The 11th of May', *The Nation*, 15 May 2014, nation.com.pk/columns/15–
May–2014/the–11th–of–may

tribune.com.pk/story/529130/imran-khan-delivers-his-own-i-have-a-dream-speech/

Tunio, H., 'Constituency profile: A fight to remember', *The Express Tribune*, 8
May 2013, tribune.com.pk/story/545949/constituency–profile–a–fight–to–
remember/; 'Electoral trends: PPP appears loosening grip on fortress', *The
Express Tribune*, 1 April 2013, tribune.com.pk/story/529372/electoral–trends–
ppp–appears–loosening–grip–on–fortress/; 'Karachi partial re–polling: PTI's Arif
Alvi wins NA–250 seat', *The Express Tribune*, 20 May 2013, epaper.tribune.
com.pk/DisplayDetails.aspx?ENI_ID=11201305200327&EN_ID=1120130
5200264&EMID=11201305200035; 'Sindh Assembly: PPP retains vice–like
grip on Sindh', *The Express Tribune*, 13 May 2013, epaper.tribune.com.pk/
DisplayDetails.aspx?ENI_ID=11201305130139&EN_ID=112013051301
10&EMID=11201305130014

Ud-Din, J., '350 small dams to be built in KP, says Imran', *Dawn*, 21 April 2014,
www.dawn.com/news/1101298

Ur-Rehman, Z., 'We could not keep our promises', *The Friday Times*, 25 April 2014,
www.thefridaytimes.com/tft/we–could–not–keep–our–promises/

Usman, A., 'Justice for Women of Pakistan: Imran Khan opposes reserved seats for
women', *The Express Tribune*, 17 December 2012, tribune.com.pk/story/480595/
justice–for–women–of–pakistan–imran–khan–opposes–reserved–seats–for–
women/; 'Rigging allegations: Imran gives three–day deadline to ECP', *The
Express Tribune*, 16 May 2013, epaper.tribune.com.pk/DisplayDetails.aspx?ENI_
ID=11201305160406&EN_ID=11201305160348&EMID=11201305160037

Usman, A., and Jafri, O., 'Imran says PTI will sit in opposition', *The Express
Tribune*, 13 May 2013, epaper.tribune.com.pk/DisplayDetails.aspx?ENI_
ID=11201305130168&EN_ID=11201305130137&EMID=11201305130017

Walsh, D., 'Imran Khan laps up acclaim in Pakistan', *The Guardian*, 31 October
2011, www.theguardian.com/world/2011/oct/31/imran–khan–acclaim–pakistan;
'In Pakistan, Drone Strike Turns a Villain into a Victim', *The New York Times*, 3
November 2013, www.nytimes.com/2013/11/04/world/asia/in–pakistan–death–
by–drone–turns–a–villain–into–a–martyr.html

Wasim, A., 'PTI condemns TTP, other terrorist groups', *Dawn*, 22 December 2014,
www.dawn.com/news/1152436

Wilkinson, I., 'Profile: Asif Ali Zardari, Pakistan's probable next president, is living the dream', *The Telegraph*, 4 September 2008, www.telegraph.co.uk/news/newstopics/profiles/2682828/Profile–Asif–Ali–Zardari–Pakistans–probable–next–president–is–living–the–dream.html

www.nytimes.com/2002/07/05/world/as-pakistani-s-popularity-slides-busharraf-is-a-figure-of-ridicule.html

Yousaf, K., 'Raymond Davis case: Men killed in Lahore were intelligence operatives, says official', *The Express Tribune*, 5 February 2011, tribune.com.pk/story/115225/raymond–davis–case–men–killed–in–lahore–were–intelligence–operatives–says–official/

Yousaf, K., and Gishkori, Z., 'Interim report: Voting at 90% of polling stations 'satisfactory'', *The Express Tribune*, 14 May 2013, epaper.tribune.com.pk/DisplayDetails.aspx?ENI_ID=11201305140466&EN_ID=112013051404 04&EMID=11201305140014

Yusuf, H., 'The youth factor', *Dawn*, 21 May 2012, www.dawn.com/news/720119

Yusufzai, A., 'Preventable cancers: govt to focus on public awareness', *Dawn*, 15 October 2013, www.dawn.com/news/1049888/preventable–cancers–govt–to–focus–on–public–awareness

Zaan, Q., 'Bitter divide: Saad challenges poll rigging claims', *The Express Tribune*, 9 May 2014, epaper.tribune.com.pk/DisplayDetails.aspx?ENI_ID=11201405090099&EN_ID=11201405090048&EMID=11201405090015

Zafar, K., 'Countdown begins: Imran to lead 'tsunami march' on August 14', *The Express Tribune*, 28 June 2014, epaper.tribune.com.pk/DisplayDetails.aspx?ENI_ID=11201406280003&EN_ID=11201406280003&EMID=11201406280001

Zafar, M., 'Election 2013: Strike, threats mar Balochistan polling', *The Express Tribune*, 12 May 2013, epaper.tribune.com.pk/DisplayDetails.aspx?ENI_ID=11201305120539&EN_ID=11201305120430&EMID=11201305120060

Zaman, Q., 'Condemning drone strikes: Former US envoy advises Pakistanis to stand up to govt', *The Express Tribune*, 1 October 2012, tribune.com.pk/story/445070/condemning–drone–strikes–former–us–envoy–advises–pakistanis–to–stand–up–to–govt/; 'Electoral reforms: PTI likely to table bill in NA', *The Express Tribune*, 1 June 2014, tribune.com.pk/story/716083/electoral–reforms–pti–likely–to–table–bill–in–na/; 'Looking for compromise: Nawaz urges PTI to give talks a chance', *The Express Tribune*, 10 August 2014, tribune.com.pk/story/746685/looking–for–compromise–nawaz–urges–pti–to–give–talks–a–chance/; 'New Govt: Energy crisis tops PML–N's priorities', *The Express Tribune*, 16 May 2013, epaper.tribune.com.pk/DisplayDetails.aspx?ENI_ID=11201305160432&EN_ID=112 01305160368&EMID=11201305160039; 'No compromise: PTI not to return to assemblies', *The Express Tribune*, 25 January 2015, epaper.tribune.com.pk/DisplayDetails.aspx?ENI_ID=11201501250152&EN_ID=11201501250 062&EMID=11201501250026; 'Rural Punjab politics: The Thana–Katcheri factor', *The Express Tribune*, 5 May 2013, tribune.com.pk/story/544639/rural–punjab–politics–the–thana–katcheri–factor/; 'Talks with govt: PTI says it cannot show more flexibility', *The Express Tribune*, 29 December 2014, epaper.tribune.com.pk/DisplayDetails.aspx?ENI_ID=11201412290085&EN_ID=112014122900 36&EMID=11201412290014

Zaman, Q., and Muhammad, P., 'Transition complete: The House that hope built', *The Express Tribune*, 1 June 2013, epaper.tribune.com.pk/DisplayDetails.aspx?ENI_ID=11201306010543&EN_ID=112013060104 98&EMID=11201305310045

Online Videos and Images

1 Billion Challenge TELETHON Imran Khan Fundraising Peshawar Hospital Part 2–8 February 2015, online video, 2015, www.youtube.com/watch?v=7WyN5e9–fuQ

A historic clip from 2008—Imran Khan protesting against Zardari, online video, 2008, www.zemtv.com/2016/10/15/a–historic–clip–from–2008–imran–khan–protesting–against–zardari–when–imran–khan–was–being–made–the–president–with–the–help–of–nawaz–sharif/

Best of Hasb e Haal (1st February 2014) Imran Khan as Exclusive Guest, online video, 2014, www.youtube.com/watch?v=vtn7djIDYS0

Biggest Democratic Exercise Begins Today, online image, *The Express Tribune*, 7 April 2014, epaper.tribune.com.pk/DisplayDetails.aspx?ENI_ID=11201404070100&EN_ID=11201404070092&EMID=11201404070014

Capital Chaos, online image, *The Express Tribune*, 24 June 2014, epaper.tribune.com.pk/DisplayDetails.aspx?ENI_ID=11201406240020&EN_ID=11201406240010&EMID=11201406240003

Durrani, N. K. (IG KPK Police), Interviewed by Saleem Safi, 2016, Geo Television Network, www.youtube.com/watch?v=TK8l7cVgbi8

Heart touching–If You are Pakistani Must Watch this Video (Why Imran Khan Great), online video, 2011, www.youtube.com/watch?v=_FteiqNzuXc

Hussain, N., Passing–out Parade, online image, *The Express Tribune*, 25 February 2015, epaper.tribune.com.pk/DisplayDetails.aspx?ENI_ID=11201502200086&EN_ID=11201502200031&EMID=11201502200013

Imran Khan and Sheikh Rasheed Press Conference outside Parliament, online video, 2014, newsbeat.pk/news/imran–khan–and–sheikh–rasheed–press–conference–outside–parliament–8th–may–2014–video_dc145532f.html

Imran Khan comments after release from jail, online video, 2007, www.youtube.com/watch?v=RYaS09YDwxU

Imran Khan demanded 100 National Assembly seats from Pervez Musharraf in 2002 elections YouTube, online video, 2012, www.youtube.com/watch?v=H9v2xibSzA0

Imran Khan in ouch Dir may 2000, online video, 2000, www.youtube.com/watch?v=s1nfYgj59jU

Imran Khan Jalsa at Bahawalpur FULL SPEECH 27th June 2014—PTI Jalsa Bahawalpur, online video, 2014, www.youtube.com/watch?v=v1ovgdm_Dow

Imran Khan Married a BBC Weather Girl Reham Khan, online video, 2015, www.youtube.com/watch?v=w–lWOfzmnoc

Imran Khan Media Talk After Wedding–9 January 2015, online video, 2015, www.youtube.com/watch?v=BomL14IfryQ

Imran Khan media talk in Peshawar, online video, 2014, www.youtube.com/watch?v=kfhPaRUh9Mw

Imran Khan on Zardari Visit, David Cameron Statement on BBC, online video, 2010, GMTV Network, www.youtube.com/watch?v=_ZxkKCxdIaQ

Imran Khan Pakhtunkhwa Radio Mardan World Radio Day–13 February 2015, online video, 2015, www.youtube.com/watch?v=zaP8beKBAyY

Imran Khan Press Conference ... exposing rigging (May 2, 2014), online video, 2014, www.youtube.com/watch?v=H9l-IpKqg4o

Imran Khan Press Conference after Nawaz Speech, online video, 2014, www.youtube.com/watch?v=r7–jsbdc168

Imran Khan Says Peshawar School Attack 'A Failure of All', online video, 2014, www.youtube.com/watch?v=xiudMyeAHSo

Imran Khan speech in Hangu | May 2002, online video, 2002, www.youtube.com/watch?v=d1ZCW_5g2ew

Imran Khan Speech warning to Nawaz Shareef and Narinder Modi 30 09 2016 Part 1, online video, 2016, www.youtube.com/watch?v=cpkIWkDGKWs

Imran Khan vs Talat Hussain Old Conversation in 2002, online video, 2002, www.currentaffairspk.com/imran–khan–vs–talat–hussain–old–conversation–in–2002/

Imran Khan, PTI Leader Message after Meeting Nawaz Sharif on 15 May 2013, online video, 2013, www.youtube.com/watch?v=F0pRDkMrwKM

Imran Khan–'Conned' by Musharraf, online video, 2008, www.youtube.com/watch?v=CJYPa79cPu4

Imran Khan–1996–Slams Kabza Group Nawaz Sharif & Asif Ali Zardari, online video, 1996, www.youtube.com/watch?v=gdUfVMMjpbk

Imran Khan's speech at National Assembly June 19, 2013 FULL Speech, online video, 2013, www.youtube.com/watch?v=VQJ6w4aH688

Imran: Civil services in Pakistan…, online image, *The Express Tribune*, 9 June 2013, epaper.tribune.com.pk/DisplayDetails.aspx?ENI_ID=11201306090467&EN_ID=11201306090397&EMID=11201306090042

Islam & America: Through the Eyes of Imran Khan–Pakistan, online video, 2001, www.youtube.com/watch?v=L9fW9jPnjgE

Javed Hashmi demanding Dope Test of Imran Khan, online video, 2016, www.youtube.com/watch?v=bJ0H1Il8Rwk

Khan, I., 'Imran Khan Address to the Nation 10 April 2016 | Dunya News', 10 April 2016, www.youtube.com/watch?v=m7F5KqD_WVY; 'Imran Khan Lahore Chairing Cross Jalsa Speech–1 May 2016–Dunya News', 1 May 2016, www.youtube.com/watch?v=06QXBNflKmU; 'Imran Khan Latest Press Conference 4 April 2016, Panama Scandal', 4 April 2016, www.youtube.com/watch?v=Wb9ObrG7ayw; 'Imran Khan Media Talk | Bashing PMLN Actions in Islamabad | Geo News', 30 October 2016, www.youtube.com/watch?v=LM15YBvyufs; 'Imran Khan Press Conference (Panama Leaks) 04 April 2016', 4 April 2016, www.youtube.com/watch?v=n080KNHXJSU; 'Imran Khan Speech Azadi March PTI Jalsa–First speech', 16 August 2014, www.youtube.com/watch?v=pfM6rVK–_nU; 'Imran Khan Speech In London Bashing Nawaz Sharif 17th April 2016', 17th April 2016, www.youtube.com/watch?v=xnroX32zyaA; 'Imran Khan Speech in Parliament Bashing Nawaz Sharif | Panama Leaks', 7 April 2016, www.youtube.com/watch?v=APKB1CfSEtM; 'Imran Khan Speech in PTI Jalsa Islamabad 24 April 2016–Express News', 24 April 2016, www.youtube.com/watch?v=vvfdSlf_L2g; 'Imran Khan's Inauguration speech at Koto HydroPower Project Timergara Dir Lower', 4 July 2015, www.youtube.com/watch?v=WNRyyid0leA; 'Imran Khan's speech in Islamabad', 11 May 2014, www.youtube.com/watch?v=_Jv5Liw_lwE; 'Imran Khan's Speech on World Teachers Day in KPK', 5 October 2016, www.youtube.com/watch?v=1ebtuIHbhbA; 'PTI Chairman Imran Khan Speech in PTI Azadi March at Islamabad—Last speech', 17 December 2014, www.dailymotion.com/video/x2crptl_pti–chairman–imran–khan–speech–in–pti–azadi–march–at–islamabad–17th–december–2014_news; 'PTI chairman Imran Khan's press conference outside Bani Gala 1ST November 2016', 1 November 2016, www.youtube.com/watch?v=hl2C–lOHzec; interviewed by Dr. Shahid Masood, 2009, Geo Television Network, www.youtube.com/watch?v=LPDKztUD0oo; interviewed by Geo Reporter, 2010, Geo Television Network, www.youtube.

com/watch?v=wWlGXiSZhwM; interviewed by Javed Chaudhry, 2014, Express News, www.youtube.com/watch?v=I6guqJJMyUA; interviewed by Kiran and George, 2009, Kiran Aur George, www.youtube.com/watch?v=zNA_bnwvo64; interviewed by Mehdi Hasan, 2016, Al–Jazeera, www.youtube.com/watch?v=AT7FV9PADf4

Khan, K., Statement on Imran Khan, online image *The Express Tribune*, 2014, epaper.tribune.com.pk/DisplayDetails.aspx?ENI_ID=11201408170143&EN_ID=11201408170070&EMID=11201408170019

Khawaja Saad Rafique Caught Rigging NA–125 Lahore in Women Polling Section, online video, 2013, www.youtube.com/watch?v=p3GjYWOmKVo

Khawaja Saad Rafique PML–N rigging DHA, online video, 2013, www.youtube.com/watch?v=qj–IanOaHGY

Maxim, online Image, The Nation, 20 January 2010, nation.com.pk/E–Paper/lahore/2010–01–20/page–6

Maxim, online Image, The Nation, 5 January 2010, nation.com.pk/E–Paper/lahore/2010–01–05/page–6

Maxim, The Royal Cutlery, online image, *The News*, 6 April 2016, nation.com.pk/E–Paper/Lahore/2016–04–06/page–6/detail–3

Musharraf votes, polls close in presidential referendum, online video, 2015, www.youtube.com/watch?v=90shS0Y9B-A

Nawaz, H., interviewed by Shahzaib Khanzada, 2016, Geo Television Network, www.youtube.com/watch?v=CQxS90Gws8c

Pakistan's Imran Khan comes to Dubai, urges investment in Khyber Pakhtunkhwa, online video, 2015, www.youtube.com/watch?v=3VP0YoU6j9I

PM Nawaz Sharif and Imran Khan, online video, 2014, www.youtube.com/watch?v=t6FqU_n6ojo

PML–N sweeps polls: merrymaking on the streets, online image, *The Express Tribune*, 13 May 2013, epaper.tribune.com.pk/DisplayDetails.aspx?ENI_ID=11201305130167&EN_ID=11201305130136&EMID=11201305130017

Saad Rafiq Speech in National Assembly, online video, 2014, www.youtube.com/watch?v=IT_euGv5cQw

Sharif, N., 'Prime Minister Nawaz Sharif Speech on Panama Leak,' 5 April 2016, www.youtube.com/watch?v=ly65Pv1Jzo4

Tonight with Moeed Pirzada 10 April 2016—Imran Khan Address amid Panama Leaks, online video, 2016, www.youtube.com/watch?v=8tltaWC_iTU

Urban Dharnas: Tsunami on the Streets, online image, *The Express Tribune*, 14 May 2013, epaper.tribune.com.pk/DisplayDetails.aspx?ENI_ID=11201305140465&EN_ID=11201305140403&EMID=11201305140014

Wasim Akram Shares How Imran Khan Achieved Target of Making Shaukat Khanum Hospital Lahore, online video, 2016, www.youtube.com/watch?v=e0MybXqxlPE

Strategic Initiatives and Institutional Reforms in Khyber Pakhtunkhwa Police 2015-16, 2016 (Government of Khyber Pakhtunkhwa).

Publications

Constitution of Pakistan: Article 6. High Treason, 1973 (Government of Pakistan)
Constitution of Pakistan: Article 245. Functions of Armed Forces, 1973 (Government of Pakistan)

Index